Edwin Abbott Abbott

Philochristus

Memoirs of a Disciple of the Lord

Edwin Abbott Abbott

Philochristus
Memoirs of a Disciple of the Lord

ISBN/EAN: 9783743344297

Manufactured in Europe, USA, Canada, Australia, Japa

Cover: Foto ©ninafisch / pixelio.de

Manufactured and distributed by brebook publishing software (www.brebook.com)

Edwin Abbott Abbott

Philochristus

PHILOCHRISTUS

Memoirs of a Disciple of the Lord

PHILOCHRISTUS

MEMOIRS

OF

A DISCIPLE OF THE LORD

ἔμαθεν ἀφ' ὧν ἔπαθεν τὴν ὑπακοήν

London
MACMILLAN AND CO
1878

[The Right of Translation and Reproduction is Reserved]

LONDON:
R. CLAY, SONS, AND TAYLOR,
BREAD STREET HILL, E.C.

TO

THE AUTHOR OF 'ECCE HOMO'

NOT MORE IN ADMIRATION OF HIS WRITINGS

THAN IN GRATITUDE

FOR THE SUGGESTIVE INFLUENCE

OF A LONG AND INTIMATE FRIENDSHIP.

PHILOCHRISTUS THE ELDER TO THE SAINTS OF THE CHURCH IN LONDINIUM, GRACE, MERCY, AND PEACE FROM THE LORD JESUS CHRIST.

Forasmuch as almost all those disciples who with me saw the Lord Jesus in the flesh, are now fallen asleep, and I myself am well stricken in years and daily expect the summons of the Lord; it hath therefore seemed good to me to bequeath unto you some memorial of Christ in writing; which, instead of my voice, shall testify to you of him for ever.

All the more need seemeth thereof because the Lord delayeth his coming. For now these ten years Jerusalem hath been trodden down of the Gentiles, and the words of the Lord concerning the destruction of the Holy City have been fulfilled; and yet he cometh not. Yea, and sometimes my mind presageth that his coming may be yet longer delayed, even till all they that knew him in the flesh have fallen asleep.

For this cause I was long ago moved, even from the second or third year after the destruction of the Holy City, to leave some record behind me to testify of the Lord. But when I adventured to write, behold, it was an hard matter and well-nigh impossible, to set forth such an image of the Lord Jesus as should be at once according to the truth, and yet not altogether too bright for mortal eye to look upon and love. Therefore at the last, when I perceived that it was not given unto me to portray any character of the Lord as he was in himself, I determined rather to set forth an history of mine own life; wherein, as in a mirror, might perchance be discerned some lineaments of the countenance of Christ, seen as by reflexion, in the life of one that loved him.

THE TABLE

Chapter
1. Of my childhood in Galilee; and how I gave myself wholly to the study of the Law.

2. Of my doubts concerning the Law; and of the Patriots or Galileans; and of the expectation concerning John the son of Zachariah.

3. Concerning the casting out of unclean Spirits; and of the nature of the Redemption of Israel; and how I first saw Jesus of Nazareth.

4. Of the doctrine of John the Prophet, how it suited with the people of the land; and how I was baptized of the Prophet.

5. Of the Greek philosophers in Alexandria; and how I had discourse with Philo the Alexandrine.

6. How I found not salvation in the worship of the Temple; nor in the teachers of Galilee; nor in the Essenes; and how I first spake with Jesus of Nazareth.

7. Of the Good News; and concerning the Kingdom of God; and how we desired of Jesus new laws.

8. Of the New Law.

9. How Quartus interpreted the New Law.

10. How some desired Jesus to mix the New Law with the Old Law; and concerning the legion of swine; and how Jesus began to teach in parables.

Chapter

11 *Concerning the new power of the Forgiveness of Sins.*

12 *How the Forgiveness of Sins is the Key that openeth the New Kingdom; and how the Old Law and the New Law must not be mixed.*

13 *Of the plotting of the Pharisees against Jesus, how they said he had a devil; and concerning the Holy Spirit.*

14 *How John the Prophet doubted concerning Jesus; and concerning them that are " born of women;" and of the beheading of John the Prophet.*

15 *How Jesus fled from Capernaum, and the Galileans at first fell away from him; and concerning the levy in Galilee; and of the visit of Jesus to Nazareth.*

16 *How, after the death of John the Prophet, Jesus foresaw that he also must be slain; and of the Bread of Life, and the feeding of the five thousand; and concerning the leaven of the Pharisees and Sadducees.*

17 *How Xanthias the Alexandrine said that the philosophy of Jesus aimed at the taking in of the Gentiles into the Kingdom, and at the enfranchisement of slaves; and how he found fault with Jesus for that he called himself the Son of man.*

18 *Of signs in heaven; and concerning the healing of the Syrophœnician maiden, how Jesus seemed to gain thereby some new knowledge.*

19 *How Jesus would work no sign in heaven; and concerning his temptation; and wherefore he denied to work signs in heaven.*

20 *How Jesus led us, in our exile, to the Rock of Salvation; and how he founded the Temple of his Congregation thereon; and how he gave the Key thereof to Simon Peter.*

21 *How Jesus, having now determined to die, spake of that which was to come, with Moses and Elias, upon the Mount Hermon.*

22 *Of our going up to Jerusalem; and of the division between parents and children; and how Jesus testified of a Day of Judgment.*

23 *Of covetousness; and of fleeing from Death into Life; and concerning the Law of Retribution.*

Chapter
24 Of the falling away of Judas of Kerioth; and of the Times and Seasons; and of the Chief Places in the Kingdom; and how Jesus did and said nothing except it were prepared for him by the Father.

25 Concerning the fire of the Lord; and of the parables of watching; and of the Holy Spirit; and how Quartus urgeth that Jesus knew not all things beforehand.

26 How Jesus went down to Jerusalem, as a king, to wage war against Satan in the Temple; and how he foresaw that the Temple must be cast down; and of the parable of the withered fig-tree.

27 How Jesus prophesied of troubles, and of a great battle against Satan; and in the end the victory of the Son of man; but, first of all, his death.

28 How Jesus, by his Testament, bequeathed himself to his disciples for ever; and how he bare the sins of men in Gethsemane.

29 Of the crucifixion of Jesus; and of his last words upon the cross.

30 How the Holy Spirit, through much sorrow, prepared the disciples to behold Jesus risen from the dead; and of the vision of angels, which appeared first of all unto the women.

31 How Jesus appeared ofttimes to his disciples; and how, after many days, he ascended up to heaven.

32 How Jesus now ruleth the world, sitting on the right hand of the Father in heaven.

PHILOCHRISTUS

CHAPTER I

My former name was Joseph the son of Simeon, and I was born in Sepphoris, the metropolis of Galilee, in the twentieth year of the reign of the Emperor Augustus, about four years before the death of King Herod. In those days Israel was grievously afflicted, and tribulation befell the righteous. Satan put it into the heart of the rulers of the land to move the people to the worship of false gods, and the Lord God had not yet raised up a Redeemer for Israel.

In my fourth year my father's brother, the Rabbi Matthias, was burned alive by Herod for causing his scholars to cast down the golden image of an eagle which the king had set up over the gate of the temple of the Lord. Not many months afterwards, the Romans marched through Sepphoris in order to bring succour to Sabinus, who was hard beset by the men of Jerusalem in the fortress called Antonia; and we fought against them, and my father was taken captive and crucified by Varus. Now as concerning my father and my father's brother, how they were slain, perchance I remember their deaths rather from my mother's often mention of them in after times than from what I heard then: but this thing can I never forget, for I saw it with mine own eyes: namely, how, when my mother brought me forth from the caves of Arbela whither we had been sent for refuge, behold, where Sepphoris had stood, there was not now one house standing; and I saw also the bodies of many of my kinsfolk, which lay unburied and crying unto the Lord for vengeance. Yet the Lord sent no avenger.

After this came tidings that the Parthians, which went with Varus, had laid waste the country in the south far and wide, and had slain our brethren with the sword; and that Varus had taken two thousand of my countrymen in Jerusalem and had crucified them, and among them Eleazar, the youngest and dearest of my mother's brethren. Then my mother led me to a rocky place not far from Sampho. There was a cave there, and only one path led to it, and that so narrow that no multitude of men could force an entrance, if one brave man withstood them. When we were come thither, my mother lifted up her voice and wept, and pointing to the cave she said, "In former times this cave was held by my mother's brother, Hezekiah by name. Six children he had; and he fled from Herod the King with them and with his wife, and here they took refuge. Now when the king could by no means drive Hezekiah hence by force, he offered much gold unto him if he would come forth from the cave quietly. But when Hezekiah refused, the king began to let down armed men by ropes from the top of the hill, with firebrands in their hands, to kindle fires at the mouth of the cave. Then when no hope of safety remained, behold, my mother's brother brought out his children, and slew the youngest with his sword in the sight of the king. Afterwards he laid his hands on his second child. But Herod, perceiving his intent, stretched out his right hand and besought Hezekiah to spare his children and to come forth in peace. But he slew the second also, heaping reproaches on Herod as an usurper and a son of Edom, sitting on David's seat; and he slew the third and the rest likewise, even to the sixth, and last of all his wife; and then he cast himself down the steep place and perished." Then spake my mother unto me and said, "The Lord do so unto thee, my son, and more likewise, if thou avenge not the blood of thy kinsfolk and of thy father." So it came to pass that, even from a child, I hated the very name of a Gentile with an exceeding hatred; insomuch that I should have accounted him blessed who should have taken the children of Rome (according as it is written) and dashed them against the stones.

There stood up at this time divers to lead Israel; but they were no true leaders of the people, and the Lord had not sent them. Athronges the shepherd, a man of great stature, and Simon, one of the servants of Herod the King, rose up in the south of Judah; but they both perished, and their followers were scattered. Again, about the time of the numbering of the people, when the decree went forth from the Emperor Augustus that all Israel should be taxed, there rose up Judas of Gamala. This was about the thirty-third year of the Emperor Augustus. The people came to him from all sides; and Judas taught them that it was not lawful to pay tribute to Cæsar, nor to call any man Master, save God alone. At that time I was some thirteen years old; and I saw him when, with a thousand men, he marched into Capernaum and burned down the house of customs there; and as I looked upon his face, and the numbers of his followers, I thought within my heart, "Surely the hand of the Lord is with this man, surely this is the Redeemer of Israel, even the Messiah to whom all the prophets bear witness, that he must arise and judge the land." But five Sabbaths had not passed away before he also had been cut off; and all the men that were with him were either scattered to their homes or slain.

Meanwhile, as I grew up, I was being trained by my mother with all care in the paths of the law of Israel; and according to the custom of my people, at five years old I had begun to learn the Scripture, and, at ten years, Mishnah; and I profited more than my companions in the study of the Traditions. But when I read how great things God had done in times past for His chosen ones, and how He had redeemed Israel by the hand of His servants Gideon and David, then did my heart burn within me; and I besought the Lord that He would repeat His mercies upon His chosen people, and that He would speedily send that Messiah of whom all the prophets spake, for the Redemption of Israel. Afterwards I questioned one of my teachers, by name Abuyah the son of Elishah, and I said unto him, "It is revealed and known before the All-seeing (blessed is He) that our will is to do His will: and what hindereth?" Then he answered and said, "The dough in the leaven" (meaning Gentile customs, which corrupt the customs of Israel even as leaven changeth bread) "and servitude to the Kingdom." Then I said, "Why therefore do we not rise up against the Gentile Kingdom?" But he answered, "Joseph, son of Simeon, busy thyself with the Law. Whosoever is busied in the Law for the Law's sake deserveth many things; and not only so, but he is worth the whole world. He is called friend, beloved; loveth God, loveth mankind; pleaseth God, pleaseth mankind. And it clotheth him with meekness and fear, and fitteth him to become righteous, pious, upright, and faithful; and removeth him from sin, and bringeth him towards the side of merit." Then said I, "But wherefore doth not the God of our Salvation bring freedom to Israel?" But he answered, "It is said, The tables were the work of God, and the writing was the writing of God, graven upon the tables. Read not *charuth*, graven, but *cheruth*, freedom; for thou wilt find none free, save only them which be occupied in the learning of the Law. For whoso is occupied in learning the Law, behold, it magnifieth him and exalteth him over all things."

Then I applied myself more diligently to the study of the Law, and I observed Sabbaths and festivals, and practised ablutions with all scruple; and I became known among my companions as a sin-fearer, instructed in the wisdom of the Law, avoiding those lesser faults which are called the "Descendants," as well as those which are called the "Fathers"; insomuch that I would not even curdle milk on the Sabbath, because that had been declared by the decisions of the Wise to be a lesser kind of building; neither would I walk upon grass during the Sabbath, because that also had been pronounced by the Rabbis to be a lesser kind of threshing.

Also in the matter of fringes and phylacteries, and in smaller matters, even to the burning of nail-parings, I walked diligently according to the decisions of the Ancients. Thus in all things I strove to bear in mind the saying that "While in the written Law there are light as well as weighty precepts, the precepts of the Scribes are all weighty." I took little sleep, little merriment; I associated myself ever with the wise, and abstained from the company of the people of the land (for by this name the Pharisees were wont to call them that gave not themselves to the study of the Law); I settled my heart to study; I asked, and answered, and whatsoever I received I strove to add thereto. And it came to pass that, because I had a strength of memory more than was usual among my fellow-students, my teacher said to me, "Joseph, son of Simeon, thou art a plastered cistern, which loseth no drop of water"; and by this name of "plastered cistern" I became known among my fellows. And when I perceived that the Traditions said little concerning a Messiah; and that my teachers also said little, and had no hope, nor so much as a desire (for the most part) that a Messiah should ever come, but were wholly given up to the study of the Law; then I endeavoured myself also to do the same, and to put away the thought of a Redeemer.

Nevertheless at times the question would arise within me, "Wherefore do I serve God for naught?" For all around I saw the wicked and the scornful seated, as kings, in high places, and the poor and the humble trampled under foot. There was the name of peace among us, but it was no peace; for Satan was making war upon us under the semblance of peace. Everywhere defilement was taking the land by force or by stealth. Many Greek cities, called by the names of the great ones among the Gentiles, were built in the midst of us, such as Tiberias, and Julias, and Cæsarea Stratonis, and Cæsarea Philippi; and even in our city of Sepphoris, now rebuilt, we were constrained to admit Greeks to be our fellow-citizens. Theatres and amphitheatres, and games, and alien rites in honour of false gods, had been brought in among us. Images of living things began to be seen on every side, and even our coinage was defiled with the uncleanness of the Gentiles;' so that, in place of the vine-clusters and wheat-sheaf and star of Israel, we were forced to handle the semblances of Thracian shields and helmets, and the winged rod of enchantments, called by the Gentiles the caduceus. Moreover, as each year passed, our fears waxed greater and greater, lest at last the eagles of the Gentiles should be brought from Cæsarea into the streets of the Holy City itself, and lest the image of the Emperor should be set up therein. For the former Emperor, even Cæsar Augustus, was now dead, and a new Emperor reigned in his stead, whose name was Tiberius. But he attained not unto the former Emperor in wisdom; wherefore the minds of many were unsettled, the common people fearing lest the Romans should take away their religion, and the Scribes fearing lest the common people should incense the Romans by fresh revolt, and so bring destruction on the nation.

So it came to pass that by reason of my continual sorrow for the burdens of Sion, my heart was pressed down with care, and my trouble became too heavy for me to bear; and I found no peace, no, not even in the study of the Law. In vain I repeated to myself the saying of the Wise, "Whoso studieth the Law, he becometh modest and long-suffering and forgiving of insult"; and again, "The Law is acquired by long-suffering, by a good heart, by faith in the Wise, by acceptance of chastisements." I looked upon my countrymen in their servitude, and I could not feel long-suffering; neither could I attain to the wisdom of the acceptance of chastisements.

When I mentioned my trouble to my teacher, Abuyah the son of Elishah, he rebuked me for presumption; for he said that such doubts came of evil, neither would he hearken unto me. Therefore I turned to another of the Scribes, whose name was Jonathan the son of Ezra. Now Jonathan was older than Abuyah the son of Elishah, but not so learned. Howbeit he was of a more gentle and loving disposition. He said to me, "Beware lest thou follow the path of Elishah the son of Solomon." "What path?" I asked. Then Jonathan answered as follows: "It is reported that Elishah the son of Solomon was once studying the Scriptures, and he saw two men taking birds' nests. The one obeyed not the Law, but took the mother with the young; yet he went his way in peace. The other obeyed the Law and took the young only, but let the mother go free; yet as he descended from the tree a serpent stung him and he died. Then said Elishah the son of Solomon, "Is it not written, The young thou mayest take to thyself, but the mother thou shalt surely let go, that it may be well with thee and that thou mayest live many days? Verily the promises of God are naught, for the man that obeyed hath not lived many days, but the man that disobeyed is unhurt." Then said I, "And what answer was made to Elishah the son of Solomon?" And my teacher replied, "Whosoever obeyeth the Law, his days will be long in the world to come." Then was my heart comforted for a while, and I devoted myself even more diligently than before to the study of the Law.

CHAPTER II

For the space of nine or ten years I was content to give myself wholly to the study of the Law; but when I had now numbered thirty years, my doubts and fears came back to me again. While I sat in the school with the Scribe, and heard his answers and asked him questions, so long I seemed to myself righteous and on the path of righteousness; but when I came forth into the streets, or back to my mother's house, then seemed my righteousness immediately to have vanished away. At such seasons the learning of the Wise seemed to me not bread, but a stone.

Moreover, my heart was turned from some of the Scribes that lived in Sepphoris, even them that were counted as props and pillars of the Law. To Jonathan the son of Ezra I ceased not to pay honour; but Abuyah the son of Elishah I could not reverence, and others also like unto him: for they had regard unto the praise of men rather than to the love of God. As, for example, Abuyah, whensoever he was delayed by the crowd so that he came not to the synagogue in time for prayer, he would stand where he chanced to be, at the hour of prayer, praying in the middle of the market-place. When he walked, he walked with a mincing gait and with his eyes half closed, feigning to be given up to

the meditation of the Law, so that he saw no passer by.
On fast days he would ever look pale and worn, as if
with watching and hunger; and whensoever he met a
woman as he went in the way, he would shiver and
turn aside. It came to pass that on a certain day one
of his pupils asked him which was the most weighty
of precepts. Then Abuyah answered, "The Law of
Tassels"; and continued he, "so do I esteem this law
that once, because I had chanced to tread upon a portion
of the fringe of my garment, going up a ladder, I
steadfastly refused to move from the spot where I
stood, till such time as the rent had been repaired."
Another day, this Abuyah chid my mother because she
wore on her dress a ribbon that was not sewn, but only
fastened to her vesture. For thus, he said, my mother
transgressed the Law by bearing burdens on the
Sabbath. But by such teaching Abuyah himself laid
upon his pupils burdens grievous to be borne; and
among the Rabbis of Israel there were more like unto
Abuyah the son of Elishah than unto Jonathan the
son of Ezra.

Many things also in the traditions of the Wise seemed
to me not worthy of wise men, nor even of honest men.
I had joined myself to a certain brotherhood (who all,
or almost all, were Pharisees), such as bound themselves
to observe the Law with special strictness, and in particular to pay tithes of all things. The brotherhood was
called Chabura, and each of the brethren was called a
Chaber. Now it was the custom of us Chaberim to
meet on the Sabbath day at one another's houses that we
might sup together. But the space between our houses
often exceeded two thousand paces, which distance was

not to be exceeded by a man journeying on the Sabbath day. Therefore to a plain man it would have seemed that we could not sup with one another on the Sabbath day and at the same time obey the Law. But the Scribes were otherwise minded; and many of them, yea even of the strictest sect, escaped from the Law after this fashion. On the evening before the Sabbath, they would place small pieces of meat, distant two thousand paces one from another, on the road whereon they desired to journey. Where a man's meat is, said they, there is his home. So when they were come in their journeying to the first piece of meat, they would say, "Now I am at my home and may walk yet another two thousand paces." And so, walking from this home to other homes if need were, they walked as far as they listed. This mixing of distances they called *erûbh*, or "mixture;" and the device remaineth unto this day.

Again, if a man's ox were dying on some holy day, and the owner thereof desired to kill it; he was forbidden. But if he slew the beast and then took of the meat and ate thereof, yea, even though it were a piece of flesh no bigger than an olive, and if he said, "I slay the beast to provide a necessary meal," then he was held excused. Likewise, though a man might not buy from a butcher on the Sabbath, yet if he abstained from mentioning the number or weight of the things bought, and the sum of money to be paid, then he might buy as much as his heart desired and be held blameless. Thus he would say, "Give me a portion, or half a portion of meat," and the butcher would give it; and the buyer would go away, paying naught. But next day the money would be paid. And this was called not a sale, but a gift. After the same manner they did away with the Law which remitteth debts in the Sabbatical year. On the day of payment the creditor would come (such was the ordinance of the Scribes) and say, "In accordance with the Sabbatical year I remit thee the debt." Then the debtor was bound to reply, "I nevertheless wish to pay it," and the debt was paid, and the Law was made of none effect.

About the thirteenth year of the Emperor Tiberius, it came to pass that I (being now thirty-three years old or a little more) discoursed with a Greek proselyte concerning the Law. He said to me that it seemed to him better to disannul such ordinances as were not convenient (just as a man might prune a too luxuriant vine); and not to say, "I will obey the ordinance, but I will make my obedience the same as disobedience." His words pleased me; but when I reported this saying to some of the Scribes my friends, they with one consent rejected it. Abuyah the son of Elishah said, scoffing at my doubts, "The Law drowneth them that cannot swim." Then said I (repeating a certain saying of the Greek), "But water groweth bad if it be kept long in one vessel." But he straightway put me to silence saying, "Is this likewise the case with the Law? Nay, it is like unto wine which groweth better as it groweth older." Jonathan the son of Ezra also added in a gentle voice, "My son, thou knowest the saying of the Elders, the first of the sayings of the Wise: Be deliberate in judgment, and raise up many disciples, and make a fence to the Law. But thou, O my son, wouldst fain pull down fences. But if we begin to destroy a part of the Law, who shall stay the hand of the destroyer?

And in the end we shall be even as the Gentiles, which have no law. Is it not better to be too careful rather than to be too careless? Is it not better to have too many fences rather than to have too few? For to what is the matter like? Even to a man watching a garden. If he watch it from without, it is all watched. But if he watch it from within, the part in front of him is watched; but the part behind him is not watched. Be thou therefore careful to go in thine obedience even beyond the things which the Law requireth at thy hands; and watch the Law not from within, but from without."

There seemed much wisdom in the sayings of Jonathan, and I knew not what answer to make. For if to transgress the Law, even in the smallest matter, was to fall into destruction, then it seemed wise to fence round the Law, even as a man would fence round a pit; and not to suffer the unwary to go near, and peradventure to stumble, and so to be swallowed up. Yet I could not but perceive that it was not well for men thus to resort to the Law and to the Traditions as to a sacred oracle, even on those occasions and in those matters wherein the voice of the Lord speaking unto the heart saith clearly, "This is right, do this. This is wrong, do not this." For thus it must needs come to pass that men would pervert even the Law to the contradicting of the voice of the Lord. And so indeed it was with us. As, for example, the Law forbade fornication, neither did it permit us to marry a woman with intent to divorce her; but one of the Traditions, making the Law of none effect, told us that "If a man first tell her that he is going to marry her for a season, then it is lawful."

Other Traditions sinned yet more grievously in the cloaking of sins and impurities. Hence also the duties of children to parents (albeit upheld indeed by the better part of the Wise) were by many diminished, or even made of none effect.

Now I have heard certain Romans say that in their Law they also use the same devices to observe the letter and to break the spirit. But the mischief was, that our Law was not as the laws of the Gentiles, which concern naught save lands, and houses, and slaves, and the like, and which have not to do with the souls and spirits of men. The Gentiles could break the letter of their laws and sin not: for what sin was it to make a slave free by feigning to sell him, or, in disputing about a farm, to treat of a clod as though it were the farm? But our Law had to do with the supreme God, the Maker of all things, the All-seeing (blessed is He). Therefore to observe the letter and to break the spirit of His Law seemed to be a profaning of His Holy Name. Now I had been trained up from my earliest years to dread the pulling down of the fences, having this precept, as it were, engraved and charactered in my memory, "Whoso pulleth down a hedge a serpent shall sting him:" and I had been taught to prefer Sinai, that is, the teacher of the Law, even to an "uprooter of mountains," that is, to a teacher which hath understanding to remove all manner of offences and stumbling-blocks from the path of the weak ones. Howbeit, at times, after discourse with the Greek proselyte whom I mentioned above, there would arise in my heart this thought, that when the words of the Law seemed to contradict that which was right, then we ought to go into the presence of God and to say, "Thou, O God of righteousness, art righteous altogether, neither can it be Thy pleasure that we should be unrighteous"; and again, "Thou art a God of truth, neither can it be Thy will that we should lie with our hands in Thy presence. Therefore permit us in this case to break Thy Law. For Thy righteousness is greater than Thy Law." But the Scribes would not so much as listen to such words as these; for they said that scarce even a prophet durst speak so exceeding boldly. But when I asked them whether it might be that a prophet should arise in Israel, then the most said that it was not possible; for the Shekinah and the Holy Spirit had departed from Israel when the first Temple had been destroyed. Thus my words were an abomination unto my teachers, so that I hid my thoughts in my heart: but it was pain and grief to me.

Yet another trouble was added to me. For as I grew older and understood more of the ways of men and perceived the thoughts of men's hearts, it seemed to me a strange and horrible thing that the Law of the Lord should be cut off from the greater part of the Lord's people: so that it was a current saying with the Rabbis that the common people were an accursed rabble which knew not the Law: insomuch that one of the most pious of our teachers, even Hillel the Great, said that no boor could be a sin-fearer, and that the people of the land (for by that name they called the common people) could not be pious. This, I say, seemed an horrible thing: yet indeed I could not deny that the Scribes must needs be right, and that the people of the land could not be pious, so long as to be pious meant to be obedient to the light precepts of the Law, such as the laws concerning the exact observance of the Sabbath, and concerning purifications, and concerning the consumption of nail-parings, and the like. For the knowledge of all these things was not to be obtained save by men of leisure, that could give their time, and settle their minds to the study of such matters: and how was this possible for them that must needs earn their bread with the sweat of their brow, to wit, the sailors and fishermen, the vine-dressers and ploughmen, the dyers and glassmakers; who all were called of the Scribes "the people of the land"? So it was borne in upon me that our Law was a Law for the schools, but not for the lives of men; and for Scribes, but not for the whole nation. Then my heart sank within me, and I remembered the words of the Prophet, how that a time shall come when men shall no longer teach each one his neighbour, saying, Know the Lord; but all shall know Him from the least even to the greatest; and I wondered if it would please the Lord to bring such a time as that to Israel, and to make His Law clear to all our nation, yea, even to the poor and simple, even to the people of the land.

Others that did not observe the Law so exactly as I did, nor felt the burdens thereof so sorely, were nevertheless ill pleased that the Scribes did naught to free them from the yoke of the Gentiles. Of these some dwelt in Judæa, and a few in Peræa; but the more part dwelt in Galilee, insomuch that the sect of Patriots was known by the name of Galileans. There were also living among us James and John, the two eldest sons of Judas of Galilee, and their youngest brother Manahem. To these, for the sake of their great father, we all had

C

respect. Many also (like myself) were ever in a readiness to avenge upon the Romans the blood of kinsfolk shed in the Galilean wars. Hence it came to pass that in Galilee more than in any region of Syria, the minds of men were ready for revolt against the Romans, and waited but for the ripening of occasion.

Now it came to pass that in the fourteenth year of Tiberius Cæsar, there arose a quarrel between the Tetrarch of Galilee and his father-in-law, the King of Arabia; because the Tetrarch had behaved ill to the King's daughter his wife, and sought to divorce her. Then it seemed good to some of my friends to join the army of Antipas the Tetrarch, to the intent that they might thereby gain experience in war; but others spake against it, saying that it was not lawful to take up arms for the unjust against the just.

At this time also a rumour went forth that a new prophet had of late appeared, John by name, the son of Zachariah a priest, who was calling the whole of Israel to repent and to be purified with baptisms, prophesying that the Lord would soon send the Deliverer of Israel, or Messiah: for by this name of Messiah, the Deliverer that was to come (of whom the prophets had prophesied) was commonly known among us. Some said that John himself was the Messiah; others denied it, but said that the Lord had sent down Elias from heaven, and that John was Elias. Many other rumours also were noised abroad, and this rumour prevailed most, that "One from the East would come forth to rule the world," which saying had spread even to Italy and Spain: and we in Galilee thought that this conqueror from the East would be our Messiah. Thus, the hearts of all men everywhere being in expectation, it came to pass that many of my friends (who were the leaders of the sect called the Patriots or Galileans), having purposed these many weeks to hold a council, determined at this time to confer together in a little valley between Sepphoris and Nazareth, there to resolve what should be done.

Most of those present were from the inland parts of Galilee: of these Barabbas, and one other, were from Jotapata. Only Hezekiah, the son of Zachariah (a Scribe, who was thought to be well affected towards the Galileans), came from Jerusalem. And from Capernaum came my cousin Baruch, the son of Manasseh, with three others. There were present also from the region of Gaulonitis James and John and Manahem, sons of the famous Judas of Galilee. James the son of Judas spake first, giving his judgment for war, and saying that Israel had slept too long: "For while we sleep," said he, "the leaven spreadeth; Greek cities cover our land; our own cities are being defiled with Gentile abominations. They are stealing from us even our language. No man may earn a living in Galilee now, unless he speak Greek. With Greek theatres and amphitheatres, and baths, and market-places; with Greek pictures and images, and feasts and games; with Greek songs, and poems, and histories, they purpose, by easy degrees, to beguile the hearts of our young men from the religion of their forefathers. Our princes are Edomites in the pay of Rome. Our rich men long for the fleshpots of Rome, and call themselves by the name of Herod. Our Scribes, our wise men, cry peace when there is no peace, and wink at the payment of tribute. Publicans and harlots bring down the wrath of God upon the nation, and go unpunished. All these things are as the meshes of the net wherein Rome is encompassing our city. And lo, the fowler layeth the net and the silly bird stayeth still." Then Baruch said: "But is it so indeed that the Romans would blot out our religion? Do they not suffer all religions? The Gauls, the Spaniards, the Numidians, Egyptians and Scythians, all worship divers gods: so have I heard from a Greek merchant at Capernaum; and this, without let or hindrance from the Romans."

"Nay," cried Barabbas, "but thou seest not that the Roman suffereth all false religions and hindereth them not; but he hateth the worship of the true God of Israel. For this alone putteth other gods to shame. The Syrians and the Egyptians scruple not to worship the Roman gods, besides Astarte and Osiris, and to offer incense to the emperor of Rome, to boot. But the children of Israel will bow down to no false god, neither offer they incense before the image of the emperor. Hence cometh it to pass that the Romans hate our religion and would fain destroy it. James therefore speaketh the words of truth; and whoso speaketh otherwise allegeth naught but pretexts of delay and cowardice."

"Peace, Barabbas," said John, the son of Judas; "we meet to hold conference, not to cast reproaches. Nevertheless, my judgment goeth with my brother, that our choice lieth between lingering perdition and speedy deliverance. Hereof this is proof. But lately I was at the Holy City, not many days before the Passover; and there went abroad a rumour that the Procurator Pilate was minded to bring the eagles of the legions from Cæsarea to Jerusalem, yea, even into the streets of the Holy City. Then the Priests, even the Chief Priests, yea, even the whole Council, fell down at Pilate's feet, if perchance he would change his purpose. Multitudes ran together round the Prætorium. In vain did they pray and were disquieted. Under the cloak of night the procurator brought in the Abomination. Then all the men of Jerusalem, and all the pilgrims which had come together from the uttermost parts of the earth, clothed themselves in sackcloth, and sat down in the streets about the palace, with ashes on their heads after the manner of suppliants; crying aloud that they would sit there for ever rather than endure the presence of the Abomination. But when Pilate saw all the streets of Jerusalem thronged, so that no one might pass night and day, and all business was at a stand, did he yield from his purpose? Nay, he gave orders that the armed cohorts should beset the streets around us, threatening to smite us with the sword if we should not straightway void the streets. And when we would not, then went the word forth from the captains to draw the swords; and the swords were drawn, and the soldiers were in act to fall upon us. But we uncovered our necks and held them out to the soldiers, crying 'Give us death rather than defilement.' So at the last, but not till blood had been shed, the procurator gave consent that the images should be sent back. Suppose ye that this was a little matter, naught but an error in judgment of the procurator? Would a procurator have dared to risk the peace of the whole province for a little matter? It was no little matter. Pilate did what he did, not of himself, but at the express instance of the emperor; to prove the limits of our slavishness, and to force us into defilement and into the worship of the Abomination."

Hereat there was a general applause; but he, not heeding it, continued, "If ye be of one mind with me that the hour is come to smite with the sword; then how and where? I say, let certain of us join ourselves to the army of the Tetrarch, which even now maketh ready to march against Aretas. Thereby we shall gain experience of war, and, as I hope, win over some of the army to our side. As for the tyrant's guards, the Gauls, Germans, and Thracians, they are bought with his money, so that we have no hope of them; but by far the larger part of the army consisteth of our own countrymen; and many of them may revolt on our side; as they did with Simon against Archelaus, and some also helped Athronges, whom men call a rebel. Meantime, let the rest of us make ready our friends in our several cities to take up arms next Passover. They in Jerusalem will attack the garrison there, others break open the armoury at Sepphoris and in Masada. On the same day our countrymen in Joppa, Cæsarea, and Ptolemais will attack and drive out the Greeks. Then will rise a flame of war from one end of Syria to the other. Our rich men, even the Herodians, seeing all the people to be of one mind, will stand with us; and having Israel with us as one man, doing battle for the name of the true God against the gods of the Gentiles, doubt not but we shall have also the sword of the Lord on our side, as in the days of Gideon."

The applause was now yet louder than before; and at first it seemed as though the whole assembly were minded with one consent to obey the words of John the son of Judas of Galilee. But one of the companions of Hezekiah, Levi by name, an old man and greybearded, rose up presently and said that the hour had not yet arrived, because, said he, the Sabbath was not yet duly observed, and the wrath of the Lord still weighed upon Israel. Then Barabbas answered with indignation, saying that it was only the rich and delicate, or else they that were enfeebled with old age, who were thus content to be the slaves of idolaters.

Upon this Hezekiah the Scribe stood up to speak: "These young men of Galilee gladly make mention of the old times of Gideon and David, yet do they not themselves imitate the old times in having respect unto old age. For even though Levi were old and enfeebled, yet what saith the Tradition? 'Old age, though it be broken, is yet to be held in reverence, even as the broken tables of the Law were kept in the ark of the Lord.' But what meaneth this youth of Jotapata, when he calleth my friend and companion Levi, the son of Ezra, delicate or enfeebled; and all because the advice of Levi is not the advice of Barabbas? Hear, O ye young men of Galilee, the words of Levi are true: the hour hath not yet arrived. 'What hindereth?' ye ask. I answer in the words of the Wise, 'The dough in the leaven.'

"I also, like John the son of Judas, will give proof of my words; but do ye, being Galileans, incline your ears to the saying of a Galilean, according to the proverb, 'A Galilean said When the shepherd is angry with his flock, he appointeth for their leader a blind bellwether.' Note therefore the leaders of Israel, which have risen up against the Romans of late. Hath God sent them in anger or in mercy? Have they been blind bell-wethers, or endowed with sight? I say naught of Judas of Gamala, in the presence of his sons: but Judas the son of the robber Hezekiah, how went it with him? He thought in his heart that he was a second Joshua, and that the waters of Jordan would part at his word. But who knoweth not his miserable end? As also the end of Athronges: who aimed at the kingdom because, forsooth, he was in stature a second Saul. Simon also, the slave of Herod the king, when he had shewn forth his valour by destroying the king's palace at Jericho, became a portion for foxes at Amathus, and his head was cast before the feet of the conqueror. Answer then unto me, ye young men. Hath the Lord sent Simon the slave, and Athronges the shepherd, and Judas the son of the robber, in mercy or in wrath?

"Nay, but since shame hindereth your answering, I, even I, a man of Judæa, will answer for you, according as it is said, 'From Judæa grain, from Galilee straw, from Peræa chaff.' The Lord sent these men in wrath. All these were blind bell-wethers, blinded by the lust of fame or gain. But do ye therefore wait for the true leaders whom the Lord your God will send? Leave it to this young man of Jotapata to follow any knave that may chance to call himself the Redeemer of Israel because, forsooth, he may be a head taller than his neighbours, or may have dreamed a dream, or may perchance have gained some knowledge of herbs or unclean spirits.

"Even now they say there hath appeared in the southern parts (so I heard, coming but now from Jericho) one John the son of Zachariah, concerning whom I judge (if he be indeed a true prophet and no deceiver) that he is either the prophet spoken of by Moses, or else Elias. For that Elias is to come again we all know, because it is so written; and that the prophet like unto Moses must needs appear, this also the Scriptures tell us: but that other prophets should appear is not written, neither is it likely; for the age of prophets is past. But whether this John be Elias or whatever else, meet it is that we go to him; for he may perchance reveal to us what it is our wisdom to do. If ye ask 'What shall be the sign of the true prophet?': I answer, it is written in our traditions, 'A false prophet may shew signs on earth and in the deep; but a sign from heaven he cannot shew.' Wait therefore till the sign from heaven shall be vouchsafed, revealing the true Prophet, whom it will be our wisdom to obey, and for whom (during this present) it is our wisdom to wait."

When Hezekiah had made an end of speaking, James the son of Judas was sore displeased at his words, and made as if he would have spoken in answer; but John (who was of a gentler disposition) prevented his brother, and said that Hezekiah gave good counsel. For he, like the rest of us, had been moved by the mention of John the Prophet. So in the end it was determined according to the words of Hezekiah the Scribe; and we brake up without resolving anything further, except that we would go straightway, so many of us as conveniently could, to Bethany beyond Jordan, where the prophet was baptizing. But on the morrow and on the day after, when I spake to my friends and acquaintance concerning John the son of Zachariah, it was a marvel to see how greatly the hearts of all men were stirred at the thought of a new prophet in Israel. For that after so many hundreds of years a prophet should arise in Israel (none having prophesied since the time of Malachi, the last of the prophets, more than four hundred years ago) this seemed a marvellous thing and well nigh impossible, and almost as if a man should rise again from the dead. For the prophets were counted as it were dead and out of mind in Israel, meet to be reverenced for their past words, but not to be hoped for in the time to come. For this cause were we much moved by the mention of the name of John the son of Zachariah. And as the Prophet Elias from the top of Carmel looking out into the Great Sea and discerning a cloud no bigger than a man's hand, foretold the imminent storm, so did all we in Galilee, on the first breath of the rumour of the coming of a prophet, begin to forebode in our hearts of the coming of one that should be no common prophet; but, in all likelihood, Elias from the dead; or else one greater than Moses, to give us perchance a new Law and a new Kingdom.

CHAPTER III

ON the fourth day, I set out in company with Baruch my cousin, the son of Manasseh, my father's brother, intending to go to Capernaum, and thence to take ship for Gamala, where we were to meet James and John the sons of Judas of Galilee ; and so to journey all together to Bethany, where the prophet was. When we were come to Capernaum, we tarried two days in the house of Manasseh : and the second day was the Sabbath. Now the house of Manasseh was nigh unto the wharf, so that nothing stood between it and the lake.

It happened that I was sitting on the house-roof and the sun wanted yet an hour or two of setting ; and a tumult arose on the beach below, between a Greek merchant and certain of the townsmen. Word had come to the Greek that his son was sick in Bethsaida and nigh unto death : so he had besought certain of the sailors that they would launch their ship and put out to sea, although the sun had not yet set ; to the intent that he might pass over with all speed, if perchance he might see his child before he died. The sailors were persuaded by the man's prayers and gifts, and were preparing their vessel to launch it. But the inhabitants, those of the more devout sort, coming together with stones and staves, threatened the sailors, and forced them to cease, declaring that not a boat should leave the strand till the Sabbath should be ended.

The air was calm and still so that the merchant's words came up even to my ears, as he pointed again and again to the coast over against us : " Surely your God will permit you to do this service of kindness. Yonder is my son, mine only son, dying as if within sight of his father. Strangers will receive his last breath, and close his eyes. I beseech you, as ye are fathers, have compassion on a father who must soon be childless." So saying the Greek beat his breast and tore his hair; but in vain. The ruler of the synagogue, who had gathered the multitude together, would not listen to his entreaties; and he departed, weeping and wailing and calling upon his gods in vain.

Then the ruler of the synagogue, seeing the crowd running together, exhorted them to a more strict observing of the Sabbath, declaring that the breaking of the Sabbath was the principal cause of the wrath of God with His people, and of the delay of the Redemption of Sion. He went on to speak of the blessing of the Redemption, and he besought the people to do what lay in them to hasten it forward, by raising up the fences of the Law, and by constant and scrupulous obedience. "Let all repent," he said, "of former slackness and misdoings; for the Lord your God is merciful, long suffering, slow to anger, and of great kindness, and repenteth Him of the evil. To Him belong mercies and forgiveness, though ye have rebelled against Him."

By this time a great multitude was come together, and in the uttermost parts of the throng stood certain tax-gatherers (among whom was the principal receiver of customs in Capernaum, by name Matthew the son of Alpheus), with certain of the looser sort, men and women, outcasts from the synagogue : which had been cast forth, some for weighty offences, but some for light, according to the custom of our Scribes. These had approached, as it seemed to me, because they had heard mention of "mercy," and "forgiveness"; and their faces were somewhat sad, as if they also would fain have drawn near unto the God of Israel, that they might receive forgiveness of sins. But the ruler of the synagogue, catching sight of them, drove them away with reproaches, reviling them as children of Satan. "Even your alms," he cried, "we trample under our feet; away, extortioners and harlots, fit food for fire and worms!"

They departed in haste amid the scoffs and curses of the crowd. But their countenances changed as they went, and there seemed no more thought of repentance in them; for they hardened their faces as flint stones because of the reproaches of the chief ruler. Then it came into my heart that the ruler of the synagogue erred, in that he drove away the sinners that would fain have drawn nigh unto the Lord. And not only he, but all our Rabbis and Scribes seemed to be in the same error, because they drove away instead of bringing nigh. For even the words of the Wise tell us that peace is to be proclaimed to the far-off as well as to the near; and to the far-off first. Moreover the words of the Prophet Ezekiel came to my mind, that if the wicked turned from his wickedness and did that which was lawful and right, he should live. Now the ruler of the synagogue had himself also used words like unto these; yet his acts had not been like unto his words. For after that he had spoken of God as merciful and forgiving, he had driven away the sinners as though God were unmerciful and unforgiving. Therefore he had on his lips the wisdom of the Law; but in the thoughts of his heart and the works of his hand there was no wisdom. Then I repeated to myself the tradition of the Wise, "Whoso hath much wisdom and little works, to what is he like? Even to a tree whereof the branches be abundant but the roots poor and thin: and the wind cometh and uprooteth it and overturneth it." Truly, said I, the wisdom of the Scribes is like unto a tree whereof the roots suffice not for the branches.

Then began I to consider with myself what would be the doctrine of John the son of Zachariah as touching forgiveness and repentance; and it was borne in upon my mind that we lacked, not the true doctrine of forgiveness (for this we had already in the Law and the Traditions), but somewhat beyond the reach of doctrine; albeit, what it was, I did not yet understand. Also methought we had need of some new kind of wisdom that should avail, not only for Scribes and lawyers but also for the people of the land, for ploughmen and fishermen, yea, perchance even for tax-gatherers and sinners. Then behold, as I mused, methought all the precepts of the Law and of the Traditions lay scattered about on the beach, like so many dry bones (according to the vision of the Prophet Ezekiel), and there they lay, awaiting, till the breath of the Spirit of God should blow upon them and give them life. And, in my musing, I saw One coming, and his face was as bright as the morning star, and the breath of the Lord breathed from his mouth, and he came forward to the bones for to breathe life into them; and I spake aloud and said, "Perchance John the son of Zachariah is the Messiah, and will breathe life into these bones."

But while I thus mused, came Baruch behind me and touched my shoulder, and pointed to the crowd and said, "See, the sun has now just set; and the people are following the exorcist yonder. Shall we not go with them? He is no common exorcist, but by means of certain herbs known only to himself he can draw an evil spirit out of the nostrils of the possessed; and this hath he done many times this week in the presence of certain of the most notable people in Capernaum, insomuch that all men here do hold him in great esteem. And even now he goeth to cast out an evil spirit from Raphael, the son of one of our neighbours: who hath been possessed now these two years."

So lost was I in thought that, while Baruch was speaking, I scarce understood the purport of his words. But shouts and shrieks from below caused me to awake out of my trance. So I looked; and behold, a great multitude below, and in the midst thereof a youth possessed with an evil spirit. The youth was led by three strong men; and as he went, he shrieked aloud and struggled against them that led him. Close after them came one whose sorrowful countenance betokened him to be the father of the youth. Before them all went the exorcist.

Here in Britain it is a rare thing to see a man possessed with a demon. Therefore it is needful to say first, that in the land of Israel (and especially in the lowlands of Galilee along the coast of the Sea of Gennesareth, and also in the valley of Jordan), the unclean spirits prevailed mightily in my days, insomuch that I have noted as many as twelve or even more in a small town, such as Bethsaida. They wandered about the country half clothed or naked, assailing their dearest friends or strangers, or even themselves, with stones or other weapons, such as they could procure. They saw strange sights, demons and flames; their ears were filled with thunderings and roarings of beasts and voices of devils. A stench, as of sulphur and brimstone, was in their nostrils. Their bellies also were beset with worms, toads, snakes, or scorpions; which nevertheless destroyed them not. Two voices, the voice of the demon and the voice of the man, issued from the mouth of the possessed. Verily of all the diseases with which Satan hath been permitted by the Unsearchable (blessed is He) to afflict the children of men, this disease is the worst and cruellest; inasmuch as it poisoneth the very springs of love, causing the son to hate even the father that begot him and the mother that gave him suck.

What were the causes of this evil, wise men have asked, and have given no certain answer. They at Jerusalem said that it was a chastisement because of men's neglect of worship in the Holy Temple; and certain it is, that Gentiles and outcasts from the synagogue were more often possessed than the devout. Nay, I have known some (more especially women) that, having been possessed, were cured by the offering of sacrifice, or by a more constant attending on the worship in the Temple. Others said that it was a punishment for eating swine's flesh; others for dwelling in houses built amid tombs or on ancient burial-places. But others said that they which lived in the lowlands about the Lake of Gennesareth and in the valley of Jordan were more under the unclean demons; for that the demons possessed and ruled over waterish and low-lying regions. And so much is undoubted, that in the inland highlands of Galilee there were few possessed, and in Jerusalem none, or at least no number worthy of mention; but down in Jericho and Capernaum the possessed could be seen at the corner of every street.

Cure there was none, or at least no certain cure. Sometimes sudden terror or sudden joy availed to drive out the unclean spirit. I have heard of one Joachim the son of Levi, that was vexed with a dumb spirit for many years; but seeing some robbers about to kill his father, the string of his tongue was unloosed, and he cried out to them not to kill him. But no physic, nor no diet, was of any certain avail. This uncertainty brought great gain to many vagrant exorcists which wandered here and there throughout Galilee, their scrips full of amulets, charms, drugs, magic roots, and books of incantations. These men, with shouts and shrieks and uncouth gestures and dances, were wont to amaze the demoniacs for a time and to drive them into a kind of torpor; which torpor they called health and peace, and boasted that they had wrought a cure. At other times, by magic arts, they would persuade Satan to go out of the man for a short time, that they might obtain a reward. But in either case, the cure lasted no long time. For in a brief space the demon would awake again out of torpor; or if he had been driven out, he would return, and sometimes bring with him other demons yet more powerful than himself; insomuch that it was a proverb among us that it was better for a possessed person that the unclean spirit should not be driven out at all, than that, having been driven out, he should be allowed to return.

But about the causes and cures of this evil let others consider and dispute: I speak now of the exorcist in Capernaum. Going down straightway with Baruch, I followed him into a house not two hundred paces from the quay. When we entered, there seemed scarce space for the exorcist and the demoniac in the middle of the chamber, so thick stood the people together; but by favour of the master of the house, who was known to Baruch, we obtained place in the inner part of the circle. The father of the boy now came up to my cousin. "I have taken Raphael," he said, "to many exorcists before, but never a man of them was to be compared with this learned man. I have described to him the nature of the unclean spirit that possesseth my son, and he protesteth to me that he hath frequently driven out the like kind of demons, and that he is assured of success." Meanwhile Raphael, the boy possessed with the unclean spirit, was seated on the ground in the middle. He no longer struggled nor shrieked, but sat quiet, though sullen withal.

Two slaves now came forth, the first carrying in one hand a bucket of water and in the other a covered basket; but the second bore a chafing-dish. Now all voices were hushed, for the exorcist stepped into the middle of the chamber. "Many," he said, "of my profession pretend to drive out evil spirits, but they do not perform what they promise. But that ye may perceive how far Theudas the son of Eleazar differeth from such common vagrants and impostors, I shall not only cast out this unclean spirit, but I shall also give you proof thereof which ye shall see with your own eyes." He then bade the slaves place the bucket upon a shelf in the room where all could see it; but the basket and chafing-dish were set in the midst of the circle.

Perchance the boy began to understand in part that the exorcist was speaking of him; or it may be that from his father's anxious mien and troubled countenance he conjectured that some new thing was at hand. For he leapt from the ground, and shrieked, and blasphemed God, uttering obscene words, tearing his hair, and marring his cheeks with his nails; and but for the two keepers on either side of him he would assuredly have rent off his garments; and even with all their efforts they had much ado to hinder him.

But the exorcist threw a few leaves and fragments of root on the chafing-dish, muttered a charm, waved his wand, and then waited as though for an answer. Then frowning, he waved his wand a second time, and repeated a louder charm, stamping his foot on the ground, and then waited again. A deep silence fell on all in the chamber, insomuch that no one ventured so much as to draw breath; and even the boy ceased from his struggles and stared amazedly at the exorcist. But he, now standing upright and manifesting in his face that he had received an answer from the unclean spirit, turned from us to the possessed, and fixing his eye full upon his face, he cried in a loud voice, "Thou unclean spirit, thine hour is come. Thy name is revealed unto me, and thy shape likewise. In vain thou wouldst evade my sight, assuming the semblance of a long black worm.

Lo! by the mysterious power of King Solomon's ring and these strong roots I will draw thee out of the poor boy's nostrils in the presence of this assembly: and when I say the word, thou, obedient to my commands, shalt leave the body which thou defilest, and, in thy passage, thou shalt overturn yonder vessel of water. Dost hear me? Thy name is Ialdabaoth."

Hereat the demoniac shrieked and raved louder than before, and a deep voice, deeper than the voice of a youth, cried out from within him, "I am Ialdabaoth, the worm of darkness; depart from me." The crowd shouted, and the sorcerer, turning to us, "Sirs," said he, "ye see how the evil spirit is already half conquered; for he hath confessed his name and nature to be even as I foretold." Then turning to the boy and applying a ring to his nostrils, he cried aloud, "Come forth, Ialdabaoth;" and with very great quickness, so that the motion could scarce be perceived, (all the time shouting charms and incantations with a loud voice,) he drew forth from the nostrils of the demoniac a shape like unto a long black worm. Now verily the crowd shrieked as if they themselves were possessed; but the boy sat, not struggling, but still and pale, as though no life were in him. But the exorcist, turning himself quickly round to the vessel of water behind him, "Away," he cried, "away, worm of darkness! Back, Ialdabaoth, to the abyss! Back through the air: and dash down yonder bucket as thou fliest!" At the word, the worm vanished, the bucket was dashed down, and the boy fell, as it seemed, lifeless.

We all pressed in upon the youth, wishing to discern whether life were still in him, or no; but the exorcist waived us back, as one having authority; and taking the boy by the hand, he raised him up, speaking kind words to him and to his father. Soon his life returned to the boy, and the exorcist restored him to his father, whole and sound (albeit weak and pale), and, as it appeared, delivered from the unclean spirit. The father, weeping for joy, placed a heavy purse in the hand of the exorcist; who, at first, put it from him, as though he would have none of it. But afterwards, while he was receiving the salutations and greetings of them that were departing, one of his slaves, being urged by the father, took the purse and placed it in the covered basket.

As for us, it being now late, we stayed not to congratulate with the father of Raphael; but with all speed, made our way through the press; all the people around us praising God and marvelling at the power which the Lord had given to Theudas the son of Eleazar. But we hasted to the house of Manasseh to make ready for our journey; for we were to set forth early on the morrow. But when the morrow came, behold, Baruch was sick of a fever, and could not travel; and I tarried for him for the space of four days. But on the fifth day after the Sabbath, Baruch being now in case to travel, we purposed to take ship for Gamala, which lieth on the southern coast of the lake. For our intent was there to join ourselves to James and John, the sons of Judas, and so to continue our journey with them till we came to Bethany in Peræa where John was baptizing.

Now it came to pass that very early in the morning when we were to set out, the sun being not yet risen, I went to the house of Joazar, the father of Raphael, to inquire concerning the boy's welfare. And when I came to the threshold, behold, another stood at the door; but his back was towards me, so that I knew not who he was. And before I could accost him, the door was opened unto us; and behold, a sound as of shrieking and lamentation. Then we both listened, and lo, a deep voice from an upper chamber, and it cried, "We are Ialdabaoth! We are Ialdabaoth, the worms of darkness!" Then came forth other words of blasphemy and filthiness, so that I loathed to listen to them; and I turned to go back. But at that instant I heard the voice of the father bewailing: and the stranger delayed not, but entered into the house; wherefore I also, albeit against my will, was moved to go in likewise.

So I went in, following the stranger till we both came to the door of the upper room: and there I stood, and durst not enter into the chamber; for my heart was empty of comfort, neither knew I how to console the old man in his affliction. But the stranger that was with me, going forward, spake first of all to Joazar the father, and said some words of kindness to him. Now so it was, that when the stranger first entered into the chamber, the evil spirits ceased not, but raged yet more fiercely than before, crying aloud and saying, "Depart from us; let us alone; let us alone"; and the youth also rent his cheeks so that the blood gushed out; and he would fain have leaped up from his bed. But the stranger (whose face I had not yet seen), hearing the voices of the spirits, turned himself round from the old man to the son: and going up to the bedside he stood there, steadfastly looking at the youth. Now when he thus turned himself, then for the first time I beheld his countenance; and, as I remember, I marvelled thereat, and also at the manner of his dealing with the youth. For, first of all, when he looked upon the youth, his face seemed swallowed up with pity; and then of a sudden it changed again, and he stretched out his arm as one having authority, and as if on the point to bid the evil spirits depart, and this he did twice; but twice again he drew back his arm, as if changing his purpose. Then, at the last, the pity came back upon his face all in an instant, so that his features seemed even melted therewith; and he stooped down and embraced the boy, and kissed him; and, as I thought, he whispered words in his ear. But this I know not for certain; howbeit the boy, in any case, ceased from his raging and no longer struggled, but lay still and quiet, only muttering and moaning a little. Hereat the stranger turned himself to Joazar to take his leave; but I (perchance because my mind misgave me that I had played the eavesdropper, albeit, unwittingly, or for whatever other reason) feared to wait and meet the stranger; so I turned my back, and went forth in haste from the house.

When I was come to Baruch again, I held my peace concerning Raphael, lest I should stir up melancholy in my cousin, since he was freshly recovered from his disease. But, when we went on board the vessel, the sailors were not yet ready to sail. So I lay down on the sleeping-cushion : but no sleep fell upon my eyes. For there appeared ever before me the image of the demoniac Raphael and his sorrowful father ; and my heart was weighed down with the thought of their affliction. But I grieved not for them alone, but also for the daughter of Sion; who seemed to be, in a manner, possessed with an evil spirit, and to cry aloud for some one that should cast it out. All the deliverers of old seemed to be even as Theudas the son of Eleazar; and even as the demon had returned into Raphael, so that his last state was worse than the first, even so it seemed with Israel; therefore I besought the Lord to hasten the time of the coming of the true Redeemer of Sion.

As I mused, I began to consider with myself what would be the manner of the true redemption. Beside the demoniac, there appeared unto me the face of Matthew the publican and the faces of the sinners. It was borne in upon my mind that, even though every legionary in Syria were slain or driven out, and though the borders of Israel should be enlarged from the Nile to the Euphrates, yet if we still had amidst us sinners unforgiven, and Priests and Rulers with no power to forgive nor to convert, then of a surety the evil spirit would not depart from us save only for a season.

By this time, as I remember, we were but just putting out into the deep, and the sun was risen. And there came down certain fishermen to the beach to prepare their tackling for fishing: and with them there came one that, as I noted, was no fisherman (for he was not girt as a fisherman): and he walked down to the brink of the waters and looked out steadfastly to the deep. And so it was that, as he looked, the sun even that instant rising above the eastern mountains, shone suddenly upon his face so that I could see it clearly (though we were by this time a full furlong from the shore); and behold, it was the countenance of the stranger that I had seen that same morning in the house of Joazar. So I called to Tobias straightway and asked him who the stranger might be: and Tobias raised himself upon his elbow where he lay on the sleeping-cushion, and he looked, and knew him, and told me his name. And then first I heard the name of Jesus of Nazareth.

Again I lay down to sleep, but still no sleep would come to me: wherefore I took forth from my bosom the book of the prophet Isaiah, which I had with me, and began to read therein. And so it was that as I unrolled it, my eyes fell upon the place where the prophet saith, "To what purpose is the multitude of your sacrifices unto me? saith the Lord: I am full of the burnt offerings of rams, and the fat of fed beasts. . . . Bring no more vain oblations; incense is an abomination unto me; the new moons and sabbaths, the calling of assemblies, I cannot away with; it is iniquity, even the solemn meeting."

Now at that word, "the new moons and sabbaths I cannot away with," I ceased from reading. For I seemed to hear the Greek merchant weeping and crying to the sailors, "Surely your God will permit you to do this service of kindness." Then I called to mind the words of the Lord, "I will have mercy, and not sacrifice;" and behold, it came in upon me all at once, as in a flood, that our exactness in the observing of the Sabbath might haply be an abomination in the eyes of the All-seeing (blessed is He) whensoever it hindereth kindness and mercy. After this my eyes again fell upon the roll, and I read aloud these words wherein the prophet prescribeth the cure for the wounds of Israel. "Cease to do evil; learn to do well; seek judgment, relieve the oppressed, judge the fatherless, plead for the widow." Then I cried aloud, "Is not this a plain and simple path even for the people of the land, that all Israel should walk therein."

Now so it was that Baruch had come up while I was thus reading and speaking aloud; and I knew it not. So he answered and said, "Thou speakest well; notwithstanding I have heard a certain Greek of mine acquaintance in Capernaum say that virtue cannot be taught; for that some men have their hearts inclined by nature to do well, but others to do ill; so that it availeth nothing to say 'Learn to do well.'" Then was I silent for a while, for methought the Greek said well, and indeed we needed, not so much that a new path should be made plain, as that a clean heart and a right spirit should be created anew within us, according as it is written, "Make me a clean heart, O God, and renew a right spirit within me." So in the end I concluded to wait till we should understand what new message the prophet John the son of Zachariah might bring to us from the Lord, if perchance he might teach us aught concerning the creating of a right spirit. But by this time our ship was come to Gamala; where we were courteously entertained by James and John the sons of Judas; and we abode with them three days. But on the fourth day we set out for Bethany of Peræa.

CHAPTER IV

As we drew near to Bethany, we noted many hundreds of travellers on the road, the most part on foot, but many on asses and camels; for rich as well as poor were journeying to the new prophet. A full score of Scribes went past us in the space of an hour; there were also some soldiers going to Machærus; here and there was a tax-gatherer; and Baruch took note of certain that were sinners, outcasts from the synagogue of Capernaum. We had now been journeying for a day and a half; and toward the end of the second day, we began to see the valley of Jordan right over against us. Going down a little further, we perceived that there was a great multitude gathered together near the bank of the river; and presently we could clearly discern the prophet himself.

Around him stood men in white garments awaiting purification; at a somewhat greater distance, the mixed multitude hearkening to his words. John himself, wearing no tunic, but clad only in a rough mantle of camel's hair with a girdle of untanned leather, was sitting upon a rock, and thence he was speaking to the people in a clear voice, whereof the sound (though not as yet the meaning) was borne up even to our ears. For a while we stood still, with one consent, marvelling at the sight; for there had not been a prophet in Israel for four hundred years and more; but presently, riding down with all speed, we came into the valley, and joined ourselves to the multitude: and, albeit, we could not come very nigh to John, for the press, yet was there such a stillness among all the assembly, that we very soon understood whatsoever he said.

He had been speaking (this I learned afterwards from one of the bystanders) concerning the old wars and troubles which the Lord had sent on Israel; how, according to the saying of the Prophet Isaiah, the Lord had brought the Assyrian against the land as an axe, whereby He had cut down our chosen nobles and princes, even as a woodman felleth the choicest trees. Also how, in the days of the Prophet Jeremiah, the Lord had sent the blast of His wrath upon the people, and had winnowed away the unstable and faithless into captivity, even as a winnower fanneth the chaff from the wheat. The same things were at hand even now, he said: "Now also the axe is laid at the root of the trees; therefore every tree which bringeth not forth good fruit is hewn down and cast into the fire."

Hereat the multitude cried aloud, saying that it was even so; for indeed we all felt in our hearts that the prophet spake the truth. As the Assyrian axe in the days of old, so now the Roman axe was laid at the root of Israel; and unless the Lord turned away His wrath from us, the nation would be destroyed. But then a stillness fell upon the multitude, as we waited till the prophet should tell us what we should do to turn away the Lord's wrath.

Then the prophet set his face toward the men in white garments, and said to them that they should cleanse their hearts and not their bodies merely, and put away the iniquity of their souls, and he called upon them to confess their sins. He bade them also not to trust in their being children of Abraham, nor in the purifications of the Law, nor in the observances of Sabbaths and feast-days. If, said he, the tree was to escape the axe, it must no longer be barren : "bring forth fruits therefore worthy of repentance, and think not to say within yourselves, We have Abraham to our father, for I say unto you that God is able of these stones to raise up children unto Abraham."

Saying these words, he beckoned to the men in white robes that they should follow him. The multitude made way for them; and he led them down to a place by the side of the river where the reeds and thickets of willow-beds had been rooted up, so that there might be free passage into the water. Then he cried in a clear voice, " Receive the baptism of Repentance," and bade them plunge themselves beneath the surface. At the same time he offered up prayers to God; and we upon the higher bank said, Amen. When he had made an end of baptizing the men, he went up again to the rock, and thence he again spoke to the people ; and as many as desired purification went up to him there.

Now while the people were going up by courses, I also began to resolve in my heart that I too would go up in the order of my course. Yet had I sore misgivings in my soul; for it seemed as if I were on the verge of a great sea, launching out into the deep I knew not whither. For the teaching of this new prophet in no wise agreed with the teaching of the Scribes and Lawyers, whom I had reverenced; and if I went with him, I perceived that I must needs go away from them. Now it came to pass that a certain Scribe (who was with our company) perceived the reasonings of my heart, and that I was desirous to receive purification at the hands of John. Therefore he took me by the cloak, and held me back, saying, "Behold, if John the son of Zachariah speaketh well, the Scribes have spoken ill, and have taught ill. Yea, and all thy study of the Law, and thy painful meditations therein, and thy nightly watchings and weariness of the flesh have all been in vain. But wilt thou lightly forsake the teaching of the Law and the Traditions of the Fathers, and all for the sake of one new prophet, concerning whom thou knowest not as yet even that he is a prophet? And wherefore shouldst thou thus seek after prophets? Knowest thou not that the Inscrutable (blessed be He) decreed that, after the destruction of the first Temple, there should be no longer with us the Shekinah, nor the Holy Spirit, nor the Urim and Thummim; wherefore it is said, 'From the fourth year of King Darius, the Holy Spirit no longer rested upon the prophets.' But in the place of the prophets (who were not always with Israel) thou hast now the Scribes always with thee, according as it is said, 'Moses received the Law from Sinai, and the elders delivered it to the prophets, and the prophets to the men of the Great Congregation;' and it is also said, 'from the time that the Temple was destroyed, the gift of prophecy was taken from the prophets and given to the Wise.'"

His words moved me, and I restrained myself for the time. Yet on the other side there rose in my heart a certain Voice, which seemed to come from the Lord, saying, "The words of John are right, and they are simple, converting the soul. Moreover, they are fit for the people of the land, and not only for Scribes and scholars and pedants. But that he is a prophet, thine own heart convinceth thee; for even when thou hearest him, thou knowest that he speaketh not from himself, but that he is taught from above. And did not also the prophets of old speak like things, saying, 'Rend your hearts, and not your garments,' and bidding Israel not to offer sacrifice, but to shew mercy, and not to observe Sabbaths, but to do judgment and relieve the oppressed?" So between the words of the Scribe and the words of the Voice within me I was in a great strait. Howbeit for the time I restrained myself and did nothing, but remained where I was, giving heed to the words of the Prophet.

Now it came to pass that certain of the soldiers from Machærus went up: and all we in the crowd waited silently expecting that the Prophet would deny purification to these men, except they should first promise to depart from the army of Herod. But he commanded them only to abstain from robbery and outrage. Upon this certain tax-gatherers (whom the Romans call publicans) took confidence, and they too went up. And now indeed all we that looked on, expected that there should have been a great outburst of wrath and of cursing upon them, as upon traitors and apostates from Israel. But the Prophet received these also, and bade them exact no more than that which was appointed to them. To others he said that they were to observe that saying in the Traditions which enjoineth the doing of kindnesses; that is to say, they were to clothe the naked and to feed the hungry, and the like.

Hereupon arose a murmuring among certain of the Scribes from Jerusalem, who were standing nigh to the place where I was: and I heard the voice of Hezekiah son of Zachariah saying in an austere manner, "It is said, 'On three things the world is stayed; on the Law, and on the Worship, and on the bestowal of Kindnesses:' what meaneth this teacher of strange things therefore, to subvert the Law and the Worship, in that he maketh no mention thereof, but he exalteth Kindnesses to the skies?" Then another said, "He allegeth the authority of no teacher; why therefore hearken we to him?" But a third said, "Peradventure he is a prophet, and is taught of God." But Hezekiah made answer, "The time of prophets hath passed. Besides, he hath wrought no sign from Heaven; how know we therefore that he is a true prophet?"

These things spake the Scribes together, as we went back from the river to the place where our tents were pitched; for by this time the sun was setting. But all that night long my thoughts still beat on the doctrine of John; and I marvelled much whence it came that the people so flocked to John as to a prophet; yea, and that my own heart also was so drawn towards him, although he had wrought no sign in heaven, nor so much as driven out any unclean spirit. But the reason seemed to me partly in himself. For his very countenance, yea, even his gesture and carriage, proclaimed him to be, not a student of books, but one that was taught of God; and yet further the hardships that he endured, and the manner of his clothing and food (for he fed on nothing but locusts and wild honey) shewed to all men that he did not prophesy for gain. But another reason lay in his doctrine. For the doctrine of John was simple and just, commending itself to the consciences of men; not flattering any nor busying itself with abstruse matters; but fit for the work of life and the paths of busy men, able, as it seemed, to carry purity and righteousness even to the side of the plough, and into the ranks of armed men, and into the shops and offices of tradesmen and tax-gatherers. For this cause the teaching of John won a way into the hearts of men of every degree, save only certain of the Pharisees. So when I thought on all these things, I began to be convinced that he was sent of God.

But when I went forth on the morrow to behold the purification of the disciples and to hear the teaching of the Prophet, my heart was even more drawn unto him. For I compared him with Abuyah the son of Elishah, and with the ruler of the synagogue, that had driven away the tax-gatherers and sinners from the teaching of repentance; and it seemed to me that John was as much better than they, as light is better than darkness. For though he were of a stern countenance and austere in aspect, yet was the austerity of John in no wise as the austerity of Abuyah the son of Elishah. For Abuyah was sour and peevish, for that he ever loved to find fault, and because he desired to obtain occasion for rebuking, to the intent that he might persuade himself that he was better than others: but John seemed to be austere only because he hated sin. So I no more delayed, but went up with the rest, about

E

the second hour of the day; and I confessed my sins and received purification.

After we had been purified, I stood with the rest, clothed in white garments, wholly given up to meditating upon the new life whereto we seemed to have risen out of the waters. But I was aroused by hearing these words spoken with a great vehemency of anger: "Ye serpents, ye generation of vipers, who hath warned you to flee from the wrath to come?" Great indeed was my astonishment when, raising myself to see what they were to whom the Prophet was thus speaking, I discerned the faces of some of the most famous Scribes in Jerusalem. It seemed that they had been questioning him who he was and by what authority he taught these things. But the Prophet rebuked them with exceeding indignation. For he said that they were even as barren trees, full of leaf, but bearing no fruit, fit for naught but to be cut down and cast into the fire. Then they went backward, being put to utter confusion; but John turned to us that had been purified, and spake to us a second time as follows:

"I am not the Christ. Call not yourselves my disciples: for I myself am naught but a herald in the wilderness preparing the way for the Great King. But verily the King cometh. Therefore weep no more for the evils of sin. The rough ways of oppression shall be made smooth; the crooked paths of deceit and violence shall be made straight. Let the daughter of Jerusalem rejoice greatly, for her salvation is nigh. For the glory of the Lord draweth near, and all flesh shall see it together. Notwithstanding think not of me as your deliverer. He that hath the bride is the bridegroom, and the Bridegroom of Sion is the Redeemer, who shall espouse her in the day of salvation. I am but the friend of the Bridegroom. Nay, I am but his servant, not worthy to follow him as slave, nor to loose the latchet of his sandal. Ye ask in your hearts who I am. But think not of me, for I am as one that is no man. I am naught but a voice, even the voice of one crying in the wilderness, 'Prepare ye the way of the Lord, make His paths straight.'"

Then he warned us that had been purified not to suppose that we needed no further purification. Speaking of the old days of Joshua the Conqueror, he brought to our minds how our fathers had two kinds of purification; one inferior, with water, wherewith they purified things perishable, such as garments and the like; but a more searching purification, wherewith they purified silver and gold and other imperishable things, and this was with fire. Even so, he said, it was given to him to purify only with the washing of water; but one would come after him, the Messiah and Redeemer; and he would purify us with fire and with the Holy Spirit.

In the evening, when we, that had received the purification, conversed together in the inn at Jericho, there was much questioning whence the Messiah should come, and by what signs he should be known. But most of the Scribes did not believe that John was a true prophet; and Hezekiah protested that he ought not to be called a prophet, for he had wrought no sign, not even on earth, much less in heaven. But this he said not openly, for fear of the multitude; for almost all believed John to be a prophet.

E 2

But on the morrow, when we turned ourselves to go northward, heaviness fell upon my heart, and all things seemed flat and unprofitable. All our counsels of action, whether to join ourselves to the army of Herod, or straightway to rise up against the Romans, behold, they now seemed no longer the wisdom of men, but rather the vain talk of children. For what could Barabbas and the sons of Judas do, in comparison with the true Redemption which had been prophesied by the Prophet; or how could they avail to bring about the day of that Redemption? It seemed to be our wisdom to wait for the Lord, who alone could send the true Redeemer. And yet, on the other hand, how was it possible for one that loved Israel and longed after righteousness, to look patiently upon the servitude of his country? Hence I loathed the thought of living in peace at home.

When I returned to Sepphoris, I applied myself to labour and to study, if perchance I might settle my thoughts; but I could not, for I was divided between two minds. At one time I was minded to obey John and his teaching, and to set no store on the teaching of the Scribes, nor to give heed to what were called the "light precepts" of the Fathers, such as those concerning tassels and fringes, and the purification of vessels, and the observance of the Sabbath for things without life, and the like; and it seemed nobler to cast these things away, and to say that mercy, and judgment, and truth, and kindness, were the great commandments, and whoso observeth these, observeth all. But then at other times, when I considered with myself how frail and fitful a thing is man, how impotent for all good ends, and how easily led aside from the right path by passion and by ignorance, then I trembled at the thought of casting down the fences which had been raised by the generations of the wise; for I feared lest I should be guilty of presumption, and should fall, and be swallowed up with an utter destruction.

But in the minds of other men (and not in me alone) there was at this time much unsettlement and many searchings of heart. For many others in Sepphoris became ill-content with the teaching of the Scribes, and with the performance of the precepts of the Law. Some men even said that, when the Messiah came, there should be no more Law. So, if, even before, men had been expecting the Messiah and looking forward to the Redemption of Sion, much more did they do so now, after the preaching of John the Prophet; insomuch that the whole of Galilee became as dry fuel ready for the flame: and nothing was wanting save a spark of fire from heaven to kindle the whole into a great blaze.

By this time I had numbered thirty-four years, or something more; and it was the fourteenth year of the Emperor Tiberius.

CHAPTER V

Now it came to pass that about this time, at the beginning of the fifteenth year of Tiberius Cæsar, very early in the spring, the only son of my mother's eldest brother died in Alexandria; and my mother's brother (whose name was Onias) sent to my mother desiring her that she would suffer me to come to Alexandria to visit him during his affliction. He was a shipwright and a man of great wealth, possessing many corn-ships; and he was desirous to have adopted me for his son. But to this I would not consent, nor did my mother urge me thereto. Howbeit out of love for her brother, and because she thought it would be for my advantage, she desired me to visit my uncle for a time. I had no mind to remain in Alexandria, nor to leave my mother for long. But at my mother's bidding I was willing to go to my uncle for a season, if perchance I might comfort him a little.

Two days I spent at Cæsarea Stratonis waiting for the sailing of our vessel; and during that time my heart was moved within me, for that I saw on all sides the signs of the power and prosperity of the Gentiles; for a Gentile city this was, insomuch that, though the wall be on holy ground, yet was the city itself esteemed of our Scribes to be defiled and in a Gentile land. For the region round about was called the land of life; but the city was called the daughter of Edom. A great breakwater here protecteth the ships from the rage of the sea. Each stone therein is thirty cubits long, six cubits deep, and seven cubits broad, let down into water twenty fathom deep. Above the waters the breakwater is of the breadth of one hundred and forty cubits. Over against the mouth of the haven standeth a temple dedicated to Cæsar, and thereon two images of marble, very large, the one of Cæsar, the other of Rome. There is also in this city a theatre, and an amphitheatre, and a market-place, after the manner of the Greeks; and in all parts of the city there were to be seen baths, and gardens, and palaces, and porticoes, and other public buildings, all adorned, after the Greek fashion, with images of living creatures. When I looked on these things, Satan tempted me and said, "God loveth the Romans more than He loveth the children of Israel; and the wisdom of the Greeks is greater than the wisdom of Sion."

More, yea much more grievously did Satan tempt me when I was come to that great city, even to Alexandria. For here the streets were broader and the public buildings also larger and goodlier than those of Cæsarea; and in the streets and public gardens, yea even in the households of the Gentiles to whom my uncle commended me, I perceived the abominations of idolatry. For on every side were to be seen images and pictures of false gods and of demons which they called demigods and heroes; insomuch that the walls of the houses and the chambers, yea even the seats, and couches, and ornaments of dress, and utensils of furniture, and instruments of music were all painted or carven with abominable devices, setting forth the doings of these demons. But when I heard the interpretation of these pictures and graven images, then sometimes indeed my heart loathed them for their lewd and profane spirit; but at other times I was constrained to confess that there was a certain wondrous beauty and delight in the songs of certain of the poets of the Gentiles.

Here also men of all nations and religions, Jews and Greeks, Romans and Egyptians, and strangers from the East, lived all together in peace, making gain, and worshipping after the traditions of their fathers; and no one vexed nor oppressed other. All this troubled me, for I said in my heart, "There is but one God: how then doth the All-powerful (blessed is He) endure that the Gentiles should live thus prosperously in the worship of gods that are no true gods?"

My uncle's house also was a snare unto me and a temptation; for although he himself reverenced the Law, yet did he consort with many of our nation which scoffed at the Scriptures and warred against all sacred things, making it their delight to have the commandments of the Lord in derision, and saying to the faithful among their countrymen, "Do ye still make account of your laws as if they contained the rules of the truth? Yet see, the Holy Scriptures, as ye call them, contain also fables, such as ye are accustomed to laugh at, when ye hear others say the like."

When I rebuked these backsliders and revolters in the presence of my uncle, he spake kindly to me; yet did his words shake my faith. As for the Scribes whose teaching I had once so prized, he described them as meaning well, but not teaching well; and he called them "puzzle-browed sophists," and "those that busy themselves with the letter." The letter of the Law, he said, was full of falsehoods, such as the Greeks call myths, which were intended to warn the wise from cleaving unto the letter of the Law.

Again, he exhorted me not to despise the learning of the Greeks, nor the teaching of the Gentile Scribes, whom they called "Philosophers." "For," said he, "they enlarge and open the mind and help to the right understanding of the Law of Israel." But when I repeated the proverb of my countrymen, "The very air of Palestine maketh wise," and said that the Scribes in Galilee eschewed the Greek learning, warning their pupils against it, as against a net that entangleth the feet, and when I appealed to the Scribes of my uncle's acquaintance, hoping that they should have been on my side, behold, they were with one consent against me and with my uncle. For they all said that the Galilean Scribes spake as unlearned men, and that there was much to be learned from a certain Gentile philosopher called Plato; and one added a line from a Greek play-writer which saith "even from enemies one may win learning." Then was I staggered in my judgment, and bent to their opinion, so that I began to frequent the schools of the philosophers.

But great indeed was my perplexity and bewilderment when I found that these philosophers treated not of such subjects as I had supposed, namely of the nature of the soul, and whether it be mortal or immortal, or whether there be many gods or one God; but they questioned whether the world came together by chance or by design, and whether there be any God or no. Yet howsoever they differed among themselves, they agreed all in believing that our God was not the true God, and that the stories of the mighty works wrought by Him for our forefathers were mere myths and fables; or, if any thought otherwise, they held that our stories were no truer than their stories, and that Æsculapius and Hercules were far more worthy of honour than Elijah and Samson. Now a certain voice within me constantly testified that they were in error; for the righteous teaching of our prophets and our lawyers far exceeded anything that the Gentiles could shew from their philosophers or lawgivers. But I had been taught by the Scribes of Galilee not to trust to this voice within me, namely to my conscience, but only to tradition and authority; and behold, my traditions and the authority whereon I set store were rejected by these Gentiles: wherefore I knew not how to answer them.

It came to pass that, on a certain day, going from lecture-room to lecture-room, I perceived a great multitude passing into a hall in the Great Library, where there was to be a dispute between two philosophers; so I followed with them. One of the two belonged to the sect called the Stoics, and the other to the sect called the Epicureans; and the dispute was concerning the government of the universe by the gods, which is affirmed by the former sect, but denied by the latter. Now the contention had endured for the space of a whole day already, and yesterday the Stoic had delivered his arguments: but to-day the dispute was to be continued by the other, and so it was that, when I entered the chamber, the Epicurean was at the point to speak.

He began with reckoning up how many unjust acts, how many oppressions and sins, how many diseases and miseries, had been let loose by the gods (if gods there were) to prey upon the children of men. He set forth the diverse gods and goddesses worshipped by diverse nations; the gods of the Grecians and Romans, wrought of marble or ivory; the sword worshipped by the Scythians; the cat and ibis by the Egyptians. What, he asked, had they all done for their servants? Then he said that in a certain region of Syria there lived a nation which professed to reject the gods of other nations and to believe in one only god: but to what end? Their god had allowed their enemies to destroy his own temple with fire, and had given up his chosen people to be the servants of the Romans. He added a story of one of our learned men, whose life had been blameless and whose teaching had been of the One True God. "Yet," said the Epicurean, "what befell this teacher of truth in his old age? His god delivered him into the hands of persecutors, who placed his tongue between the teeth of a dog which had been made exceeding fierce with hunger; and so the dog bit off the tongue of the pious teacher, even that tongue which had ever spoken words of truth. What say we then? If there be a god, then he suffered this wickedness (for without him is naught); and therefore he is wicked. But if there be no god, then at least we are delivered from the constraint to believe that the Supreme Governor of the world is worse than the worst of men."

The people, who had been on the side of the Epicurean from the first, in despite of the interruptions of the Stoic, now loudly applauded; and when it fell to the Stoic to speak, he had little to say. If he discoursed of oracles as proofs of the divine foreknowledge, then the Epicurean asked who had ever been profited by oracles, bringing forward many dark sayings of the gods, which had led men to destruction ; and other sayings that savoured of manifest folly ; adding thereto jests and flouts of oracles drawn from the plays of the comedians. When the Stoic spake of a life after death, and alleged apparitions of the dead, then his adversary answered that the said apparitions were mere unsubstantial phantasms, such as appear to madmen and drunkards when they see all things twofold. Lastly, when the Stoic spake of judgment after death, and a final consumption of the world by fire, then the Epicurean demanded proof hereof; and he laughed at the stories of Minos and Rhadamanthus as nursery fables and bugbears to frighten babes withal. He also compared the Supreme Being of the Stoics burning up the world, to an unskilful cook that burneth the cake that he is baking.

Again the people laughed loudly, and shouted applause; but the Stoic, touched with choler, left reasoning with his adversary and began to revile him, calling him atheist and sacrilegious wretch, and other names ; which only made the people laugh the more. But I came forth from the theatre sick at heart and saddened, not more by the arguments of the Epicurean than by the faithlessness of the multitude. Then said I, "How know I that there is a life after death ? or who hath returned from the grave to bring back word thereof ? For it is written, 'Whatsoever thy hand findeth to do, do it with thy might.' But wherefore ? 'Even because,' saith the Scripture, 'there is no work, nor device, nor knowledge, nor wisdom in the grave whither thou goest.'" Then again I lamented that I had wasted my years in labour, and much study had been to me a weariness in the flesh, and I said, "It would have been wiser to have preferred mirth, for it is written, 'A man hath no better thing under the sun than to eat and drink, and to be merry: for that shall abide with him of his labour the days of his life, which God giveth him under the sun.'"

From henceforth my days and nights were busied with such questions as these, which crept into my soul against my will, and would not be driven out: After death shall I live no more, and will no one even once think of me, since infinite time burieth all things in forgetfulness? Will it be even as though I had never been born? When was the world created, and what was in the beginning before the world? If the world was from all eternity, then it will always be; but if it had a beginning, then must it likewise have an end. And, after the end of the world, what will be then? What perhaps but the silence of death?

Being constantly given up to such thoughts, I resorted yet more diligently to the schools of the philosophers, hoping to obtain some deliverance from my doubts: but I saw nothing but the contentions of orators, and the foyning and thrusting of rhetoricians, fighting not for the truth, but each desiring to prove himself more skilful than his adversaries. So it came to pass that I inclined, now to one, now to another. As, for example, at one time they that taught the immortality of the soul seemed to prevail; then again they that would have the soul to be mortal. When the former doctrine had the upper hand, I rejoiced: when the latter, I was downcast. Thus was I driven to and fro by differing opinions, and was forced to conclude that things appear not as they are in themselves, but as they happen to be presented on this side, or on that. My brain was in a greater whirl than ever, and I sighed from the bottom of my heart.

At the last I went to my uncle in my distress, and poured forth my troubles in his ear. But when he had hearkened to my complaints, he said, "It will be well that thou shouldst have speech with Philo; for he is our principal teacher here, and he will answer thy doubts." But I said in my haste and impatience, "Behold, I have resorted unto the wisest teachers in Galilee, and now, at thy word, I have frequented the lectures of these Gentile philosophers; but they have added nothing to me, for they are as dried-up springs." At this my uncle laughed, and said, "Suppose not, O son of my sister, that our Philo is like unto the Scribes of Galilee: for as well might a dog hope to lap up the Nile as that thou shouldst drain dry the wisdom of Philo the Alexandrine." So without more ado I accompanied him to the house of Philo.

When we entered the house of Philo, I admired first of all the homely plainness of his household. For though he were one of the foremost Jews in Alexandria (and there were nigh unto a hundred myriads of our countrymen in the city and the country round about) and kinsman also to Alexander the Alabarch, whose wealth was known to all, yet were there no signs of luxury, nor of pride in his house, nor in his furniture nor in his clothing: and his wife also wore a plain and simple garment without plaiting of the hair, or painting, or adornment with gold and precious stones; and in all the house there was naught whereat the strictest Pharisee could have been offended.

Philo received us courteously; and when I had opened to him at large all my doubts, he replied fully to them. I cannot at this time set down exactly all that we spake together; but this was the substance. First, I said that I was loth to be as one of the backsliders among my countrymen, who in effect gave up the Law, deriding it as a heap of fables; yet on the other hand, I confessed that after much study of the Law I had not been able to attain to righteousness nor peace. Thereto Philo made answer that he was not one of them that rejected the Law of Israel; for he diligently observed it, believing that it contained all knowledge and all wisdom; "and," said he, "I consider that Moses was the greatest and most perfect of men, and that he attained unto the very pinnacle of wisdom.[1] But as for the wisdom of the Greeks, it is but as a handmaid in respect of our wisdom; even as the slave Hagar was, in respect of her mistress and queen, Sarah. "Notwithstanding," added he, "when I speak of our Scriptures, I mean that there are two interpretations of every Scripture. There is first the outer meaning, which is as it were the body; but there is, next, the inner spiritual meaning, which is, as it were, the soul. Thus, for example, when thou readest that Eve was made out of the rib of Adam, or that the world was made in six days, or that God talked with Moses in a thorn-bush, the letter of these Scriptures is indeed fable, but the spiritual meaning is truth and life." Then said I, "If the letter be fable,

[1] See Note II.

why retain the letter?" But he said, "And if the body be unspiritual, why retain the body? As well cast away the body because it is not soul, as cast away the letter because it is not spirit."

Then I asked, "But how shall I attain righteousness?" Philo replied, "All men have in them a certain spiritual nature, in virtue whereof they are allied with the Word of God. Whosoever recogniseth the sins wherewith he is defiled, hath the power (if he will use it) of rising above his passions, and conquering his lusts, so that in the end, by repentance and by constant struggling after righteousness, he can follow after the virtues of the Father in heaven who begat him." Then said I, "All this have I done; for I have now these many years observed not only the words of the Law, but also the Traditions of the Elders; yet have I not attained peace." But he said, "Thou puttest first that which should come second; first aim after the virtues that have to do with men; afterward shalt thou attain the virtue that hath to do with God." "It would seem therefore," said I, "that thou dost not advise thy disciples to withdraw themselves from the world, after the manner of hermits." "Yea, but I do advise them," said Philo; "only first men should attain to the lower step before aiming at the higher. For first, they should study truthfulness, striving to love their neighbours, and to be helpful and gentle to all; for man should be gentle, and not savage, being fitted by nature for fellowship and concord. But after that thou hast attained to this lower stage, my counsel is that thou forsake thy home and thy friends, and thy wealth, and all that thou hast, and that thou abstain from business of state, and from all traffic, and that thou give thyself entirely to the contemplation of the divine essence."

Then said I, "Methinks, many of our Scribes in Galilee would not please thee; for they seek after righteousness by other ways, observing the smallest matters of the Law, and afflicting the flesh." "Tell such an one from me," said Philo, "when thou shalt see him perchance abstaining from food or drink at the times of eating, or disdaining the bath and the use of oil, or tormenting himself with a hard couch or with night-watchings, deceiving himself with this show of abstinence, that he is not in the true way to continence, and that all his labour is in vain."

"But what," asked I, "is this highest revelation of the essence of the Supreme (blessed is He) to which the soul shall at last attain?" Philo paused a moment and then answered, "Thou shalt attain to the knowledge of God, as mere being or existence." But I, not understanding him aright, said, "Thou sayest 'existence:' dost thou mean 'holy existence'?" But Philo answered with a smile, "How can we call Him holy who is holier than all holiness? But by 'mere existence,' I mean that which is known as existence and in no other way." Then I said, "May we not therefore call Him good? or loving?" "Call Him so," replied Philo, "if thou dost not believe that He is better than all goodness, more loving than all love."

Hereat my heart sank within me; for such a God as this "mere existence" seemed to me not a being able to love me nor to be loved by me, no more than if it had been a triangle or a circle. But presently I called to mind that Moses had named God the Father of the spirits of all flesh: and the prophets also had named God Father. Therefore said I to Philo, "And the name Father also? May we not give this name to God?" "No," said Philo, "except in order to teach the common folk; as when the Scripture saith that God chasteneth those whom He loveth, like as a father chasteneth his son. For God cannot change; neither can He feel anger, nor love, nor joy. But when the Scripture sayeth such words as these, it speaketh for the common multitude, even as when it saith that God spake or heard; or that He smelled a sweet savour; or that He awaked from sleep; or that He repented of that which He had done."

When I heard this, it seemed to me that I had come to Philo for naught; but I said to him, "Thou speakest of that revelation of God, which thou callest mere existence, as being the highest revelation. Is there then a lower revelation?" "Certainly," he replied, "for just as there is, in human life, the thing and the word that revealeth the thing, even so is there also on the one hand God, the true God, THAT WHICH IS, and on the other hand the Word of God, which revealeth God to the minds of men." Then I questioned him concerning this Word of God, or Logos (as he called it, using a Greek name): and he answered me fully, yet not so that I could altogether understand him. But this I gathered, that the Word or Logos was a second divine being, inseparable from the Father; and that by the Word was the world made. But sometimes he said that the world, as conceived by the intellect, *was* the Word, ("for," said he, "as a city, not yet being, is in the mind or reason of the architect thereof, so the world, albeit not being, was in the mind or reason of God";) and with these exact words he made an end of this part of his discourse, for I set them down at the time : "If any one should desire to use still plainer terms, he would not call the world (regarded as perceptible only to the intellect) as anything else but the Reason of God busied with the creation of the world; for neither is a city, while only perceptible to the intellect, anything else except the reason of the architect."

Then said, I "But how do men attain to the revelation of the Word?" "By the exercise of the divine Word or Reason within them," said Philo; "for all men have in themselves a ray of light from the archetypal Light, the Word of the Supreme Being. For no mortal thing is framed, nor could have been framed, in the similitude of the Supreme Father; but only after the pattern of the second deity, the Word. Now this Word can be received of all them that will live according to it. For the race of mankind is twofold, the one being the race of them that live by the Divine Spirit and reason; the other, of such as live according to the pleasures of the flesh. The universe therefore, apprehended by the reason of man, conveyeth the revelation of the Word. And this revelation, this heavenly food of the soul (which Moses calleth manna), the Word of God meteth out in equal portions among all them which are to use it. For the blessed soul proffereth her own reason as the holy goblet of true joy. But who can pour forth the wine of life, save only the Cup-bearer of God, the Master of the Feast, the Word? And indeed the Cup-bearer differeth in no wise from the draught. For the Word is the draught itself, pure and unpolluted."

Then it was borne in upon my mind, that in all his discourse (which inforced attention by reason of the beauty of his sayings, and because of his exceeding earnestness) he had left no place for the Messiah or Redeemer of Israel, whose coming had been prophesied by John, the son of Zachariah. Therefore I questioned him of this matter. But he smiled and said, "Trouble not thyself on this matter; for it is likely that no Messiah is to come. But it will come to pass, in the day of Redemption, that the children of Israel, which be now scattered over the earth, will be led from all parts back to the Sacred Land, by the light of a great light invisible to all others, but visible only to such as are to be saved." Then, seeing that I was of a sad countenance, he added, "Dost thou not perceive that the revelation of a Messiah would be as much inferior to the revelation of the Word, or Logos, as the revelation of the Logos is itself inferior to the revelation of mere existence, τὸ ὄν, or THAT WHICH IS? For the revelation of the Logos (that is of God known by creation) is through hope and fear; but the revelation of τὸ ὄν (that is God in itself) is through love. And the revelation of a Messiah must needs be a poor and low thing as compared with either of these. But thou shouldst aspire towards the highest revelation of all, even the Father of all, with a divinely inspired passion not inferior to the *enthousiasmos* wherewith the worshippers of the gods of the Gentiles celebrate their inferior rites."

The day was now far spent: so my uncle arose to bid Philo farewell. I thanked him with my whole heart: for righteousness and goodness breathed in his presence; and my spirit was refreshed while I heard him speak.

For the very voice of the Lord seemed to sound from him when he said that to afflict the flesh was of no avail without afflicting the spirit, and that the practice of virtue with men should go before the practice of virtue with God. But when I was departed from him, musing as I returned home, then I saw that the philosophy of Philo could in no wise give me peace. For it was not possible that I should feel that *enthousiasmos*, or divine passion, whereof he made mention, for such a being as Mere Existence : and methought I could feel this *enthousiasmos* for none save a man, or some similitude of a man.

Therefore my heart went back to that lower revelation whereof he spake, to wit, to God revealed through the world; that is, the Word : and this seemed to me more likely to give peace. But as for Mere Existence, albeit Philo called it the Father of all, yet had he plainly told me he meant this only for the unlearned multitude. And whereas he used one word, God, to signify two things, one thing for the learned, and another for the unlearned; herein, to say truth, his doctrine brought to my mind a certain tale of the poet Homer, which my uncle had but yesternight related unto me ; how a certain mighty man of valour, and a wise counsellor among the Greeks, Ulysses by name, deceived the giant Polyphemus, saying that his name was NOMAN. Wherefore, when Polyphemus said that NOMAN had blinded him, his brethren, the giants, thought that he meant to say that not ⁀a man, but a god, had blinded him. And even so Philo seemed to me, when he spake to the wise and learned, to call God *no man;* but when he spake to the foolish and unlearned, he called Him NOMAN, making them think He was a person.

But what troubled me in this revelation was, that it seemed not to leave any room or place for the Messiah, the Redeemer of Israel. And "Why," thought I, "should the Word reveal himself only through the world, and not through mankind? But if he revealed himself through mankind (which Philo also would allow), why might he not reveal himself through a Messiah?" All that night I lay awake musing on the same thing, and asking whether it might not be that Philo spake truth in proclaiming the revelation of the Word, and yet John the son of Zachariah might also speak truth in proclaiming the revelation of the Messiah. But after long tossing of the matter in my mind I concluded that there was no cause why the one should destroy the other: so I prayed that both might be true.

But as for my former studies, and my old strict observances of the Sabbath and of the precepts concerning the use of purifications and concerning the consumption of nail-parings, and concerning the wearing of tassels, behold, all these matters began to seem unto me things far off, forgotten, and childish. And though I knew not clearly whither to turn, yet I felt at least that to them I could return no more; for I perceived that, even if I became as perfect in these matters as Abuyah the son of Elishah himself, yet should I none the more attain to peace, nor could I find in them that food for want whereof my soul was an-hungered. Wherefore I was now resolved in my mind of this one thing, in any case, namely, that the observance of the smaller precepts of the Law could not gain for me that Banquet, or Manna, or heavenly Draught of the Word of God whereof Philo had made mention. But what the true Manna might be, or how I might attain to it, this I did not as yet perceive. For I was, at that time, even as a little child in a boat without oars or sail, which hath drifted out unawares far into the open sea.

CHAPTER VI

Not many days after my discourse with Philo the Alexandrine, when I returned from the Great Library to my uncle's house, a messenger was waiting for me, bearing a letter from Rabbi Jonathan. Opening it I read that my mother was suffering under a grievous disease, and being, as she thought, nigh unto death, she would fain see me before she died. So I straightway made all things ready for my journey, and having bidden farewell to my uncle, I set sail on the morrow from Alexandria, and on the fifth day arrived in Jerusalem; where, according to my mother's desire, I purposed to offer sacrifice unto the Lord, and to make vows for my mother's health.

The sun was well nigh set when I came to Jerusalem. But on the morrow, as I went up to the Temple through the narrow ways, amid the throng of them that sold oxen and sheep and doves, new thoughts and doubts rose in my heart, such as I had never felt before when I had gone up to sacrifice during the three great feasts. Methought the Lord must needs turn His face from so much traffic and disorder and defilement of His Holy House. On both sides of the gate Horæa, as far as Solomon's porch, were shops of merchants and stalls of money-changers. Even in the Court of the Gentiles, which is a part of the Temple itself, there were penned flocks of sheep and oxen, with drovers and salesmen. Pilgrims and proselytes from all parts pressed and thronged; buyer reviled seller, and seller buyer; from the stalls of the money-changers one might hear the clink of money mixed with the sounds of contention. The stench also of so many cattle, being increased by reason of the great heat, made the ill-savour of the place almost past bearing. Also I could not but marvel at the greediness of the sellers. For the Chief Priests had let out the right of selling offerings at a great price, to make profit thereof for themselves, insomuch that a single dove was sold for a gold piece.

Then, again, when it came to the offering of the sacrifice, I must needs wait for the space of an hour whilst others were offering up their sacrifices; and the Levites and priests seemed all in haste, and did their work rather as an handicraft than as worship; and many others were sacrificing at the same time, and the cries and struggles of the victims, and the smoke and reek of the fat, and the blood flowing on all sides, caused the place to seem rather like a butcher's shambles than like the House of the Lord. Now all this I had known and seen aforetime, yet had I never taken it to heart. But now there came to my mind certain words of Philo touching the sect called the Essenes, how they worship the Lord with an exceeding carefulness of purity: wherefore they think it not meet to sacrifice the blood of beasts unto the Lord, but they offer up their own hearts, purified so as to be a fit offering for Him. Also at this time (perchance because

I was but freshly come from the lecture-rooms of the philosophers of Alexandria, or belike because the Lord would have it so to be, willing by easy degrees to open mine eyes, and to reveal unto me His Messiah) so it was that I could think of naught but the words of Isaiah the Prophet wherein the Lord saith, "I am full of the burnt offerings of rams, and the fat of fed beasts, and I delight not in the blood of bullocks, or of lambs, or of he-goats." These words, I say, so possessed my soul that, even when the victim was being slain, I could not refrain from repeating them to myself again and again; albeit against my will, being fearful to pollute the sacrifice of the Lord. But though I made shift to dissemble my trouble until the sacrifice was ended, for fear of offending the priests, yet when I had returned to my lodging in the city, I could not forbear weeping; for behold, all worship seemed as vanity, and the children of men were in mine eyes as beasts of the field, void of understanding and given over to all folly; and God was He that had made them thus. Therefore I cried aloud in the fervency of my passion and said, "It is written, 'On three things the world is stayed: on the Law, and on the Worship, and on the Bestowal of Kindnesses;' and lo, I know not the interpretation of the Law; and worship is naught but vanity; and as for kindness, my heart is dry and empty of love, so that there is no kindness in me."

On the third day after the sacrifice, I came to Sepphoris. My mother was so far recovered of her sickness that she was no longer despaired of by the physicians. For the time, my joy thereat, and our rejoicing together (because the Lord had suffered us to look on one another again) drove away my former searchings of heart: which notwithstanding presently came back upon me. My mother took a delight in my continual presence, and that I should sit by her bed, expounding unto her passages of the Law; and many a time, while I was doing this, she would make mention of the title wherewith I had been honoured by Rabbi Jonathan, who had called me "the plastered cistern." But oftentimes it was not in my heart to find any words of comfort or hope, and when my mother longed for the draughts of the Law I felt that I was a dried-up cistern, and no longer full.

At the last, on a certain morning, my mother, having (as I suppose) noted my silence before, spake aloud reproving me, albeit gently, and saying, "Why flow not the drops of refreshment from the plastered cistern as in former days?" But I replied in haste, "Call me no longer, O my mother, a cistern. For lo, I am become even as a strainer, which letteth out the wine and keepeth in itself nothing but the dregs." Then my mother wept bitterly, thinking that she had angered me, and that I had spoken falsely; and I also wept, partly for that I had made her weep, but still more because my words were true.

Then went I forth hastily into the street; and meeting Jonathan the son of Ezra, and Abuyah the son of Elishah, I accompanied them. And we came to the well that is on the road to Nazareth, about a thousand paces from the town, and there we sat down to rest. For a time we were silent. Then I turned to Rabbi Jonathan and said, "Simeon the Just was of the remnant of the Great Synagogue. He used to say,

'On three things the world is stayed: on the Law, and on the Worship, and on the Bestowal of Kindnesses.' Now there was a certain young man which observed the Law, and worshipped duly in the temple. Also he clothed the naked, and buried them that lay unburied, and fed the hungry: but there was no kindness in his heart. Is such an one, therefore, in the path of righteousness?" Then Abuyah replied at once, "He is righteous. For it is written concerning the statutes and judgments of the Law of the Lord that whosoever doeth them shall live in them; but whether he shall do them easily or with difficulty, or gladly or sorrowfully, concerning this, behold, nothing is written." But Jonathan the son of Ezra was silent for a while, and said at last, "Antigonus of Soko used to say, 'Be not as slaves that minister to their lord with intent to receive recompense; but be ye as slaves that minister to their lord without thought of recompense; and let the fear of Heaven be upon you.'"

Then I replied, "True, oh my Master; but ought not the love of Heaven as well as the fear of Heaven to be upon us? For is it not said, 'Learn for love, and honour will come in the end'?" "Thou speakest well," said Jonathan, "and it is written also as the chief of all the commandments, 'Thou shalt love the Lord thy God, and Him only shalt thou serve.'" Then I said, "But what if a man feel no love of God in his heart? For I have met lately certain of the Gentiles, yea, and some also of our own nation, which have no love of God; whereof some even constantly say that there is no God. Yea, and even in mine own heart arise strange questionings as to whence I came into this world, and whither I am going, and before whom I am to give account and reckoning."

Then Abuyah brake forth again: "Joseph son of Simeon, busy not thyself with questions that are too high for thee: for it is said 'Whosoever shall consider four things, what is above, below, before, behind, it were better for him that he had not come into the world.'"

"Yea, but," said I, smiling, "it is said by the Wise, 'Consider three things, and thou wilt not come into transgression, Know whence thou camest; and whither thou art going; and before whom thou art to give account and reckoning.'" Hereat Abuyah arose hastily from his seat in sore displeasure, and he said, "Child, thou hast defiled thyself by going to a city of the Gentiles which is not a place of the Law; for it is said, 'Two that sit together without words of the Law are a session of scorners;' and again, 'Betake thyself to a place of the Law, and say not that it shall come after thee, for thine associates will confirm it unto thee: and lean not unto thine own understanding.' Howbeit, I thank thee, O Lord my God and God of my fathers, that Thou hast cast my lot among them that do frequent the schools and synagogues, and not among such as frequent the theatre and the circus. For both I and they work and watch: I to inherit eternal life, but they for eternal destruction." So saying he departed, and left me alone with Jonathan the son of Ezra.

Jonathan sat still by my side saying naught, but gazing up into the heaven, or else upon the trees round about us. For all around us were orange-trees and pomegranate-trees; the leaves thereof scarce to be seen for the multitude of white and scarlet blossoms; for the spring was now something worn. The fields also and the gardens and the hedges of cactus, by reason of the rains, were of a marvellous verdure, even above their wont. Behind us, at a little distance, stood a grove of olive-trees, wherein the doves made a pleasant murmuring: and birds of divers colours fluttered to and fro around the well. Nigh over our heads there were passing larger birds, flying in a long train towards the country of the Lake; and far off I could discern an eagle, like a spot, high up in the sky. Then Jonathan spake unto me and said, "My son, dost thou not remember the words of the Psalmist, how he praiseth the name of God because 'He sendeth the springs into the valleys, which run among the hills. They give drink to every beast of the field: the wild asses quench their thirst. By them shall the fowls of the heaven have their habitation, which sing among the branches. He causeth the grass to grow for the cattle and herb for the service of man: that he may bring forth food out of the earth; and wine that maketh glad the heart of man, and oil to make his face to shine, and bread which strengtheneth man's heart.' Doth not the sight of all this glory and beauty cause thee also to say with the Singer of Israel, 'O Lord, how manifold are Thy works! in wisdom hast Thou made them all'?"

But I made answer, in the bitterness of my heart, according to the words of the same Psalm, saying, "Thou hidest Thy face, they are troubled: Thou takest away their breath, they die, and return to their dust." Then Jonathan bowed his head and answered nothing, but I continued, "Did not the same hand which made the dove make also yonder eagle to destroy the dove? Did not the God which chose out Israel from among the Gentiles to serve Him, choose out Rome also to rend Israel in pieces? Thou speakest after the manner of Philo the Alexandrine, who saith that God revealeth Himself to us through His Word in the universe. But verily He revealeth Himself not so unto me. Nay rather, unsearchable are the paths of the Creator in the universe, and His ways in the world are past finding out."

Then the old man covered his face with his hands and wept; but soon raising his head he said, "Is it seemly that a son of Abraham should have so little trust in the Lord? Bethink thee of the times when the Holy Temple was burned with fire, and Judah led into captivity: did not all the Gentiles say in those days, 'God hath forsaken them'? Yet did the Lord save Israel out of the hand of the daughter of Babylon, and out of the hand of the Assyrian and the Philistine, as also out of the hand of the Egyptian, in the days of old. Commit thy way therefore unto the Lord, and trust in Him, and He shall bring the word of His prophets to pass.

"Is not the Lord our God perchance even now on the point to stop the mouths of them that complained? Is there not even now, after four hundred years, a prophet again in Israel? But if the Lord sendeth unto us a prophet after so long a time, as it were from the dead, surely it is like that He hath some great redemption in store for Sion. Even during this week have I heard that John the prophet, who hath these six months prophesied of a Deliverer shortly to come, hath of late prophesied that the Reedemer is even now amongst us; and some say that it is a certain Jesus, the son of Joseph, of the town of Nazareth, one famous in word and deed. This Jesus, as they report the matter, being baptized of John, beheld a vision of the Lord; and in that instant the Spirit of the Lord fell upon him; insomuch that, since that time, he both speaketh as a prophet and worketh signs as a man of God. Moreover, I had speech but yesterday with some that say he is come into Galilee, and is even now in these parts. Who knoweth whether this may not be true? But whether it be true or false, trust thou in the Lord God of Abraham and of Isaac and Jacob, whose arm is not shortened, and who is not a man that He should lie."

For an instant, my heart leaped up at the mention of the name of that Jesus whom I had seen in the house of the father of Raphael; but then it seemed not possible that one of so gentle an aspect should be the Redeemer of Israel. Howbeit, I asked Jonathan concerning the vision that had been reported to have been seen of Jesus; and he told me that it had not been a vision of flames of fire, nor of angels, nor of thrones, nor of seraphim, nor any such vision as had been seen of the prophets in times past, but a vision of a dove descending from heaven. Hereat I marvelled and I said, as I remember, in the bitterness and folly of my heart, that the times needed an eagle, and, lo, the new prophet brought a dove.

But Jonathan rose up from his seat to depart, and paying no heed to my last words, he spake kindly unto me and said, "If thy heart inclineth thee, my child, to prove whether there be any avail for thee in a life of contemplation, and whether thou mayest thereby attain peace; wherefore goest thou not unto the village of Jotapata where the Essenes dwell? Menahem the son of Barachiah is their chief ruler, a man that followeth after holiness and seeth things to come; who, being my friend, will for my sake receive thee kindly. Finally my child, offer up prayers unto God and pour forth thy troubles before Him; neither think too evil of thyself nor give place unto dark thoughts; and let not thy prayers be uttered at set times and in set words, but let them express thy heart's desire, according as it is said, 'Make not thy prayer an ordinance, but an entreaty before Him who filleth all space (blessed is He).' Think not also too evil of thine own heart; but remember the saying, 'Be not wicked unto thyself.' And now farewell, for I must needs go back to the city."

Saying these words, the old man departed and left me still sitting by the well. But, as it was not yet the third hour of the day (and the Essene village was distant not much more than a two hours' journey, or three hours' at the most), it came into my mind that I would hearken unto the voice of Jonathan, and visit the village of the Essenes that very day. So I arose straightway and set out on my journey. I rested often during the heat of the day, for I was weary with long watching and fasting; but a little before noontide, I was come to the top of the mountain which looketh down upon the village.

Then I looked, and lo, in the valley the Essenes busy at their labours, even as the ants that move to and fro in an ant-hill; and as near as I could conjecture, they were to the number of three or four hundred thus labouring together. But as I looked, behold, a sound as of one proclaiming the hour of prayer; and lo, the fields were empty, neither was any one anywhere to be seen. Presently they appeared again in white robes thronging to the house of prayer. Then a sound, as of psalms sung by many voices, rose up to my ears, and filled my heart with a deep peace. I waited for the space of nearly an hour, till the assembly had broken up, returning in their white robes to their several cottages. When I had beheld all this, my heart rejoiced, and I said, "If only all Israel could thus return to the Lord, then would the dough be no longer corrupt with leaven, according to the saying; and the wrath of the Lord would be turned from His people." But then came into my mind the saying of Philo, that the virtue towards man must come before the virtue towards God. I remembered also that which I had often before heard of the Essenes, how they neither marry nor give in marriage, but replenish their community by adopting the children of others and by admitting of strangers into their number. Then I bethought myself that if all the children of Israel should become Essenes, Israel would speedily perish; neither could there be any Redemption. For even now, though there had been Essenes these thirty or forty years, or even more, yet did they number no more than three thousand or four thousand men in all Israel; and of these almost all lived in the country, avoiding towns for fear of defilement, and exceeding even the Pharisees in the strictness wherewith they observe Sabbaths and obey the precepts of the Law (save only in the matter of sacrifice). So, as I looked down upon the village, and round upon the hills which shut it in and hid it from the sight of men, the proverb came to my mind which sayeth that "a city that is set upon a hill cannot be hid:" but said I, "the city of the Essenes lieth in a valley." Then I turned my back upon the place and would not go down to see Menahem, but set out to return to Sepphoris.

But as I went, my burden grew heavier than I could bear, and I cried unto the Lord in the sore grief of my heart. For all Israel seemed unto me even as sheep without a shepherd, a nation given over to servitude. For behold, the Scribes, and Lawyers, and all the Pharisees, had set their thought on vanity, and fed the people with chaff and not with wheat. Yea, they despised the poor and simple, and said that the "people of the land" could not attain to the knowledge of the Law. But as for the Priests and Sadducees, they were given over to the pursuit of wealth and to the pleasures of this world. And last of all, these Essenes were as naught save for themselves alone. For they took for their watchword the saying, "Withdraw thyself from an evil neighbour and consort not with the wicked:" therefore were they of no avail to the sinners of my people. For albeit that saying of Hillel was often in their mouths, which saith, "Be of the disciples of Aaron, loving peace and pursuing peace;" yet did they forget the last words of that saying, which bid us also to "love mankind and bring men nigh unto the Law." For the Essenes bring no man nigh unto the Law save themselves only.

But when I came in my journey back to the well where Rabbi Jonathan and I had discoursed together, then did my despair so weigh upon me that I could not so much as cry unto the Lord; for the Lord seemed as one that heard not; and even as I had made a circle in my journey that day, and was now come back to the same place whence I had set forth at the first, and all in vain, even so did I seem to have journeyed these many years in a circle of vain thoughts, searching and groping after God; and all for naught. "For," said I, "I have gone from the Scribes of Galilee to the teaching of John the Prophet, and from John the Prophet to the wisdom of the Greeks, and from the wisdom of the Greeks to the teaching of Philo the Wise; and yet seem I no nearer to God than before, but even where I was at the first. And they which did profess to guide, have been unto me as no guides. Therefore the foundations of my life are broken up, and the rock of my trust is become as unstable as water. Whithersoever I look, I see no one to avenge, no one to deliver; for the ways of the world are crooked, and sin is stronger than righteousness."

Then a Voice of the Lord spake unto me, and rebuked me in that, albeit I compassed sea and land in search of guides, and had made much of them which explain the Law and the Prophets, yet I had not given myself so zealously to the true guides of Israel, even the Prophets themselves, of whom John the son of Zachariah was one. Now they all with one consent prophesied of a day of Redemption, and of a Redeemer; and without a Redeemer their prophecies seemed maimed and void of fulfilment. Moreover John the son of Zachariah had prophesied that the Redeemer should come speedily, and that the rough places should be made smooth, and the crooked places straight; and Jonathan the son of Ezra had spoken as if the Redeemer were even now among us, yea in our own country of Galilee. So falling on my face before the Lord, I besought the

Almighty (blessed is He) to make no long tarrying, but to have mercy upon me and either to take away my life, or else to send the Redeemer unto me, even me, and to grant me His salvation.

But as I arose, there came one behind me unperceived and touched my shoulder; and he said unto me, "Wherefore weepest thou?" I started at his voice, for there was a power in it; but I looked not up for weeping, but made answer and said, "Because of the yoke of the Law; for it is written 'Whoso receiveth upon him the yoke of the Law, THEY remove from him the yoke of oppression and the yoke of the path of the world.' But it is not so with me. For from a child I have settled my heart to study the Law, and to take upon me the yoke thereof, yet have I not attained to the knowledge thereof. But the yoke of the world and the yoke of the oppression of Israel weigheth heavily upon me." Then he that spake said unto me, "Cast away the heavy yoke and take upon thee the light yoke."[1] So I looked up, marvelling at such words, and behold, it was not the face of a stranger, for I knew it; and yet again I knew it not, neither could I bring to mind the name of him that spake to me. But I saw strength in his countenance, and his face was as the morning-star in brightness; and I rejoiced with a great joy, for I knew that the Lord had sent unto me a teacher to guide my feet into the path of life. So I replied, "What yoke, O Master?" And he answered and said, "Take my yoke upon thee, and learn of me; for I am meek and lowly of heart." When I heard that, I was speechless and as one astonied to hear such a saying, which seemed in

[1] See Note I.

part the words of a king, and in part the words of a child. But when speech came back to me, I said, "My heart is afflicted because of the wonder of the ways of the Lord, and because His paths are past finding out." But he answered, "They that wonder shall reign, and they that reign shall rest."[1] Now I perceived not all the meaning of his words at the time; but thus much I did most clearly perceive, that here was one that could guide me through all wonderment and perplexity, even unto the haven of rest. But a sudden fear fell upon me that peace would depart from my soul, if my Master should depart; therefore with many entreaties I besought him to tarry that night at my mother's house. So when he had consented we straightway went to the city. But, as we went, my mind still beat upon the thought that I had seen my Master's countenance before; yet could I not call to mind the when and where.

But even as we entered into the house, behold, my mother was crying aloud, being tormented beyond measure by her disease: and when my Master heard it, he asked who cried thus, and I answered and told him concerning my mother's condition. Then straightway he desired to go into the upper chamber where she lay; and having gone in, he looked steadfastly at her, and took her by the hand, and said, as one having authority, "Arise:" and immediately my mother arose and went about as one whole. Now it came to pass, that when he looked steadfastly at my mother, even in that instant I knew his face, that it was the face of the stranger that had looked after the like manner upon Raphael the son of Joazar, even the face of Jesus

[1] See Note I.

of Nazareth; and then also in that same instant it was borne to my mind that this was he of whom Jonathan had spoken, concerning whom John the son of Zachariah had prophesied, saying that he was the Messiah of Israel: and I marvelled that I had not known him before; but I perceived that, albeit the same, yet was he not the same; so great a glory and a brightness, as of power from heaven, now reigned in his countenance. All this, I say, I perceived even when he was gazing on my mother; but I durst not for my life speak to him then. But when my mother was made whole and arose from her bed, then straightway I fell down on my knees and bowed before him; and I spake also to my mother all the words of Jonathan the son of Ezra, how that John had affirmed my Master to be the Redeemer of Israel: and I believed, and my mother also, and all our household.

On the morrow, when I would fain have accompanied Jesus to Capernaum (for he was journeying thither), he suffered me not, but said that he must needs go to Capernaum alone; but I was to remain for nine days at Sepphoris with my mother, and on the tenth day I might go down to Capernaum. But he suffered me to go with him about twelve or thirteen furlongs out of the town, and there I was to bid him farewell.

He did not speak many words to me by the way; but what I noted especially in him (as being that wherein he differed from all my former teachers) was that he spake not according to rule, nor out of any books, nor traditions, but as it were out of himself. For he taught as one having authority. There was also yet another difference. For most of the Pharisees were wont to walk with their faces turned up to the sky, or else with their eyes half shut, repeating, as they went, certain passages of the Law, or prayers, or precepts of the Elders; and if they met women they would avoid them; and of children also they took no note, except it were to instruct them or question them in the Law and the Traditions; moreover they walked with a sour and austere countenance. But Jesus was in all respects different from these. For he looked on all things, and in all things seemed to see joy and gladness, taking note even of the smallest matters, such as the flowers of the field, and the birds of the air, and also of the trees, and the cornfields. Moreover, as often as we met women on the way, he saluted them courteously and shunned them not.

But most marvellous of all, in my judgment, was the manner of his dealing with children. For so it was, as I remember, that when we were passing by a hamlet, about six furlongs from Sepphoris, a little child ran out from the door of a house, even under the feet of our asses, insomuch that we had much ado to prevent the asses from trampling down the child. But when I rebuked the child somewhat vehemently, Jesus chid me; and presently, after we had ridden on awhile in silence, he turned to me and bade me always have respect unto little children; "For," said he, "their angels do always behold the face of my Father which is in heaven." Then he added words still stranger and harder for me to understand, that "Except a man were born again and become as a little child, he could in no wise enter into the Kingdom of Heaven."

But I returned, marvelling greatly at his words and

pondering them in my mind. For I could in no wise perceive how we could redeem Israel and drive out the Tetrarch from Tiberias, and the Romans from Jerusalem, and set up the Kingdom of God, and all this by becoming as little children.

CHAPTER VII

WHEN I drew nigh to Capernaum, it was about the eleventh hour; so I hasted that I might inquire where Jesus of Nazareth abode, before the sun went down: for it was the day before the Sabbath. But as I journeyed down the valley, called the Valley of the Doves, and came to the place where the road turneth round to the right, I could not forbear to draw rein for a while, so beautiful was the sight; and though I had seen it often-times before, yet never before, methought, had it seemed so beautiful as now.

On the tops of the hills were walnut-trees; lower down fig-trees; and below them grew luxuriant palms. For the place hath, as it were, several climates suiting several trees and plants; corn also aboundeth in those parts, and flax is not wanting; but the olive-trees (as elsewhere in Galilee) stand so thick together, and so thriving, that it was a common saying, "Thou mayest sooner rear a forest of olive-trees in Galilee than one child in Judæa;" fruit-trees also of all sorts grew there without number, laden with the goodliest fruits, exceeding the fruit-trees of any other part of Galilee; insomuch that the place was justly wont to be called the Garden of Abundance. But the city itself was as a half-circle of pearls, encompassed with gardens as with a circlet of emerald. A multitude of ships and fishing-boats bestrewed the surface of the lake, which was of a deep blue colour, as blue as sapphire; and the waves thereof were very still, because no wind at all was blowing. But as I looked towards Chorazin, the sight in the surface of the waters surpassed the sight of the land. For there, as in a mirror, one might see by reflexion in the water below, all that was on the land above; the walnut-trees and fig-trees and palm-trees, and the oleanders on the border of the waters, and the white pelicans watching for their prey upon the brink thereof, and the hedges of cactus, and the cottages of the husbandmen; all these things were to be clearly seen as if painted on the waters of the lake.

Then came into my mind certain words which my Master had said to me when we went forth from Sepphoris together; how that our Father in heaven provideth for the adornment even of the grass of the fields, and how He hath made the simple flowers of the fields more beautiful than Solomon in his glory. And so it was that, as I thought on these words, I praised the Lord of Hosts, who hath made the world so beautiful; and though I had seen this sight many times before when I had come down from Sepphoris, yet now mine eyes seemed, as it were, to be opened to discern a new beauty therein. But I thought also on Israel and of the blessedness that was in store for this goodly land, if only the Roman could be driven forth. As I thought on these things, an east wind sprang up; and lo, where there had been but a moment ago so fair a sight, naught was now to be seen save troubled waters of many divers colours.

Then I hasted onward, purposing to inquire concerning Jesus of Nazareth first, and afterwards to go to the house of my uncle.

But when I was now at the going down to the city, my cousin Baruch was come forth to meet me, saying I was stayed for at a feast in the house of Manasseh. So I went straightway with him, and the sun set and the Sabbath was begun; and I had not yet seen Jesus of Nazareth. During supper time I would have inquired of Manasseh concerning Jesus; but Baruch had forewarned me that I should be silent. For my uncle, (he was a dyer by trade, and had many slaves and more than one house of merchandise, there and at Magdala, and elsewhere round about the Lake,) being fond of peace and wholly given to traffic, feared Jesus, lest he should beguile the people of Capernaum to take up arms against the Romans. Also he feared for Baruch, lest he too should be led away by Jesus. This I learned from my cousin after supper; howbeit he said not much about Jesus, for my uncle watched us. Only he said that Jesus had been now a full week in Capernaum, and that he was said to be able to work signs, and that certain of the fishermen had joined themselves unto him; but the most part still held with John the Prophet, saying that John was greater than Jesus; neither believed they that Jesus was the Messiah.

On the morrow, about the sixth hour, we went to the synagogue. There was a great throng, so that we were fain to sit in the farthest seats from the Ark of the Law; neither could we discern who sat in the chief seats, nor who read, because a pillar stood between us and the pulpit. Now first the Law was read and prayers were offered up according to custom; but by reason of my sadness, because I desired to have seen Jesus again, I was even as the parched ground, and no moisture fell upon my soul. But when the Prophets were read, then it was as a shower of heaven on the congregation, and the dew of the Lord upon our souls; for the voice of him that read was the voice of Jesus of Nazareth.

When he had made an end of reading, Jesus began to exhort the people, saying that he was sent to proclaim good news, to release the captive, give health to the sick, and light to the blind, and to bring Redemption to Israel. God, he said, loved all; not the good alone, but even the bad: yea, God was in very truth our Father in heaven. Therefore how much soever the kindest father on earth may love his children, albeit they transgress against him, much more is the love of God toward us though we be sinners. He did not tell us that we were not sinful; nay rather, he made it clear to us that our sins were as red as blood in the sight of the All-seeing; but none the less, he called us the children of God. As many as would repent should be forgiven; and he spake as if he himself had a certain divine power of forgiveness whereby he might purify the soul and bring us close to God, one family in the presence of our Father. One thing was needful, that we should trust in him and in his message. This day, he said, this very day, are the prophecies of Redemption fulfilled in your ears. Then he cried aloud unto all that were hungering or thirsting for righteousness, all that were weary of the burden of their sins, all that felt themselves utterly hopeless, friendless, and vile, bidding them resort to him as their refuge : " Come unto me all ye that are weary and heavy laden, and I will give you rest."

While he was speaking, methought I was not hearing words, but seeing somewhat that might be seen and touched ; so solid seemed the mercies of God, even as a rock whereon one standeth. For Jesus ever testified of the Father as one testifieth that knoweth by experience, and spake of heaven as of that which he had known and felt. Yea, and more than that ; a certain strange power was in him to make things invisible to seem visible by his discourse. Wherefore, albeit Moses had called God the Father of the spirits of all flesh, and the Prophets also had taught Israel to say unto God, " Thou art our Father," and all this doctrine was well known and trite among us ; yet now, for the first time, the doctrine seemed to be no more a mere dead letter, but a living word. Such a life did Jesus of Nazareth breathe into it, insomuch that his Good News (for so he called it) came upon our hearts as news indeed, never heard before among the children of men.

This long while (since Jesus had first begun to speak), a certain youth whom I had before noted, sitting not far from me, had been muttering and moaning gently to himself ; but I was rapt in the words of Jesus, wherefore I had given the less heed to the boy. But now, he stood up, and cried aloud in a deep hollow voice, as of a full-grown man, " What hast thou to do with us ? Let us alone, let us alone." Then in his own voice he cried again, " I know thee who thou art, the Holy One of God." Immediately I perceived that it was the demoniac, even Raphael the son of Joazar, whom Theudas the Exorcist had adventured to heal; but a great fear fell on all the congregation, and the women rose up from their places, shrieking for terror. But Jesus, without use of charm or gesture, rebuked the unclean spirits and bade them come forth. Then they tare the youth, so that he shrieked with a piercing shriek; and so they came forth. And Jesus delivered the boy to his father; who would scarce suffer Jesus out of his sight, between joy that the devils were gone forth, and fear lest they might return. Howbeit, now the spirits were driven out so that they returned no more. For the boy lived to be a man; nor did he die (as it hath been reported to me) till he numbered fifty years, dying about twelve years ago, two years before destruction came upon the Holy City.

When Jesus departed from the synagogue, the people thronged him, bringing to him divers requests, some concerning their friends that were diseased or lunatic, or afflicted with devils; others begging him to come and bless their children; others asking him that he would lodge in their houses, or at the least sup with them. For at this time all men, rich and poor, Pharisees, Sadducees, and Galileans, inclined to follow Jesus. But he would go to none of the rich men's houses, but only to the house of Simon the son of Jonah (whom he afterwards called Peter); he was one of the fishermen of the place and had joined himself to Jesus. But Jesus suffered me to accompany him.

But when we were now entering into the house, behold all things were full of disorder and lamentation. For Simon's wife's mother (who abode in the house) had been suddenly afflicted with a grievous sickness, so that, instead of serving the guests, she was laid speechless upon a bed in an upper room. Then they spake to Jesus concerning her. Now I was not myself present when the thing took place; but (as it was reported to me) Jesus healed her after the same manner as he had healed my mother; for he took her by the hand and lifted her up, and she arose whole and free from her disease, and ministered unto the guests.

Jesus straitly charged us that we should tell no man; whereat we marvelled not a little. But howsoever we obeyed him, it could not be hid. And besides this, the fame of the healing of Raphael the son of Joazar had been noised abroad through the whole of the city, insomuch that at sunset, when we went forth, the Sabbath being now ended, we saw great multitudes of demoniacs, lunatics, and some also sick of the palsy and of fever, laid in their beds along the road through which we would have passed. Some also, that were afflicted with incurable diseases, had been brought notwithstanding, because of their entreaties; if perchance Jesus might heal them; and I saw one man that had been blind from his birth.

Now it came to pass that when Jesus came forth from Simon Peter's house, and saw the faces of all these sick people, and the faces of their friends, all waiting if perchance he would help them, his countenance was altered, and the shadow of sorrow fell upon him, and he sighed and said, "Verily for the sorrowful I am sorrowful, and for the sick I am sick."[1] Then he passed along the ranks of the sick people; and wheresoever he perceived that any could be healed, he laid his hands on them,

[1] See Note I.

and lo, they were at once freed from their infirmities; and many unclean spirits were driven out from those whom they had possessed. Now most of them that were healed had been possessed with evil spirits; but others were lunatic, or sick of the palsy, or of fever, or had impediment in their speech. But Jesus had a marvellous power to discern, methought, not only them that had faith from them that had not, but also such diseases as were to be cured, from such as were not to be cured, because it was not prepared for him that he should cure them. But when Jesus had made an end of healing, the multitude still followed us; and the friends of such as had not been cured, vexed us with importunities; and others, whose friends had been cured, called down blessings on Jesus, and refused to leave him. Thus, go whither we would, we could not be alone. So Jesus returned to the house, and I went back to the house of Manasseh.

I opened my mind to my uncle that night, and said to him that I purposed to go with Jesus of Nazareth whithersoever he went; and Baruch said the same. But my uncle no longer opposed himself against our wills; only he forewarned us that evil was in store for us; "For," said he, "I have sojourned in Italy among the Romans three years, and I know well that nothing can withstand their power. But whoso gainsayeth them gainsayeth the strength of a king: according as it is written, 'Where the word of a king is, there is power; and who may say unto him, What doest thou?'"

All the night long no sleep came to my eyes for musing on all the things that I had seen and heard that day: "For this day," said I, "is, as it were, the birthday of the Redemption of Israel." But when I thought thereon, and considered with myself that I had now joined myself unto Jesus as the Redeemer, and when I compared Jesus with the image of the Redeemer of Sion (such as I had framed it in my mind from the reading of the Prophets, and such as my countrymen expected), then was I as one astonied and amazed to find myself believing in Jesus, and standing on his side. For I had imagined unto myself one that should perchance appear, riding on the clouds of heaven, encompassed by thousands of angels, taking vengeance upon the enemies of Sion, according to the word of the prophet Daniel ; or else I had thought to see a royal deliverer, even such another as David himself, mighty with the sword, riding at the head of his ten thousands, ruling the Gentiles with a rod of iron, or breaking them in pieces like a potter's vessel ; or else I had fashioned in my mind a Deliverer after the manner of Elias, rebuking kings in their pride, and calling down fire from heaven for a sign, or for the destruction of the Gentiles.

Now before this time, I had had no leisure to consider the matter; for, in the presence of Jesus, I had been drawn towards him as by an enchantment: but in the stillness of the night, Jesus being no more before my face, I thought on all the signs and wonders wrought by Moses and Elias aforetime, and doubt fell upon me ; and it seemed to me not possible that Jesus of Nazareth could be greater than they, so as to be the Messiah. But when I asked myself, "Could it then be that Jesus is a deceiver?" my heart made answer, "Nay, that could not be. And if thou trust not in Jesus, there is not any one in the world in whom thou canst trust." So I comforted myself in my perplexity, saying to myself,

"Perchance the time hath not yet come for Jesus to manifest himself as the son of David, nor as the Son of man spoken of by the prophet Daniel: but doubtless that time will come; and then shalt thou see Jesus, as the Messiah indeed, in power."

But on the morrow, very early, when we went forth to the house of Simon Peter, behold, a mixed multitude had gathered round the doors waiting for the coming of Jesus. And I also waited, standing with them, and heard how they conversed with each other. But it seemed that one had but now come forth from the house of Peter, saying that Jesus could not be found in the house. Then arose a murmur in the crowd; and a certain man from Antioch said that Simon had set a snare for Jesus of Nazareth, and had betrayed him to Herod the Tetrarch. But there was in the press one Gorgias the son of Philip, a man well known to Simon; and he laughed the man of Antioch to scorn. He had been in the army of Herod the King in former times, and his father was a Greek; but he conformed himself to the Law and joined himself to the sect of the Galileans; and his word prevailed greatly with them, because he was versed in warlike matters. This man declared that Jesus had withdrawn himself, that he might not be shut up in prison by the Tetrarch: "And no marvel," said he, "for, seeing that the tyrant hath but now taken John the son of Zachariah, why should he not also adventure to take the new prophet?"

Others, beside myself, had not heard before that John had been cast into prison. So we questioned Gorgias, and heard that the prophet had been cast into prison in the Black Castle at Machærus three days ago. Many of them that were in the crowd had been disciples of John; and they cried aloud that the men of Galilee ought to rise up and deliver the prophet. But Gorgias beckoned with his hand that they should be silent, and when silence was made, he said, "Let us rise up, indeed, but not without a leader. Now the Lord hath sent to us this Jesus of Nazareth: and that he is a prophet sent from God none can deny." The multitude shouted that it was even so, and one or other uttered praises of Jesus; and a certain man said, "Yea, never man spake as this spake." But Gorgias answered and said, "It is known to all that I am a soldier, neither do words prevail with me without deeds. Wherefore I also, until yesterday, did but lightly esteem Jesus of Nazareth. But now he hath shown forth his power in deeds. And he that can do such deeds as Jesus hath wrought in our streets, shall he not do even greater deeds than these when the time shall come for them? Yea, doubtless, all things are possible to him. And what will avail squadrons of horse, or legions of foot, against one that can call down fire from heaven, or cause the walls of a city to fall to the ground? Choose we therefore Jesus to be our leader, and no one shall be able to stand against us."

At this instant Simon Peter came forth, and he confirmed what had been said, to wit, that Jesus of Nazareth was not in the house: but he thought that he was gone forth to be alone. And so it was. For when we had made diligent search for him we found him alone on a mountain, about three miles from the town. We besought him to return; but he answered that he must proclaim the Good News in other villages also, for to that end he had been sent. So Simon Peter and the rest of the disciples accompanied him, and Baruch and I went with them; and for the space of four or five weeks we continued with him, going from town to town in Galilee; and Jesus preached the Good News, and healed the sick; and a great multitude of all sorts was added to our number.

Now the greater part of our band were honest people, hungering and thirsting for the Redemption of Sion: but some were vain men, children of iniquity, seeking the wages of unrighteousness. Especially they that had been formerly soldiers resorted to Jesus, as to a prince or general, like vultures hasting to the prey, supposing that they should gain much spoil if he prevailed against the Romans. And so it was that once when Jesus spake to his disciples, saying that they must be "fishers of men," then Baruch, being offended by the presence of these children of mammon among us, answered and said, "But must the fishers catch vile fish as well as good?"

Hereat Jesus turned and looked sorrowfully on Baruch, and said, "The kingdom of heaven is like unto a net that was cast into the sea, and gathered of every kind: which, when it was full they drew to shore, and sat down, and gathered the good into vessels, but cast the bad away. So shall it be at the end of the age. The messengers of God shall come forth and sever the wicked from among the just, and shall cast them into the furnace of fire. There shall be wailing and gnashing of teeth."

Another parable spake he to the same effect, that the tares must needs grow with the wheat till the day of harvest, for not till then can the division be made between good and evil. When we heard this, we grieved thereat; for we had supposed that none save the faithful should have been admitted into the Kingdom, and we marvelled why Jesus should first suffer the bad to enter, and then drive them forth. Howbeit, we besought him that he would give us ordinances which we might observe, to the intent that we might not be cast out of the Kingdom. For some of our number had begun to say that Jesus had come to destroy the Law, so that every one might do what he listed; as though Jesus had said that God loveth the wicked as much as the righteous, even though the wicked abide in wickedness. Thus they brought shame upon us, and they set stumblingblocks in the path of many that had otherwise believed. Moreover the disciples of John the Baptist compared us with themselves, and asked us concerning our laws and customs and prayers; and, when they found that we had none of these things, then they despised us, saying that our Master was not equal to John. For at this time the fame of John the son of Zachariah overshadowed the fame of Jesus; yea, and for some time after this, even after John had been cast into prison. For this cause we intreated Jesus that he would both teach us how to pray, as John also had taught his disciples, and also that he would lay down laws for the new Kingdom, even as Moses had laid down laws for the kingdom in old times.

Jesus hearkened to our petition in silence. Then he said that he must depart from us for a season and go to the top of a certain mountain; but he appointed the third hour of the following day that we should come to him.

Certain of the Scribes that followed with us murmured at Jesus, because he had appointed that we should come to him on the mountain: and one, finding fault for that Jesus was often wont to spend the whole night praying alone on some mountain, said, "It is written, 'Out of the depths have I cried unto thee, O Lord;' therefore it is good to pray from a low place, and not from a high place." But Nathaniel answered and said that Jesus loved to be alone on the mountain by night, to meditate on the greatness of the Lord and how He hath exalted the Son of man, according as it is written, "I will consider thy heavens, even the works of thy fingers, the moon and stars which thou hast ordained:" and "these very words," said Nathanael, "I heard the Prophet but yesterday repeat, when we were upon the top of yonder mountain." Hereat the Scribes murmured the more, saying that it was not written that any prophet in old times thus took counsel with the heavens after the manner of a Chaldean. But Gorgias the son of Philip murmured for another cause, saying that the Prophet ought not thus to mistrust his followers, nor to be so fearful for his own safety, and that it behoved the friends of Jesus to take him by force, if need be, and to make him a king. And to this Judas of Kerioth consented and some others.

But to the most of us the words of Gorgias seemed an abomination; for we knew that Jesus did not depart for fear: for indeed fear was not in him. But he desired to be alone because he wished to pray, and because of the burden of his heart. For it grieved him, more than can be told, to see the misery and wretchedness, yea, and the ignorance and the sinfulness of the mixed multitude which pressed round him. All their pains pained him and all their sufferings he suffered, insomuch that more than once I have heard him saying in a low voice to himself, "For them that are hungry I hunger, and for them that are athirst I thirst, and for them that are sick I am sick."[1]

Notwithstanding he was not so much distressed with the pains and diseases of the body as with the pains and diseases of the soul. For the sins of souls seemed to him as real and loathsome as the diseases of the flesh to us; and oftentimes a transgression that would appear slight to us, he counted as a work of Satan; so that whithersoever he moved, he saw sins more than could be seen of common men, yea, a very sea of sinfulness; albeit, underlying the sea of sin and sorrow, he still discerned the Everlasting Arms.

Moreover, because he loved all men with an exceeding great love, for this cause every hour in his life brought unto him a burden passing the power of words to describe. For the sins of men were not unto him as the sins of aliens and strangers, but as the sins of his own brethren: yea, they were even as his own sins; for, although he himself sinned not, neither knew sin, yet what pain cometh from the bearing of a brother's sin, that he knew full well. Wherefore in him was fulfilled the saying of the prophet Isaiah; who prophesied that the Messiah should be a man of sorrows and acquainted with griefs, and that he should carry our sins and bear our iniquities.

[1] See Note I.

CHAPTER VIII

On the morrow, about the second hour, we began to go up the mountain which Jesus had appointed. But having strayed from the path, we knocked at the door of a house which was near the foot of the mountain, and besought the goodman of the house that he would guide us. There opened the door a man of churlish appearance; but he would neither come out, nor so much as speak with us. This delayed us for a time, but we soon found the path, and the way became steep. The sun shone, but not with too fervent a heat, and the north wind blew gently from Hermon, whose top we saw clearly toward the north, clad in snow. On the west was the Mount Carmel, shining with a brightness as of purple; and further off the Great Sea, resembling a blue plain, whereon appeared many sails, almost too small for sight by reason of the distance. We climbed upward through groves of terebinth and oak. As often as we turned round to recover breath, the houses and fields grew smaller, till, at the last, when we drew nigh unto the top, the whole plain of Esdraelon seemed but as a small ground-plat; and large towns appeared as little hamlets, and all the works of man became very small in our eyes, as though we were leaving earth and approaching heaven.

Then said Baruch, "Is not this a second Sinai? For verily Jesus of Nazareth is about to give us a new law." But Eliezer the son of Arak, the principal Scribe of Capernaum (for he at this time followed Jesus and was now with us) rebuked him, saying, "Even though Jesus of Nazareth were the greatest of prophets, yet were he not equal to Moses; for it is said, Sinai is to be preferred even to the uprooter of mountains!" And another said, "Behold, the Word of God, when it went forth from Sinai from the mouth of the Holy One (blessed be His Name), was like sparks, and lightnings, and flames of fire; a torch of flame was on his right hand, and a torch of flame on his left hand: it flew and hovered in the air of the heavens, and returned and graved itself upon the tables of the covenant which were given into the hands of Moses. How then is it possible that the like wonders should be wrought on this mountain?"

Then said Nathanael to Simon Peter that it might perchance please the Lord not always to speak by the whirlwind or by the fire, but, as in the days of Elias, by the still small voice. And to this Peter agreed, but others did not agree: for though they inclined not to Eliezer the son of Arak, yet it was because they thought that Jesus would of a surety soon work some sign in heaven to prove that he was the Redeemer. But Judas of Kerioth affirmed that Jesus would not, at this present time, lay down laws for the Kingdom, but only ordinances for a season, to instruct the host in the journey towards Jerusalem; but until Jerusalem should be ours, lasting laws would not be made.

While we were disputing among ourselves concerning the saying of Judas, Peter cried "Peace:" for, said he, "yonder is the Prophet:" and looking upward, we saw Jesus on a rock stretching out his hands in prayer. When he had made an end of praying, Peter approached him and besought him a second time to teach us to pray; and Jesus gave us that well-known prayer which is used in all the churches. Afterwards he beckoned to us to follow him, and he came down and stood in the bed of a torrent, which was dry by reason of the drought. While we were following him, I heard the companion of Eliezer murmuring because there were no words in the prayer concerning the Redemption of Israel; "moreover," said he, "albeit the prayer asketh for bread, yet is there no mention of wine, nor oil, nor even of raiment. But how can a man sit and search the Law and the Traditions, and know not whence he is to drink as well as eat, and whence to be clad and covered?" To this I would have made reply; but Peter again cried to us to hold our peace, for Jesus was beginning to speak.

When he opened his lips, every one was silent for expectation; but, as he proceeded, the silence was a silence as of them that are astonished and disappointed. For he began with setting forth in his discourse a character and image of a citizen of the New Kingdom; and lo, it was not the image of a conqueror, but of one conquered. Also he drew as it were a model of the palace of the Great King, and of the princes and nobles which stand about His throne; and behold, when we compared the model with that which we had imagined in our hearts, and with that which we had read of in histories, the model of Jesus was in all things contrary to the model in our hearts. For in old times men had done reverence unto the valiant, the proud, the strong, the rich and the wise; but Jesus said that the chief places about the throne of God should be given to the hungry and thirsty, and poor; to them that were innocent and simple; to them that made not war, but peace; yea, even to them which resisted not evil, but rewarded evil with good. Upon all these, as being the nobles and princes of the New Kingdom, Jesus pronounced a blessing; to wit, that all things should work together for good to them, so that they should have all that they needed, according to the words of the prophet, "Behold, my servants shall eat, but ye shall be hungry; behold, my servants shall drink, but ye shall be thirsty; behold, my servants shall rejoice, but ye shall be ashamed." Even so did Jesus ordain that they which hungered should be satisfied, and that the makers of peace should conquer and inherit the earth.

Next, he described the statutes and judgments of the New Kingdom; and, behold, instead of an easier yoke, he seemed to be placing upon us a yoke even heavier than the yoke of the ancient Law, too heavy to be borne. For the old Law forbade us to commit murder; but the new Law forbade us even to hate our enemies. Again, the old Law forbade us to commit adultery; but the new Law forbade us even to entertain a lustful thought in our hearts. In a word, the old Law laid down certain ordinances, which if a man obeyed, he should live therein; but the new Law laid down nothing fixed nor certain for us, so that we might say "I have done this or that, and therefore I have fulfilled the Law of Christ." For the Law of Moses touched the life of man, as it were, in certain points; as for example, in sacrifices, and feasts, and purifications, and

Sabbaths, and in the obeying of the Ten Commandments: but the Law of Christ covered the whole of the state of man, the thoughts as well as the deeds; even as the encompassing air, which pierceth into every corner and cavern of the earth, wheresoever human life is. In fine, whereas the Law of Moses commanded us what we should do, the Law of Christ commanded what we should be. For this cause Jesus set himself against all bookishness, and against all worship of Traditions, and even of the precepts of the Scriptures; for he taught that precepts, howsoever they may shape the outward action, shape not the inner man.

Again, as concerning the laws, and the judgments, and the rewards, and the punishments, in the New Kingdom, he spake as if they were not laws of man's device, but rather Laws according to the nature of things, like unto the ordinances of the rain and the sunshine, the harvest and the seed-time. For he said that righteousness was not any such thing as could be attained by a price, nor by the doing of deeds; but that it consisted in a seeing of that which may be seen of God. He also spake of a certain eye of the soul, which, if it were clear, the man would be righteous; but if it were darkened, the man would be unrighteous. Also he spake of a certain law of retributions, which decreeth that whoso judgeth shall be judged, whoso forgiveth shall be forgiven, whoso giveth shall receive: adding thereunto this most strange doctrine, that if we would go forth into the world, giving and ready to give, then, from all sides, the world would give to us again; yea, the angels of God, and the elements of the world (which are His ministers) and even the children of men, should make us marvel by reason of their gratitude, giving us back good measure pressed down and running over. Now there is a saying in the Traditions that, "Whensoever a poor man standeth at thy door, the Holy One (blessed is He) standeth at his right hand. If thou givest him alms, know that thou shalt receive a reward from Him who standeth at his right hand." Jesus therefore added to this doctrine, teaching that God standeth at the right hand not of the poor only, but of every one that is in need of aught, that is to say, of every one of the children of men : wherefore whatsoever is given to men, is given to God, and from God cometh back multiplied to the giver. Howbeit, we were neither to give alms, nor to do aught else, for hope of reward; but only out of love.

Concerning citizenship in the Kingdom and how men should become citizens therein, he spake little to us, as being already citizens therein : save only this, that whoso would come, must come unto him ; and through him, as through a door, they should pass into the Kingdom. And behold, the Kingdom was no other than a family, wherein God was at once Father and King, and all men were as children of the Father in Heaven. For the foundation of all was, that the heart and not the hands shaped the goodness and badness of all deeds, and made men to become citizens of the Kingdom : wherefore the heart and not the hands must be purified; nor could any be in truth citizens of the Kingdom except they had the thought of the Kingdom always in their hearts, so that their hopes and treasures were all stored up, not in the banks of money-changers, but in the Kingdom of Heaven.

Then he spake of the exceeding joys of the citizens of the Kingdom of God, and how they are free from all troubles and all disquietudes. But none, he said, could serve God and Mammon at one time; neither was it possible to serve God aright and yet to be distracted and torn asunder by cares concerning meat or raiment. Hereat the companion of Eliezer murmured again, saying that Jesus had before spoken blasphemously in joining the forgiving of sins by God with the forgiving of sins by men, and now he had spoken as a madman, in forbidding us to be careful about food and raiment; "Can a man sit," said he, "and search the Law, and not know whence he is to eat, and drink, and to be clad?" Now whether Jesus perceived his murmuring I know not: but he pointed, first upwards to the birds (for even at that instant there was a flight of pelicans above us) and then downward to the flowers, which bestrewed the side of the brook, and he said that our Father in Heaven fed the birds and clothed the flowers; and should He not much more care for us? Then he bade us seek first the Kingdom of God and His righteousness, and all things else should be added unto us.

Now concerning this Kingdom of God (or Kingdom of Heaven, for he called it by both names) we understood not much at this time: but my judgment now is that Jesus desired that all the Lord's people should be as Prophets, not teaching one the other and saying "Know the Lord," but all knowing the Lord from the least to the greatest. For he perceived that all the tribes of the earth were joined together under one emperor through desire of wealth and ease, and that Israel was joined together through hatred of the Romans and through desire to be rescued from them; but he saw that neither love of ease nor hatred of enemies could bind men together in an enduring Kingdom: but that which bindeth men together is the Spirit of love, which is a Spirit of brotherhood among men and of childhood unto God. For all nations begin with being first families, and then many families together; helping one another by reason of kindred, and not by reason of manhood. Now such a nation as this, and all men of such a nation, Jesus called "born of flesh and blood:" and he said that no nation could leave off to be a tribe and become a nation indeed, except it were born again, not of flesh and blood, but of the Spirit; so as to enter into a certain government of God, which the Greeks called *theocratia*, but Jesus called it the Kingdom of God. Such a *theocratia* Moses had partly established in old times; howbeit the King in the kingdom of Moses was the God of Abraham, but the King in the kingdom of Jesus was the Father of the Son of man.

But now to return to the words of Jesus. He ended his discourse with warning. First he warned us to beware of the common saying, "Give judgment according to the greater number"; for he said that the path to destruction is broad, and many go thereby. He bade us also try teachers and prophets by their works. Last of all, he spake very earnestly against certain which pretended to obey him but obeyed him not. We were the salt of the earth, he said, but if we lost our savour, how could the world be salted, and to what end could we serve, but to be cast out and trampled under foot? Whoso heard him and obeyed him not, such an one he likened unto a foolish shepherd (and even as he spake, there was nigh, within a bow-shot of us, a sheep-cote that had been cast down by the swollen waters of the brook) which built his house upon the sand, so that it fell: but whoso heard and obeyed, he likened him unto a wise shepherd, which built his house upon a rock so that it fell not. This parable Jesus did not at this time interpret to us, but afterwards he made it clear. For even as the Psalmists of Israel spake often of a certain Rock of Salvation, even so was it afterwards a common saying with Jesus both that each citizen of the New Kingdom must build his house upon a Rock, and that the Kingdom itself must be founded on a Rock, so that the gates of Hades or Destruction should not prevail against it. Howbeit what this Rock might be, we did not as yet understand; for he had not at this time revealed it unto us.

CHAPTER IX

WHEN Jesus had ended all these words, he came down from the mountain, and we followed, reasoning much among ourselves. Baruch spake first, complaining that the new Law was full of hard sayings. "For," said he, "when the Prophet proclaimed a blessing on the poor and hungry, that was easy to understand, and I rejoiced thereat: but afterwards, when he bade us bless them that cursed us, and do good to those that injured us, yea, and turn the left cheek to him that had smitten us on the right, and give our coat to him that had taken away our cloak, then indeed his doctrine seemed too wonderful for the mind of man to fathom." Then a certain Essene (who at that time followed with us) made answer and said, "This world is but as a vestibule before the world to come: therefore the Prophet's intent is to instruct us how to prepare ourselves at the vestibule so that we may find grace to come into the King's presence: and his words enjoin on us to abstain from all earthly cares and pleasures, and to withdraw ourselves from the cities of men." But to this Simon Peter made answer that Jesus had taught us to live in the sight of all men, like a city on an hill or like a candle on a candlestick: moreover, he had promised that we should inherit the earth.

But here Eliezer the son of Arak could no longer constrain himself. "I marvel," he said, "that we listen so long without first asking this Prophet by what authority he sayeth these things, or what sign he can work in Heaven to prove his authority. For other teachers received of teachers before them; as, for example, Hillel and Shammai received from Shemaiah and Abtalion; and Shemaiah and Abtalion received from Jehudah the son of Tabai, and Simeon the son of Shatach; and so on successively; but this teacher maketh mention of no teachers from whom he hath received his doctrine: neither worketh he any sign in Heaven. But whence doth he draw his knowledge about the Unapproachable (blessed is He)? Even from the creatures; even from the weeds of the field, and the silly birds that are caught in the snare of the fowler; from the senseless rain and from the shining of the sun; yea, and from the nature of the heart of man, which is evil from his youth! But how much better than all these is the Law, whereby was created all that is; according as it is said, 'Beloved are the children of Israel, in that there was given to them the instrument by which the world was created.'"

No answer was made to the words of Eliezer: but Barabbas took up the words of Baruch, and said, "If we are to turn the left cheek to him which hath smitten the right, and if we are to do good unto them which do us harm, who shall cause injustice to cease in the world? For verily the unjust will wax fat in their injustice and will go on from oppression to oppression." But said Judas of Kerioth, "Listen unto me, O foolish ones, and take counsel from me: for is it not even as I foretold?

Did not I say unto you that the Prophet would not at this time make laws that should endure for ever, but only ordinances for a season, till we had gained the upper hand? Wherefore ye must know that it is in the mind of the Prophet to draw unto himself the hearts of all people by fair words and gentle dealing: but when the time is come for different policy, then we shall take fresh counsel according to our needs. But now hearken. Did not the Prophet prophesy woe to the rich and the powerful? These are the Romans; and in foretelling woe to them, he foretold woe against the Romans. Again, did he not prophesy blessing for the poor? And we are poor: and in every city of Israel the poor are the greater part, and will fight on our side, and will have a part in our blessing. I grant, he said not that we should be judges and princes: but he promised that we should have that for which we asked; and is not this enough for us? Yea, and albeit he mentioned not expressly money, or lands, or houses, yet he said that our reward should be great. But if persecution or the shedding of some of our blood must needs come before our success, who is so fainthearted and womanish as to draw back for such a cause? Therefore, I say, be of good heart; and though there be some dark sayings of the Prophet, let us be content to stand fast on those sayings which are plain. But as touching the words of Eliezer, we all know in our hearts that Jesus is not a man as other men, but that he is a leader sent from God; and howsoever he teacheth, and whithersoever he leadeth, it is our wisdom to obey him and to follow him."

The words of Judas pleased us: and we all agreed

to them. Only a certain Alexandrine (whose name was Quartus) said to Baruch that he judged not that the words of Jesus were intended to be merely transitory ordinances. Now this Quartus was a man of no common understanding and discernment; and inasmuch as his father had been a Greek and had caused him to be trained in the Greek learning and philosophy, he spake with more art and subtlety than most of my companions. Howbeit he lacked not faith and the love of righteousness; and, his mother being of our nation, he had been circumcised, and had conformed himself to the worship of Israel; but having been bred up in the schools of the Greeks and in the school of Philo, he was at all times desirous to compare the teaching of other philosophers with the teaching of Jesus. He was a merchant, and his business brought him oftentimes to Capernaum, where I had met him; but I had also met him before in the house of my uncle at Alexandria. So when I overheard Quartus saying these words to my cousin, I questioned him how he interpreted the sayings of Jesus, and in particular, that saying concerning the turning of the cheek to the smiter.

Then said Quartus unto me, after some pause, " Be not displeased if I speak in a parable. Many times in Capernaum have I seen mariners (such as know not your waters) grievously tossed by a storm while they strove to enter into the harbour by a straight course, and toiling hard for many hours, but all to no purpose; but others (which know the secret) leave the straight course on one side, and stand far out to Taricheæ. Thence floweth a current toward Capernaum, strong at all times; but in stormy weather it cannot be resisted.

Falling into this current therefore, the wise mariner needeth but to row softly, or scarce at all, and lo, he entereth into Capernaum as it were upon wings. Now even such a wise mariner doth Jesus seem unto me."

I marvelled at his words. But Quartus perceived that I understood him not; and he continued, "I speak as one groping in the dark. But the meaning of my parable is this: The lake is the world; the vessel is Israel; and Capernaum is redemption. Other pilots have striven to guide Israel to redemption by dint of force, but they have failed: Jesus is the true pilot, and knoweth the currents and streams in the nature of men and things; and by his wisdom he thinketh to guide us aright."

"But what," I asked, "are these streams and currents?" Again Quartus was silent for a while, and longer than before, so that by this time we were almost come down from the mountain; but at last he said unto me, "What seemeth to thee the strongest current in the nature of men?" But, when I held my peace, not knowing what to answer, he spake again very earnestly, "Thou art a student of the sayings of the Wise, O Joseph, and canst answer with discerning. Tell me, then, on what standeth the earth?" Then I replied according to the saying, "Upon the pillars; and the pillars upon the waters." "Yea," replied Quartus; "and after these cometh the wind; and what after the wind?" Then I said, "Beneath the wind is the storm, and beneath the storm is the arm of the Holy One; for it is said, 'Underneath are the Everlasting Arms.'" Then said Quartus, "It is so; and verily the foundations of earth are the Everlasting Arms of the Father in Heaven: but if the Fatherhood of God be the strongest thing on earth, and if this be the mightiest stream or current in the nature of men, then how may we best sail with that current?" I remembered the words which Jesus had spoken that we were to become as little children; so I answered, "I suppose, by approaching Him as children."

Here Judas interrupted us and said, "Nay, but wisdom is the strongest thing in the world, for it is written of wisdom, 'The Lord possessed me in the beginning of His way, before His works of old. When He appointed the foundations of the earth, then I was by Him as one brought up with Him.'" "Thou sayest well," said Quartus, "but what human wisdom is like unto that wisdom which revealeth God to men? Now as no child can understand his father unless he love his father, so no man can know God (who is our Father in Heaven) unless he love Him; but whoso loveth, understandeth; therefore to love God is the highest wisdom of man." Then Judas scoffed at him and said, "This is nothing but repeating in new words the old saying of the Law, 'Thou shalt love the Lord thy God with all thy heart, and with all thy soul, and with all thy mind, and with all thy strength.' What! do ye then deem our Master to be naught but a merchant that retaileth old wares as if they were new?" So he left us and went on before.

But Quartus continued, "Judas saith truly that the new Law aimeth at the same mark as the old Law. But the means are diverse. For the old Law worketh by purifications and feasts and sabbaths; but the new Law belike worketh in part by these means, but in greater part by other means. And, as I judge, Jesus goeth toward the end of the old Law; but by a path that is new, yea, altogether new. For I have myself heard him say that the redeemers of old were like unto thieves and robbers, using force and violence; but he himself cometh not like a thief over the wall, but like the true shepherd through the door of the fold, that is to say, through the path of Redemption which God hath appointed. Now this path is kindness or love. And Jesus saith that the former redeemers failed of their purpose, for they thought to redeem men by force; but he will not fail, for he purposeth to redeem men by gentleness. And he saith that God ordaineth strength out of babes and sucklings, and that the spirit of childhood is the conquering spirit of the world. Rememberest thou not how our teacher Philo said some things not much unlike to these, teaching that the highest revelation of God is through love? Howbeit, none methinks, save Jesus only, can reveal this revelation. For Philo testifieth of that which is behind the veil; but Jesus of Nazareth hath power to lift up the veil."

By this time we had overtaken the others, whom we found all sitting, and Jesus in the midst of them. By the side of Jesus was a man bearing in his arms a little child. He was come forth from a house nigh to the place where Jesus sat, bringing a cup of water for Jesus to drink. While Jesus was drinking, the father still kept his eyes upon the child in his arms, and his face was full of compassion and tenderness; for the child was very sickly. We soon perceived that it was the same man that had denied to give us guidance in the morning; but at first we knew him not; pity and love had so transformed his countenance. Now it came to pass that when Jesus had given back the cup to the man, he laid his hands on the child and blessed him. And as he blessed him, his face shone as with the glory of the Lord; and the little one also seemed to rejoice and to partake in the brightness of our Master's countenance.

We both stood still, beholding Jesus. Then said Quartus unto me, "Did not Eliezer the son of Arak say truly, that 'Jesus looketh upon the book of the world as well as upon the book of the Law, and seeth in all things God'? For even as Elias the Prophet loved to commune with God on the tops of mountains, and in deserts, and in caves, and received revelations of the Lord from earthquakes and fires, but most of all from the still small voice; even so doth our Master look upon all things that are, yea even on the smallest things that live or grow, and from all, he heareth a still small voice that speaketh of the Father. Yea, and there is yet more than this. For whithersoever he turneth his face, methinks he giveth of his love to all things, whether they be the flowers of the field, or the birds, or the mountains, or the children of men: and because he thus giveth, it is given to him again; yea, wisdom and joy and peace are given back to him, even from things that have not life; but most of all from the children of men, which are made in the image of God. Therefore said I that Jesus seemeth as the wise mariner of whom we spake but now; for, by the Word of God in himself, he hath haply hit upon a certain current in the nature of created things, whereby he will easily prevail over the blasts of all opposing storms, and be carried into the haven of God, both he and all they that put their trust in him."

"Thy words are fair," I replied, "but they do not persuade me. That the love of children doth bind husband and wife together, and that the bond of families is the bond of nations, this I deny not. Perchance also the love that parents have to their children may have lifted up the hearts of many in Israel, during many generations, to the true God. But how we are to take Jerusalem or thrust forth the Romans from Syria by becoming as little children, this passeth my understanding. Or dost thou not believe that Jesus will lead us against the Romans in Jerusalem?"

"I know not," replied Quartus (who spoke as one musing, and not giving heed to my question); "but what troubleth me most of all is the fear lest the knowledge of Jesus may haply perish with him; for if he hath (as I judge that he hath) a certain inborn power of winning men over to his will by kindness and gentleness, then, as it seemeth to me, this power may be likened unto the fabled ring of Solomon, which gave unto the owner well nigh whatsoever he desired. But there is this difference. The ring could be delivered from one man to another; but the art or secret of Jesus is, in all likelihood, not able to be delivered to them that shall come after; but it will perish with him. And then what becometh of his Kingdom of God?"

As long as Quartus was speaking I heard him gladly: but when he had ceased, his words seemed like mist in the morning sun; but the words of Judas seemed as the solid ground from which the mist rolleth away. For what Quartus said was hard to understand; but the words of Judas seemed according to reason, and very plain to be understood; to wit, that the ordinances given on the mountain of blessing were transitory, and that we were still to wait for the New Law: and to this I agreed, and not I only, but the most part of the disciples.

CHAPTER X

IT came to pass, not many days afterwards (about a month after the Feast of the Harvest), that we journeyed to Capernaum; and Nathanael, and Gorgias the son of Philip, and I, had been sent on before to prepare a lodging. Now when we were standing at the door of the house where we were to lodge, we heard a sound as of many feet; and, looking up, Gorgias said, "See, hither cometh the Tetrarch's Thracian guard." I looked and saw a band of about three hundred men, of a wild and savage aspect, bearing targets and girt with scimitars. But Gorgias, noting as I suppose the anger in my countenance, answered, "These dogs (may the Lord destroy them root and branch!) are swift indeed to shed the blood of women and children, but they are as naught compared with the Romans. Could'st thou but see a Roman legion how they march, these would seem unto thee but as jackals at the lion's tail. Mark but how the dogs straggle. But when the Romans march, the spears in their hands all point one way, and the swords by their sides hang all after one fashion, and even their stakes and tools (which they carry behind their backs) do all swing to one time, and their feet, arms, and heads, yea, even to the winking of their eyes, go all together after the manner of a five-banked corn-ship of Alexandria, with her five hundred oars all keeping time; and when they charge, they charge like ten thousand elephants clad in iron. Moreover, they add to their power so much wisdom, that when they halt for the night, each man setteth up his stake in the ground, and taketh his spade, and diggeth his portion of trench before his stake, and behold, the solitary place becometh in a trice a fortified city, with streets and walls and ditches. Verily these Roman swine are all as children of Satan; but a Roman legion is as Satan himself." By this time our Master had arrived; so I was silent. But when he went into the house, I remained without, musing; for the words of Jesus came into my mind again, concerning the entering into the Kingdom; and methought it would be very hard to overthrow these Thracians, and much more the Romans, by becoming as little children.

While I thought on these things there came to the door of the house Jonathan the son of Ezra; for he knew that I was coming to Capernaum, and he had appointed to meet me there. When he had greeted me in loving terms, he said that he desired to speak with me touching Jesus of Nazareth; "For," said he, "I hear that he turneth from him the minds of many, in that he observeth not the Sabbath." I could not deny this; for indeed Jesus had oftentimes, during our journey in Galilee, broken the Sabbath. Sometimes he had healed the sick on the Sabbath; and but lately on the Sabbath before the Feast of the Harvest, he had healed one that had an impediment in his speech; and when certain of the Pharisees had blamed it, he had said aloud, before all the people, that it was right to do good on the Sabbath, but not to do evil. Moreover, he had not rebuked them that carried the sick to him on the Sabbath, though the bearing of burdens be forbidden. Once, indeed, he had even commanded a sick man to carry with him the bed whereon he lay. I therefore held my peace, but Jonathan added, "Even though he cure the sick on the Sabbath, yet why need he offend the learned and the pious by bidding the sick bear burdens on the day of rest? Moreover, if he desire to go more than a Sabbath day's journey on some errand of mercy, why doth he not use the device of meat, so that he may keep the letter of the Law? Therefore, speak thou unto him, as one that loveth him; and warn him that the Pharisees are wroth."

Then there came into my mind how, on the last Sabbath day, Jesus had passed by a house in a certain village, which was the house of a poor widow; and a great storm of wind and rain, which had arisen in the night, had washed away some part of the wall thereof, so that the rest was in danger to fall. And behold, a man, a mason by trade, was working diligently to repair the breach. When we saw it we were ready to take up stones for to stone him; but Jesus forbade us, and said to the man, "Man, if thou knowest what thou doest, blessed art thou; but if thou knowest not what thou doest, cursed art thou."[1] Thereat we all marvelled, and there was much questioning among us. But when we had considered the matter, we perceived no more but this; that Jesus would not have us to observe the Sabbath as the Scribes observed it.

[1] See Note I.

I therefore replied that I durst not speak to Jesus, nor did I believe that he would give heed to my speech: for that I thought he brake the Sabbath, not out of heedlessness, but of set purpose. Jonathan was astonished at these words, but I continued, "Not that our Master aimeth at breaking the Sabbath: but if a sick man needeth to be healed, he thinketh it right that the Sabbath should be broken for the sick man's sake." Then Jonathan said, "Then what new rule doth he teach? Doth he suffer you to go four thousand paces or even five thousand paces on the Sabbath, instead of two thousand, which the Law alloweth?" But I replied, "Neither four thousand paces, nor five thousand; for our Master maketh no rules. But, as it seemeth to me, there is in him a certain spirit from God which prompteth him to do this or that, and forbiddeth him to do otherwise: and if the spirit of kindness say unto him 'Go,' then he will go and bid us go, though it be ten thousand or twenty thousand paces; and this, even on the Sabbath. For, in fine, he saith that the Sabbath is made for man, and not man for the Sabbath."

Hereat Jonathan was sorely grieved, and said, "If this be so, I fear lest counsel be of no avail." But after that he had weighed the matter, he said, "Even though he be a prophet, and have a message from God, yet are there seasons and ways of delivering a message; and in these matters the experience and counsel of old age may have weight. Therefore I will adventure to speak to him." I was glad that he had thus determined: for many of us had desired to speak with Jesus. Yet I feared lest Jonathan might not prevail. For I had noted that Jesus at first brake the Sabbath, only when a kindness compelled; but when the Scribes and Pharisees were wroth, and strove to place the yoke on his neck, so as to cause him to cease from good works on the Sabbath, then he not only rebelled against it, but made as if he would break the yoke from off the necks of all, especially the poorer sort, to whom the Sabbath was rather a burden than a joy. For the more the Pharisees raged against him, the more he made war against the Sabbath. Therefore I did not forebode well for Jonathan: howbeit, I accompanied him into the presence of Jesus.

When we entered into the house, behold, Barabbas was with Jesus, beseeching him that he would not go into the synagogue on the next Sabbath: "For," said he, "the chief ruler of the synagogue hath a plot against thee, and desireth to question thee touching the Sabbath, that he may raise up a tumult of the people against thee. For all the Pharisees and elders of the synagogue are wroth with thee for the sake of the Sabbath, saying that thou dost both break it and teach others also to break it."

Hereon Jonathan, finding his occasion, spake to the same effect, saying that all the Scribes in the country round about Sepphoris had been turned away from Jesus because it had been noised abroad that he observed not the Sabbath. So he besought Jesus to consider his course well: "Despise not instruction from an elder, O my son, even though thou art a prophet. Art thou confident in thine heart that it is a spirit from God, and not a spirit from Satan, that tempteth thee thus to break the Sabbath? Bethink thee also how thou wilt cause the people of the land to go astray. For the simple walk by rules, and straighten their path by ordinances. But lo, thou takest away rules and ordinances; and what dost thou leave in the place thereof? I have heard from Eliezer the son of Arak that a certain man was working even at his handicraft on the Sabbath day, and thou sawest him, and didst not rebuke him: but didst say, that if he had knowledge of that which he did, he was blessed; but if he had not that knowledge, he was accursed. Whence, O my son, should the simple and unlearned gain this knowledge whereof thou speakest? But if thou sayest, 'I am a prophet and will give them this knowledge,' then remember that thou too art mortal, and as the grass of the field; and when thou shalt pass away, thy knowledge shall perish with thee, unless it be set forth in rules. But thou givest no rules to thy disciples.

"But come, let us reason together as though thou wert altogether right in this matter, having a message from God to us touching the Sabbath. Notwithstanding, is there not a place and a time for delivering a message, and a place and a time for concealing it? There is a time to go forward; but is there not also a time to make a stand? It is good to set thy face toward the light, that thou ·mayest advance; but it is good also to turn thy face from the light, that thou mayest see whither thou hast advanced. Moreover, why dost thou cause the Pharisees to stumble, and the rich to take offence at thy doctrine? Art thou not the Redeemer of all Israel? Are not the Pharisees also thy brethren, and the rich also sheep of the flock? Why therefore dost thou drive them from the fold and cast them forth into the wilderness? If thou sayest, 'They

K

are weak,' then take pity, O my son, on the weak ones of Israel, yea and perchance on thine own disciples, lest they that may come after thee drink of thy doctrine and die, and the Name of Heaven be profaned."

Now at the first the face of Jesus was not altered toward Jonathan the son of Ezra, and he heard him kindly, yet patiently withal, and as if he knew what the old man would say, before he said it. But when Jonathan begged him for compassion's sake not to cause the weak ones to stumble, then the fashion of his countenance was changed as if he would have wept, and he seemed to us like one in sore straits, for he changed colour and was silent. Judge, therefore, how great was our astonishment when he stood up and rebuked Jonathan as though his words were from Satan.

Perplexity and sore grief fell upon us all, and the old man would have retired abashed. But Jesus took him by the hand and constrained him to stay, and made him sit down by his side and spake kindly unto him. Yet he began to speak again of the words of Jonathan as being a sore temptation, telling us how in former times he had undergone a like temptation from Satan. He had been in the wilderness, he said, and lo, in a moment of time he had been borne to the top of a mountain, whence he saw the kingdoms of the earth and the glory thereof, and Satan said to him, "All these things will I give unto thee, if thou wilt fall down and worship me."

While we marvelled at the words of Jesus, and disputed among ourselves how that temptation in the wilderness could be like unto this temptation, behold, Judas of Kerioth came into the chamber, saying the same things which Barabbas had said, to wit that the Pharisees in Capernaum were laying a snare for Jesus, for to catch him in his teaching, that they might cause the people to stone him. But Jesus gave command that we should pass over on the morrow to the other side of the lake.

On the morrow, while we rowed across the lake, I asked Nathanael what seemed to him the nature of the temptation of Satan whereof Jesus had spoken. Nathanael made answer and said, "Thou perceivest that the heart of our Master overfloweth with pity for the miseries of men; and even to redeem them from these miseries he hath been sent by the Lord. Now as for silver and gold, or fame, or wisdom, none of these things can in any wise tempt him once to go aside either to the right hand or to the left from the straight path of Redemption. Howbeit, pity and love can tempt him. Wherefore the only temptation that can befal him is from the Voice that saith, Be pitiful, even though thou transgress in pitying ; Do evil that thou mayest do good ; Gain power by crooked ways, that thou mayest straighten the paths of salvation for them which wander astray ; Wink thou at falsehood, that they which err may be guided toward truth." Now this Voice, as it seemeth to me, is to our Master the Voice of Satan; and to listen to it is to bow down to Satan. And Satan, perchance, knowing that in this way alone can our Master be tempted, hath caused Jonathan the son of Ezra to tempt him. But I know no more than thou ; only such is my conjecture."

While we thus conversed together the boat drew nigh unto the eastern shore. The mountains came down to the water's edge, so close, and so precipitous withal, that there was scarce space enough to land: and, because the sun still lay low in the east, all was dark before us, though the waters behind us shone fair and bright. But when we were now entering under the shadow of the cliffs, so that we could discern things more clearly, we perceived that there was a margin of shore, but narrow and exceeding rocky, strewn all over with large and small fragments of black rock, which had fallen from the mountain above. Then suddenly there fell on our ears a marvellous strange cry, neither as of a man nor yet as of a wild beast; and while we ceased rowing for to listen, behold, yet another cry, more piercing and strange than the first, and then straightway another: and withal the rocks and cliffs took up the sound and multiplied it, and tossed it this way and that way till all the land seemed alive with the clamour. But Gorgias trembled and said it was an evil spirit, for, said he, "There be burial-places in this part of the coast." Then Peter cried aloud and said, "I see a form as of a man, lank and lean, coming out from the rocks; and it is naked." Then some of us bade steer towards another part of the coast; but Jesus commanded to keep on our course.

Now when we landed, we perceived that it was a man, but he was one possessed with evil spirits. For he had chains about his body; and he had cut and lanced his flesh with grievous wounds. When he saw us, he took up stones to cast at us, so that we feared to approach him; and certain shepherds from afar off beckoned to us to go back from him. But Jesus went before the rest of us and accosted him. And lo, at the voice of Jesus, the man straightway let the stones fall from his hands; and, for a moment, he stood as one astonied and in a trance. Then he shrieked aloud and made answer to Jesus in two voices, after the manner of those possessed with unclean spirits. For at one time the man spake, and at another the devils. But the devils, speaking in a deep hollow voice, declared that they were swine, and three thousand in number, and that their name was Legion. Moreover they besought Jesus that he would not send them into the abyss (for by this name do the evil spirits use to call that place wherein they must needs wander so long as they have no bodies of men to dwell in), but that he would suffer them to remain in the man's body. But Jesus drove them out, and the Legion went forth into the abyss, to the number of three thousand, and in the shapes of swine. But Jesus did not suffer the man to accompany him, but bade him return to his friends, and to tell them what great things the Lord had done for him.

This mighty work of Jesus I have set down the more exactly, because no such unclean spirit as this was ever cast out by any other exorcist. For other men have been possessed with swine, or toads, or scorpions, or serpents, but not with many in number, seldom with more than seven. But this man was possessed with three thousand swine. For I not only heard him say this to Jesus, but he also repeated it to me; for I conversed with him. He told me also that he himself saw the three thousand swine go forth and run, first upward, and then violently down from the cliff, even to the abyss. Now the man was a Gadarene, a Jew by birth, and a patriot, one of the sect of the Galileans. Howbeit, living in Gadara, which is a Greek city, he had suffered himself to become defiled, and had rejected the Law and the Worship, and had eaten swine's flesh. But it came to pass that on a certain day, even at the hour of prayer, when he thought on these things, a darkness fell upon his soul, and he saw sights of demons; and sometimes also he saw the sun as though it were red as blood; and he loathed his food as it had been poison. And this continued for the space of six months. But at the end of the six months, on a certain Sabbath, as he stood in the streets of Gadara, so it was that there came a cohort, which is the tenth part of a Roman legion, marching through the town. And he turned and cursed them in the name of the Lord; and lo, as the curse went forth from his mouth, the devils entered into him in the shape of a legion of swine; and they possessed him even to the day when Jesus healed him. All this I heard from the demoniac himself.

When Jesus had worked this miracle we all rejoiced greatly; for we thought that whoso could do so mighty a work, to him all things were possible; and we desired Jesus to go back to the other side of the lake, and there to work miracles that he might convince the Pharisees. But we marvelled that Jesus set so little store on his mighty works, insomuch that he even seemed oftentimes unwilling to work them. Many also he wrought in private; and many he would fain have kept secret, but he could not. Now when I asked Nathanael (for he was as it were an interpreter unto me to explain such sayings of Jesus as were hard to understand) for what cause Jesus lightly esteemed his own miracles, he asked me whether I had not noted how the common folk resorted to Jesus as a mere worker of wonders, so that sometimes they even interrupted his discourse, being desirous that Jesus should cease to teach that he might begin to work cures. "Now Jesus," he said, "doth not desire that men should come to him merely as the healer of their bodies, but as the healer also of their souls."

"For this cause," said Nathanael, "Jesus often biddeth such as he healeth in Galilee to keep silence, although he suffered the Gadarene in these distant parts to make it known. For he deemeth it his especial work not so much to drive out diseases and evil spirits from the body, as rather to heal the soul, ministering bread to the hungry and wine to them that are athirst, loosing the tongue of the dumb, and causing the deaf to hear, opening the eyes of the blind, and making the lame to leap as a hart in the paths of salvation."

We made no long stay on the eastern side of the lake; but when we came again to Capernaum we found the hearts of the people turned from us. For not only did the chief ruler and the elders of the synagogue watch us, as before, if perchance they could take us at an advantage; but the zeal of the townsmen also seemed to have waxed cold. Scarcely had our boat touched the strand at Capernaum when my uncle Manasseh met me. He took me aside and spake with me very earnestly, saying that he had rebuked his son Baruch for his slackness at business, because poverty was coming upon them as an armed man, by reason of his constant attending on Jesus; and he added, "It is true also of thee as of Baruch, 'He becometh poor that dealeth with a slack hand; but the hand of the diligent maketh rich. He that gathereth in summer is a wise son; but he that sleepeth in harvest is a son that causeth shame.'" "And what said Baruch?" I asked. "He hath consented to my words," said Manasseh, "and hath promised that he will no longer accompany this Jesus of Nazareth in his wanderings: and do thou the like." But this I would not do; so we parted in anger.

Not a few left Jesus at this time, mostly they of the wealthier sort, as were Baruch and Manasseh; some going back to their vineyards, others to their olive-presses, others to the dye-works and glass-furnaces, whereof there were many in Galilee. But the poorer sort joined themselves to Jesus as much as before, being drawn unto him by the fame of his mighty works. Howbeit they also began to wax impatient that Jesus should give the sign for war. Nor did they give now much heed to the words of Jesus; but they paid regard to him as to some great exorcist and sorcerer, who useth his art for good ends. Therefore the heart of our Master was sad at this time; and he was grieved that the simple folk knew him not: and their words of praise were an abomination to him.

Now it came to pass that on the third day after we had returned to Capernaum, the fame of Jesus, how he had driven out the legion of swine into the abyss, having been now noised abroad on our side of the lake, behold, the common people thronged him more than before; insomuch that, when he began to teach the people on the shore after his manner, during the cool of the evening, they pressed in upon him and interrupted him, so that he was not able to continue his discourse. But Jesus, being grieved thereat, gave command to Peter and to Andrew that they should straightway launch a boat; and he went on board. When the people saw it, they made lamentation; but the boat was stayed at about fifty paces from the land; and Jesus sat in the boat and taught us while we stood on the shore.

When he opened his mouth, we perceived that he taught after a new fashion. For he no longer said "Do this," "Do not that"; but he spake in parables. Now almost all the teaching of the Wise is in parables, and Jesus also had before taught in parables; but these parables had been short, and along with the parables there had been added the interpretation thereof. But it was not so now; for the parable was naught but a tale about a certain sower, how he sowed seed on several kinds of ground: of the seeds, some falling on rock were destroyed by birds; others by heat and the shallowness of the soil; others by weeds; but some brought forth fruit.

Hereat certain murmured, and Gorgias said aloud, "Doth he think to redeem Sion with a tale? Lo, the prophet John is in prison, and the men of Galilee wait but for a nod from Jesus to rescue him; and our Master rescueth him not, but openeth his mouth in dark sayings." But the greater number listened all agape, as though spell-bound; for the very voice of Jesus had power to bind the souls of a multitude. Howbeit, when evening, or at the most when the morrow came, the parable had clean vanished out of the minds of the greater part. Notwithstanding some (but these only a very few) stored up the words of Jesus in their hearts, and diligently pondered them.

In the evening I went with the rest to Jesus; and we besought him to tell us what the parable might mean, and also why he taught thus in parables. When he had answered, I perceived the meaning of the parable, how that Abuyah the son of Elishah, and Eliezer the son of Arak, were the rocky ground from which the birds picked up the seed; but Baruch, and such as Baruch, were the shallow ground; and Manasseh and the rich merchants and artificers were the fertile ground wherein weeds choked the seed. But still we were fain to know why he spake in parables.

When we again questioned him of this, behold, Jesus cried aloud with an exceeding bitter cry, saying, in the words of the Prophet Isaiah: "I heard the voice of the Lord saying, Whom shall I send, and who will go for us? Then said I, Here am I; send me. And the Lord said, 'Go and tell this people, Hear ye indeed, but understand not; and see ye indeed, but perceive not. Make the heart of this people fat, and make their ears heavy, and shut their eyes; lest they see with their eyes, and hear with their ears, and understand with their heart, and be converted, and be healed.'"

Then were we all sad, and sat silent for a while; for our Master's face was full of sorrow, and this was, as it were, the first shadow of evil that had fallen upon our path. Moreover we began to fear that, as in the days of Isaiah, so it would be now. The Lord had sent his prophet, even Jesus of Nazareth; but the hearts of the people would be hardened against the words of the prophet; yea, the prophet himself would seem to make the hearts of the people hard and not soft, as it was with Abuyah the son of Elishah and Eliezer the son of Arak, whose hearts were made fat and their ears heavy by the words of Jesus of Nazareth.

For we perceived in part his meaning, to wit, not that he desired in truth to shut the eyes of the people, but that he was constrained of the Lord to preach the Gospel, and all pressed to hear it; yet could he in no wise preach it so as to make it plain to all, but only to a few. For behold, he had made trial of the plain way of teaching, and men had thought they had understood him, but they had understood him not; but had esteemed him lightly, as little better than an exorcist. For his words had not pierced into their hearts, but had rested without, as seeds on the wayside; insomuch that they had been carried away by the angels of Satan. Therefore must he now adventure a new path of teaching to the end that, at the least, some few of us might be convinced of our want of understanding, so that we might seek and find the truth; but, to the most, all things should be in darkness, yea, the light itself should be as darkness unto the most.

All this the Lord Jesus spake more clearly afterwards, when he perceived the will of the Father that only a few should be chosen, though many were called: but at this time (perchance because it had been but newly revealed to him) he spake more darkly and with a greater bitterness of sorrow. Howbeit when he had lifted up his head and perceived that we also were weighed down with his affliction, then straightway he made himself to be of a cheerful countenance, and comforted us, saying, "Unto you it is given to know the mysteries of the kingdom of God; but unto them that are without, all things are done in parables." Then he bade us take heed that we taught others even as he had taught us; for, said he, "with what measure ye mete, it shall be measured to you." He said also, "Take heed how ye hear; for whosoever hath, to him shall be given, and whosoever hath not, from him shall be taken even that which he hath." These latter words we understood not then; but, as I take it, the meaning of Jesus was twofold; first, that whoso had not faith nor honesty would receive damage (even as Judas received damage, and not advantage) from the doctrine of Jesus; but, secondly, he seemed to mean that the doctrine was, as it were, lent to each of the disciples, as money upon usury; each being bound to traffic with the doctrine in the commerce of his own thoughts, so as to add thereto. In the same way he told us, at another time, that we were to bring forth out of our treasuries things new as well as old; and he also bade us to "be trustworthy bankers."[1] For of all things Jesus misliked that we should repeat his words by rote; nor did he even bid us copy his actions exactly (but he even said that a time should come when we should do greater works than he had done); and the like also of his words. For this cause perchance, Jesus spake afterwards to us also, even to us his disciples, sometimes in dark sayings; to the intent that we might ponder, and ask and know the

[1] See Note I.

truth. For albeit we often feared to ask him questions (because of our folly and our want of faith), yet did he ever desire us to question him; teaching us that only to them that knock, is the door opened; and only to them that hunger, is given of the bread of Life.

When we went forth from the chamber, Gorgias said, "What meaneth the Prophet? Doth he say that whosoever is rich, he shall be made richer? And whosoever is poor, shall he also be made poorer?" Hereat we all smiled; for we knew that our Master spake not of money, but of wisdom: and one made answer to Gorgias to this effect. Then said Judas, "But if Jesus mean wisdom, then how sayeth he 'With what measure ye mete, it shall be measured to you?'" But Jonathan the son of Ezra replied, "Is not this even according to the saying of the Wise, 'Man is born to learn in order to teach?' And again, 'He that learneth the Law and doth not teach it, he it is that despiseth the Name of the Lord.' Therefore the meaning of Jesus is, that if a man teach others what he hath learned, the angels give into his bosom a hundredfold reward." To this Nathanael agreed, and he added, "The reward is not as a price that is paid, so many shekels for so much teaching; but it is even as the rain cometh from the cloud, or as heat cometh from the fire. Even so doth wisdom come from teaching. For wisdom is not as a dead block that wasteth with the using, but as a living thing that groweth with exercise. But most of all is this true of that kind of wisdom whereof our Master speaketh."

Then Judas said, "But I would to God that our Master would leave off to speak of wisdom and would do somewhat." And Gorgias said Amen to that. But Simon Peter replied: "It is said, 'Take to thyself a master, and be quit of doubt.' Now my Master is Jesus of Nazareth, and I purpose not to spend the time in doubting, nor to halt between many opinions. For the man that is given to much doubting, to what is he like? He is like unto a ship with many pilots, which attaineth not to the harbour. Therefore have I settled my mind to believe that whatsoever Jesus doeth, that is righteousness, and whatsoever he purposeth, that is wisdom."

To this we agreed, and no more was said. Howbeit many of us could not so far constrain ourselves, but we had some searchings of heart; and passing clouds of trouble sometimes crossed our souls for that the Pharisees were set against us, and because Jesus himself had that day seemed like unto one bearing a burden of the Lord. Notwithstanding on the morrow, when we looked upon his countenance, full of brightness and cheerfulness, and when we heard him speak, after his wont, of the greatness and the glory of the Kingdom that was to come, behold, all our dark thoughts had immediately vanished away.

CHAPTER XI

AMONG them that came to Jesus, a few were outcasts from the synagogues, or, as they were called, "sinners"; and it grieved the chief ruler of the synagogue in Capernaum and the elders of that synagogue that Jesus should receive such people. But Jesus received them gladly, and his anger waxed daily hotter against the rulers of the synagogues and against the Scribes, "because," said he, "they kept the key of the Kingdom, and yet they would neither enter in themselves nor suffer others to enter in." He also spake sometimes of a new Key which he must give to his disciples; but this, as yet, he spake not clearly. But as I remember, these words concerning the Scribes were spoken when Jesus first heard of the story of Hannah; which I will set down here, though the matter occurred some days before.

There lived in Capernaum a certain woman whose name was Hannah, sister of the mother of Nathanael. This woman was afflicted by Satan, so that she could not stand upright, but was bowed down to the earth. Now it came to pass that on a certain day when Nathanael visited her in her affliction, behold, the Rabbi Eliezer was in her house, questioning her touching her sins. And Eliezer had persuaded the woman that she was guilty of many sins; for enquiring whether she had visited any of her acquaintance on the Sabbath, he found that one of them, a widow, old and bed-ridden, lived somewhat more than two thousand paces from her house; wherefore he declared that Hannah had broken the Law in visiting this poor widow on the Sabbath. Moreover he reproved Hannah because she had borne burdens on the Sabbath, in that she had worn ribbons upon her garment during the Sabbath, which ribbons were not sewn to her garment; neither had she observed the Law of the Sabbath as touching things that are not living. Many other like sins did Eliezer reprove in Nathanael's kinswoman.

But when she sought how to be forgiven, he said, "Thou hast not sinned against man, but against God. If a man sin against men, the judge shall judge him: but if a man sin against the Lord, who shall entreat for him? But give of thy substance to the treasury of the synagogue, and I will entreat for thee if perchance the Lord will deal mercifully with thee. Howbeit thou must needs wait till the Day of Atonement: for until that day thou mayest not be forgiven. But in the mean season fast, and eat no pleasant food, nor drink wine: but afflict thy soul before the face of the All-merciful (blessed is He) if perchance He may incline His ear unto thy prayer."

Now when Hannah heard these things, her spirit fainted within her, and she knew not what to do, and she cried aloud to Eliezer, "Alas! the Angel of Death is even now upon my threshold, and my sins weigh heavily upon me. I beseech thee therefore, entreat the

Lord for me, that He may forgive me immediately, lest I die unforgiven." But he made answer, as before, that she must needs wait till the Day of Atonement; and he made ready to depart. Then she caught him by the garment to entreat him; but he would not stay, but went out.

On the third day after these things, it came to pass that seven evil spirits entered into Hannah and possessed her in the shapes of swine; and Eliezer heard it, and said that it was a judgment of the Lord. Then was Nathanael sorely grieved, and he came to Jesus and told him everything; both that which Eliezer had said, and how Hannah had cried unto him, and afterwards how the evil spirits had entered into her. But Jesus (as it was reported to me by Nathanael), being exceeding wroth, arose in haste upon hearing of this story; and he went forth straightway to the house of Hannah and cast out the seven devils, and bade her be of good cheer and live in peace. And then it was that he uttered this saying against the Scribes, whereof I made mention above, namely that they kept the key of the Kingdom of God, but would neither enter in themselves, nor suffer others to enter in.

Now it happened that, soon after these things, I brought Nathanael to visit the Rabbi Jonathan at his lodging in Capernaum; and we found there the aforesaid Eliezer the son of Arak conversing with him. When Eliezer saw us, he complained sorely of the light-mindedness (so he called it) which our Master manifested in receiving sinners. But Jonathan replied saying that the cause lay in the exceeding gentleness of our Master, because he knew not the evil nature of man.

L

"For," said he, "from his birth upward, Jesus of Nazareth hath moved in Paradise; and being himself good, pure, and gentle, he believeth that others also are in their thoughts like unto himself, and that they need but a little help to make them in their deeds like unto himself. For he esteemeth of sin as being naught but an infirmity. But time and experience will open his eyes."

Then answered Nathanael and said to Eliezer, "But is it not truly said, O son of Arak, that 'The perfection of wisdom is repentance?' and again, 'When a man hath been wholly wicked, and hath repented at last, the Holy One receiveth him'? Nay, it is added that, 'If a sinner repent, all the transgressions which he hath committed are imputed to him as merits,' and that 'Repentance was created before the world.' How then is our Master wrong in receiving them that repent?" But Eliezer answered, with an austere countenance, that repentance availed nothing without works; and he quoted the saying, "No boor is a sin-fearer; nor is the vulgar pious"; and another saying which warneth men "Not to frequent the company of the unlearned." "Moreover," he added, "the All-seeing (blessed is He) alone knoweth the hearts of men, and discerneth the true repentance from the false. Wherefore none can forgive sins but God alone."

Then Nathanael, remembering how great an evil had befallen his kinswoman through the hardness of Eliezer, became exceeding wroth, and brake out into bitter accusations against the Scribes, because they despised the people of the land: "For lo," he said, "more than half of Israel even now goeth down to the pit of destruction, and ye raise no hand to save them. Yea, when the drowning ones lift up their heads from the waters and cry saying, 'We are alive, help us,' then stand ye on the bank and answer, saying, 'Down, down, ye ought not to be alive, ye are not alive.' For ye say that ye make fences to keep in the Law; but ye make fences indeed to keep out the people from the Law. Wherefore your fences are as offences, and ye are guilty of the blood of half the nation of Israel in the sight of the Lord."

Then Eliezer arose in wrath, and as he went to the door, he turned and looked on Nathanael and said, "Like master, like scholar:" and so he went out. But when he was departed, Jonathan said to us, "Eliezer spake unadvisedly and harshly; yet is there truth in his words. For when we shun the 'unlearned' and the 'vulgar,' or the people of the land, we mean such as have not learned their duties toward God and man, which also are wholly given up to the things of earth. Such men are lovers of self, wallowing in carnal lusts: and are they not to be blamed?"

To this Nathanael replied, "True, O my father; and if all the teachers of Israel were as thou art, verily Israel would be blessed. But do not the Scribes cast out many from the synagogues for small matters, even though they perform the weightier duties? Yea, I myself have heard Eliezer say many times, 'Hasten to a light precept'; and I have seen him to be more angered for a light transgression than a heavy one. Also many of them say that a 'vulgar' person is one that repeateth not the daily Krishma, or weareth not phylacteries, or fringes, or doth not wait on the learned.

These things do the Scribes exalt, but they pass over justice, mercy, righteousness, and truth."

Jonathan made no answer to this at first; but presently he sighed and said, "Truly we have need of a discerning spirit; and we should pray unto the All-seeing (blessed is He) that we may not make defiled the pure, nor make pure the defiled, and that we may not bind the loosed nor loose the bound." No one spake further about this matter. But Nathanael sat musing, while I conversed with Jonathan concerning his return to Sepphoris and concerning certain messages which I desired that he should deliver to my mother. Presently we bade farewell to Jonathan and departed.

But as we passed through the street together, Nathanael still mused, and, as it seemed to me, was repeating to himself the words of Jonathan, "That we may not bind the loosed nor loose the bound." Then he turned to me and said, "Joseph, is there not a certain saying touching the destroying of the Evil Nature?" "Yes, of a truth is there," replied I; "for it is said that it shall come to pass, in the time to come, that the Holy One will bring the Evil Nature, and slay him in the presence of the righteous and in the presence of the wicked." Then Nathanael smote his hands together for joy, and lifted up his voice and said "Perchance, therefore, in the day of the Redemption of Sion, the Evil Nature shall be utterly destroyed, and we shall no longer pray according to the prayer of Jonathan the son of Ezra, that we may not loose the bound; for all shall be loosed."

While he spake thus, somewhat loudly, behold, a certain Barachiah the son of Zadok heard the last words of Nathanael; and he cried after us and mocked at us and our Nazarene prophet, for so he called Jesus. Now this man was a beggar, crook-backed and lame, and of a malignant disposition, one that took pleasure in slander and mischief: and oftentimes he had thrust himself in the path of Jesus and had besought Jesus to heal him of his deformity. But Jesus would not. So this man called after us, mocking us and imitating the voice of Jesus and saying, "Go in peace, go in peace."

Then I began to question Nathanael why Jesus had not healed this Barachiah: Nathanael answered and said, "Because he hath not faith. Moreover, as thou knowest, Jesus doth not adventure to heal all afflictions and all diseases. And even if the affliction be such as can be healed, yet he healeth not, except there be first faith." Then I said, "But how doth he discern such as have faith from such as have not faith?" But Nathanael answered, "I know not; and indeed it is a marvel to me to see how he healeth the sick. But he speaketh of these mighty works as being prepared for him beforehand in heaven. And indeed it seemeth to me that whensoever Jesus doeth a mighty work on earth, he seeth it also done, in that instant, in heaven. For he looketh upon the body of the sick man with his eyes; but with his spirit methinks he looketh on the spirit of the man in heaven; and there he seeth a Hand, even the Hand of the Everlasting Arm; and whatsoever the Hand worketh in heaven, even that doth Jesus work on earth; and if he seeth the Hand unloosing the chain from the spirit of the man in heaven, then Jesus unlooseth the chain on earth. But if he seeth that the Hand in heaven moveth not, then his hand also is stayed on earth."

But I said, "When Jesus hath healed the sick, he biddeth them go in peace, as Barachiah but now cried after us. Now if there be no peace in the man's heart, how can he go in peace? Doth Jesus therefore make peace in the man's heart? Or is it that he merely seeth peace in the man's heart, and speaketh aloud that which he seeth?" "Both," replied Nathanael; "at least, so it seemeth to me. For I judge that Jesus not only discerneth peace, but also maketh peace. Likewise also he seemeth to me to make faith. I know not how it is, but of late a certain Mattathias described to me the manner in which Jesus had dealt with him. Now this Mattathias was afflicted with a disease in his feet, insomuch that he had not walked for these three years: and he was carried by his friends into the presence of Jesus. 'And,' said he, 'before I saw Jesus, I had scarce any hope that he might be able to help me; but when I looked upon Jesus, and saw what a strength shone in his countenance, then I began to have faith, but not much; for still I feared more than I hoped. Yet as Jesus healed first one and then another (for there were many waiting to be healed before me) my faith grew stronger and stronger. But when Jesus was come to the bed whereon I lay, he fixed his eyes steadfastly upon me, so that the brightness thereof passed like purifying fire into my soul; and he looked up unto heaven and then down upon me, and it was as if he had been wrestling with the evil spirit of faithlessness in my heart and had quite driven it out. For now, behold, of a sudden, my doubts and fears and troubles were all clean gone, and my heart was as light as air, and a certain irresistible faith possessed me; insomuch that, though I lay still on my bed, I knew that I had been made whole and that I needed naught save the bidding of Jesus to tell me when to arise. And when the word came, I arose.' Now," said Nathanael, "thus spake Mattathias to me. But if he spake aright, then methinks Jesus hath a power to create faith in the heart as well as to heal the diseases of the body."

All that night I meditated upon the words of Nathanael and upon the story of Mattathias: for that a prophet should cure diseases seemed possible, though wonderful; but that any one, yea, even though he were the Redeemer of Israel himself, should have power to create peace and faith, this indeed seemed a marvellous and almost an impossible thing. But it came to pass that on the morning of the very next day, as I remember, we went into the house of a certain rich man with Jesus; and a great company was assembled (some because of the mighty work that Jesus had wrought on the Gadarene, but others, of the richer sort, because they desired to abet the plotting of the Pharisees against him), and Jesus was now on the point to speak to the people, when a noise was heard from the roof above. There had been no small stir, even before, near the door of the house, and none had taken heed thereof; but now we looked up, and behold, one sick of the palsy in a bed was let down by ropes, until the bed reached the place where Jesus was; for he sat in the gallery that ran round the court-yard, but we stood in the court-yard below. Now many of us thought that Jesus would not heal one that thus thrust himself into the midst of the people, interrupting his exhortation and doctrine; and some cried out to remove the man, but others cried out Nay. Howbeit, when Jesus gave command that there should be silence, there was silence, even such a silence that men feared almost to breathe; so great was the expectation of all to see what Jesus would do.

Then sounded forth these words above the heads of all the congregation, full of pity, yet like unto the sound of a silver trumpet in clearness: "Thy sins be forgiven thee." I myself was so far off that I heard the words, but could not see the countenance of Jesus. But they that saw him told me that it was even as Nathanael had described unto me the healing of Mattathias. For Jesus fixed his eyes steadfastly on the man, as if he saw, not the man himself, but the man's angel standing in heaven bound before the throne of God, with the chains of Satan round him, and all the host of heaven looking thereon. "His countenance also shone as the sun: pity and sorrow were there, but pity and sorrow swallowed up in the brightness and glory of joy and triumph; and the sick man's face gave back the brightness. But when Jesus perceived that the time had come, and that the word of God had gone forth, and that the chains in heaven had been broken, then Jesus spake and broke the chains on earth." So spake one unto me afterwards, describing the manner of Jesus, how he forgave the palsied man.

But after the first silence there arose a great murmuring and the sound of many voices disputing. The voice of Eliezer was clearly heard saying, "This man blasphemeth; who can forgive sins but God alone?" "Yea," said another, "and sins are forgiven not on earth, but in heaven, at the last day." But others mocking said that the sick man seemed not yet to have gained much profit, albeit his sins had been forgiven. All this noise and stir ceased at once when Jesus began to speak. He said, "Why reason ye these things in your hearts? Whether is it easier to say to the sick of the palsy, 'Thy sins be forgiven thee,' or to say 'Arise, and take up thy bed and walk'? But that ye may know that the Son of Man hath authority even upon earth to forgive sins"—here he paused and stood up, and behold, the whole of the congregation was constrained to stand up with one consent; insomuch that I saw even Eliezer the son of Arak standing up with the rest, and his face was kindling as the faces of the rest, and the silence was even such as could be felt, and the palsied man himself seemed half to raise himself in his bed in expectation: and, like a shock, there fell on us the word "Arise." And lo, the man arose at once, and stood straight up, and Jesus said to him, "Take up thy bed, and go thy way into thy house." And immediately he arose, took up his bed, and went forth whole before them all.

Then were all amazed, and glorified God, and some said, "We never saw it in this fashion." But others praised and magnified the All-merciful because He had given this new authority to men, so as to forgive sins, and this too not hereafter in heaven, but at once and upon earth. But Eliezer and the chief ruler and others of the elders of the synagogue, when they had recovered from their first astonishment, took counsel how they might again catch Jesus in his doctrine. For they said, "None can forgive sins, except God only: therefore it is certain that this man maketh himself God." Howbeit they veiled their thoughts with a smooth countenance, for fear of the multitude; and going up to Jesus they saluted him before they departed from the synagogue. But Jesus looked wistfully at them, like unto one hoping for good news; for he thought that they would have understood that God had sent him, perceiving the finger of God in the healing of the man that was sick of the palsy. But when he perceived their dissimulation, he was silent until he had come forth from the synagogue: and then I heard him sigh, and he said in a low voice to himself, "For judgment am I come into this world, that those who see may see not."

During the rest of that day Jesus sat musing: and at one time he seemed to be sad, but at another time to rejoice. But even when he was sad, there always appeared a joy beneath the sadness; so that his sadness was but as the cloud that dappleth the side of a mountain, the summit whereof shineth bright in the sunlight. For it was the nature of Jesus always to be cheerful and to rejoice; insomuch that peace and joy seemed to go forth from him to all men and things around him, and from them to come back with increase to him again. But now he was sorrowful, as we gathered, because of the hardness of heart of the Pharisees. For howsoever they might outwardly dissemble, yet did he discern their hearts, that they were inwardly grieved, yea, at the goodness of God; wherefore now indeed, after this second token of their hardness, it seemed to be indeed the will of God that the Good News should be of no avail unto the Scribes, save only to make their eyes blind, and their hearts fat, and their ears hard of hearing. For this cause our Master sorrowed: but for some other cause he rejoiced, or seemed in expectation of some joy to come.

But as for the rest of us, we disputed among ourselves touching this new power which Jesus had brought into the world; for it seemed more than human, and such as no prophet before him had ever used or so much as sought from God. Only Judas was silent more than was his custom: and he seemed disturbed and doubtful, as one uncertain of his path and not knowing whether to go forward or backward. For when Nathanael spake about our Master's authority to forgive sins, and how in the day of Redemption he would destroy the Evil Nature, then Judas at times heard him gladly, as if he earnestly desired that this should be true; but at another time he scoffed and said that "No forgiveness of sins would drive out Herod from Tiberias, nor the Romans from Jerusalem."

CHAPTER XII

By this time the autumn was come round, and it wanted but a few days to the tenth day of the month Tisri, which is the Great Day of Atonement. Now so it was that, when we arose on a certain morning (in the first week, as I remember, of the month Tisri), behold, Jesus was not in the house, and when we sought him, we found him on the shore musing; insomuch that at first he was not aware of our presence. But when he saw us, he bade Simon Peter prepare his fishing-boat, for he desired to go out into the deep. So Simon Peter and Andrew launched the boat, and I with them; and Jesus went on board, and there he sat, still musing, while we made ready the tackling and the nets. While we busied ourselves herein, many of the sailors and fishermen of the town came down to the coast and began to launch their vessels; for the day was fair for fishing.

Now there was standing on the beach the hunchback Barachiah, the son of Zadok: for his custom was to beg of the sailors, and to do for them such small services as he was able. But he was hated of the most part of the sailors by reason of his envious and malignant disposition, and because he could not refrain from reproaches and revilings. Moreover they accused him that he had sometimes mislaid or hurt their tackling. Others also said that he had an evil eye and brought evil fortune. Wherefore he fared ill with the sailors, and even when they gave him alms, it was as to a dog or an unclean creature: and oftentimes they struck him when he crossed them. Now it chanced that while we made ready our nets, behold, a certain merchant, coming down to the water, stumbled upon a stone and fell against Barachiah. Then Barachiah cried out in anger, "Wast thou born with a bridle in thy hand that thou shouldst treat thy brethren as if they were mules or asses?" But the other replied, "Yea, and thou wast born with a saddle on thy back, that I might ride upon thee." So saying, he spurned Barachiah out of his path, so that he fell to the ground: and hereat all the sailors laughed.

Not long after this there came down two sailors, nigh to the place where Barachiah sat wiping the blood from his face; and one of them spake to the hunchback some words, I know not what, but, as it appeared, of kindness. Then straightway Barachiah rose up and went with the man, and willingly helped him to launch his boat and to prepare his tackling. And the man's companion laughed and said, "Whence hast thou the power to soften the heart of that child of Satan?" But when Barachiah was departed, the sailor answered that he had in times past shown kindness to a brother of Barachiah, that was now dead; and he added in jest, "In all men there be two hearts, a heart of stone and a heart of flesh: and Barachiah hath his heart of flesh, even as others, though he be a child of Satan." "Nay," replied the other, "but if there be a heart of flesh in Barachiah, it would need Solomon's ring to find out where it is hid." And so jesting they rowed out into the deep.

Now I perceived that Jesus noted all these words of the two sailors, and likewise that which had befallen Barachiah, and while he listened and looked, the appearance of his countenance was altered; for before, he had seemed in his musing like one waiting for an answer to a question, but now like one that had received an answer. Howbeit still he mused and ceased not, while we rowed out into the deep, and busied ourselves with casting our nets.

But so it was that, as we rowed and drifted hither and thither in our fishing, we were carried very close to the coast, where the rocks came straight down to the sea after the manner of a wall; and suddenly we heard a piteous sound as of bleating. When we looked up, we saw a lamb, which had strayed from the flock, and had come to a stand upon a ledge in the rock, exceeding narrow, so that it could not go forward, neither knew it how to turn back: but there it stood, and bleated often and piteously, so that our hearts were sorry for the creature, and we would fain have helped it, but knew not how; for there was not space to land. But while we hung upon our oars not knowing what to do, Peter cried out, "The shepherd cometh"; and presently we all discerned him, very high up, and clambering from rock to rock for to reach the lamb. And when we all shouted and beckoned to him, he straightway understood us, and coming down, though with much ado, took the lamb on his shoulders and bore it safely away. Hereat we were all well content; but when I looked on Jesus, his face shone with an exceeding joy, too great, methought, for so small a matter, so that I marvelled. For there was no more in his countenance the look of one questioning, but rather of one gazing upon the glory of God. Then when we had hauled in the net, he gave command that we should row back to Capernaum.

Now the next day Jesus showed forth what he had on his mind. For about noon he went down to the place where one Matthew a tax-gatherer was sitting at the house of customs near the quay. And for a while Jesus beheld him, how he bore himself amid all the concourse and stir of that busy place; then he drew nigh, and called Matthew to be one of his disciples, saying unto him, "Follow me." And Matthew arose and followed him and bade him to a great feast in his house on the same day, and thereto he called many of his acquaintance, both tax-gatherers and sinners, and others of the poorer sort; and Jesus promised that he would come to the feast. But when this was noised about the town, the anger of the Pharisees was great; for they counted it as a sign that Jesus would not join himself to them, nor do anything to gain their favour. But as for the sailors and common people, some rejoiced, others marvelled; insomuch that when we came to Matthew's house, we found a great concourse of people both round the doors and in the feast-chamber.

Now as we entered the chamber, I could not but chafe somewhat for the baseness of the company with whom we were forced to consort. For they were all unlearned men, and given to vain conversation; and many of them had not washed before supper; and the savour of their garments and the heat of the room were scarce to be borne. Moreover I saw at one of the tables Barachiah the son of Zadok, and others with whom I should never have expected to sit at meat. Then the words of Jonathan the son of Ezra came back to my mind, how he had said that Jesus was misled, in that he knew not the evil nature of men; nor could I refrain from imparting these words to Nathanael, who was my companion at the table.

But Nathanael answered that I erred greatly, for that Jesus knew the evil that was in men better than any man, and hated it more than any man: "But," said he, "the evil of unwashed hands and unsavoury garments doth not seem to Jesus the greatest of evils." "But," said I, "these men are given to other sins; and how cometh it to pass that Jesus beareth with the sins of these men, but doth not bear with the Scribes, who do not commit such sins?" Then said Nathanael, "As it seemeth to me, there is a certain light in the hearts of men; and whoso hath this light in him, loveth light, and is drawn towards the light whenever the light is placed near to him, even though he may have turned his back upon the light: and thus these sinners are drawn towards Jesus. But if a man for many years make it his business to quench the light in himself, because he feareth it; then he cannot love the light, nor can he be drawn towards it, even though it be very close to him. Even as the Pharisees fear the light in themselves, and say there is no light save in the Law and the Traditions. Therefore they quench the light in their hearts and cannot see the true light; and they destroy the Word of God in their hearts, and cannot hear the true Word." "But," said I, "if there be stripped off fine-sounding words from thy speech, to what is the matter like? It is as though thou shouldst say, 'It is better that a man should commit murder and adultery and theft (provided that he love righteousness), than that he should abstain from all these sins, but not love righteousness.'" "Thou knowest well," replied Nathanael, "that according to a man's love of righteousness will be his hatred of sin; and whoso really hateth sin, he cannot live therein. Yet what thou sayest is true; there is more hope of the vilest sinner than of the man that hath in his heart no love of righteousness."

I mused for a while, and then I said, "Thou speakest of hope: but doth it seem to thee truthful, looking upon a bad man, to say, this man is good, merely because thou mayest have hopes that he may become good?" But before Nathanael could make answer, there came into my mind the words of the sailor, that "If Barachiah the son of Zadok had a heart of flesh as well as a heart of stone, it would need Solomon's ring to find out where the heart of flesh was hid;" so I told the words to Nathanael. Straightway Nathanael looked toward the place were Barachiah was sitting at table; and then he turned to me and said, "And hath not our Master the ring of Solomon?" Then I also looked at Barachiah; and I marvelled to see what a gentleness there was in his countenance. But Jesus was at that instant beginning a discourse; so we ceased conversing that we might hearken unto it.

The discourse told of a certain son of a kind father, who, taking his patrimony, wandered into a distant city, where he squandered his substance in riotous living, so that he was forced to keep swine like an hireling; but

M

returning to his father he was welcomed. Other like parables he spake: and all the people were marvellously attentive to hear him. Notwithstanding, Jesus would not always discourse himself alone: for he gladly heard others, and by questions led many to speak, questioning them with courtesy in no way akin to condescension (even as a brother meeting brothers after long absence); the merchants concerning foreign countries; the officers of the customs concerning the commerce and wares of the place; the mariners and soldiers concerning the ships and currents and strong places and fortresses whereof they severally had knowledge. With all these common people did Jesus converse, and to each, methought, he added somewhat of his own nature. And so it was that amid all that concourse of vulgar and unlearned people and boors (as the Scribes would have called them), not one did or said anything unworthy of the presence of our Master. Thus did Jesus give to others, and lo, they gave back to him good measure into his bosom, pressed down and running over, according to his own saying.

But when he rose up to go, behold, Barachiah the son of Zadok also rose up in haste, and coming to Jesus he fell down on his knees before him, and besought him that he would forgive all the slanders and revilings which he had used concerning Jesus and concerning his disciples. And Jesus both forgave him and blessed him. And from that hour even to the day of his death Barachiah was a new creature; insomuch that he was no longer known among them of Capernaum as the viper, or the child of Satan, but they called him "the changed man."

But as Jesus was now going forth, two of the disciples of John the son of Zachariah came unto him. For they had been present in the chamber, though they had not partaken of the feast; and they marvelled at the cheerfulness of Jesus, because he ate bread and drank wine and conversed freely with the common people, not after the manner of their master. So they were offended at Jesus, and said to him, "Master, why do we and the Pharisees fast oft, but thy disciples fast not?" Now John himself had called Jesus the Bridegroom of Israel. Jesus therefore, using these same words, answered and said, "Can the children of the bride-chamber mourn as long as the bridegroom is with them?" Then he turned and looked at us, and his face was sorrowful; and he added, "But the days will come when the bridegroom shall be taken from them, and then shall they fast in those days." Then first did Jesus speak concerning his departure from his disciples: and he meant, perchance, that as John the Prophet had been taken from the midst of his disciples, so also would he himself be taken away from us; for the Lord had revealed unto him that Israel was not to be redeemed easily, nor without much tribulation. But by what power he should be thus taken, whether by imprisonment (as had befallen John), or by death of violence (as was shortly to befall John), or by death in course of nature, concerning these things he said naught at this time. But we neither understood his words, neither took we thought of them.

But as we came forth, we met Eliezer the son of Arak, and the chief ruler of the synagogue, and many of the elders of the synagogue; and they looked at us with sore displeasure. And the chief ruler did not restrain himself, but said to Jesus aloud in the presence of us all, "Is it even so that thou wouldst fain be Ruler over Israel? Behold, on thy side are Matthew the tax-gatherer, and Barachiah the child of Satan, and Mary the sinner; but on my side are Eliezer the son of Arak and all the elders of the synagogue. Is it not better to be the tail of a lion rather than the head of a dog?"

But when Jesus noted how certain of the sinners feared to stand before the faces of Eliezer the son of Arak, and of the ruler of the synagogue, and how they were shaken in their faith and abashed (for that they were accustomed to be despised and to be trampled on, as being without all hope of redemption); then was he exceeding wrath, and he answered and said unto the ruler of the synagogue, "Woe unto the world because of offences: for it must needs be that offences come: but woe to that man by whom the offence cometh." Then he pointed to the sinners behind him (whom he was wont to call "little ones," because they were babes in faith), and he spake again to the chief ruler and his party, saying, "Take heed that ye despise not one of these little ones; for I say unto you that in heaven their angels do always behold the face of my Father which is in heaven. For the Son of Man is come to save that which was lost."

Then Eliezer the son of Arak interrupted him and said, "Why eatest thou, contrary to the Traditions, with tax-gatherers and sinners?" But Jesus answered and said, "How think ye? If a man have an hundred sheep, and one of them be gone astray, doth he not leave the ninety-and-nine, and goeth into the mountains, and seeketh that which is gone astray? And if so be that he find it, verily I say unto you, he rejoiceth more of that sheep than of the ninety-and-nine which went not astray." "But," said another of the Scribes, "why dost thou shun and rebuke the righteous? What evil is it not to be a sinner?" When Jesus heard that, he said unto him, "They that be whole need not a physician, but they that be sick. But go ye and learn what that meaneth, I will have mercy and not sacrifice. For I am not come to call the righteous, but sinners to repentance." So saying, he passed on and left the Pharisees, and we followed him.

Now Andrew and Simon Peter had been disciples of John the son of Zachariah, before they had joined themselves to Jesus. In the evening, therefore, they resorted to Jesus to question him touching the answer he had that day given to John's disciples concerning fasting. I was with them, and also Judas of Kerioth, and a certain Eleazar the son of Azariah, a Scribe of Sepphoris and a friend of Jonathan. Now Eleazar did not venture to advise Jesus to use shifts and subterfuges so as to keep friendship with the Pharisees; but he said that perchance such sinners as might be converted to the path of righteousness might not be able to continue therein, unless the path were fenced in by rules and laws, feasts, fasts, and other like ordinances. He also bade Jesus not separate himself from the congregation; for said he, "Whatsoever is decreed by the congregation below, that is decreed by the congregation above; and what is ratified on earth is ratified in heaven; and with whomsoever the spirit of men is pleased the Spirit of God is pleased."

But Jesus answered that as new wine was not like unto old wine, nor a new garment like an old garment, even so the doctrine of John was not like unto his doctrine; neither could the two be mixed. The doctrine of the Pharisees also, he said, was not like his doctrine, and the two kinds of doctrine needed two several and distinct shapes, even as several kinds of wine need several bottles. When Eleazar heard this, he went out; for these words seemed to him (as he said to John the son of Zebedee) to be a kind of proclaiming of war against the Pharisees; so that there appeared no longer any hope of concord between Jesus and them. Judas also, although he still seemed strangely perturbed, and spake less than was his wont, nevertheless said that a great gulf was opening itself between our Master and the Pharisees; "and," said he, "unless something is speedily done, this gulf will be impassable." Many also that had been disciples of John the Prophet murmured against Jesus, because he had promised to fulfil the Law and had been expected to follow in the course of John, but now he went contrary to the Law and was for choosing a path of his own. For at that time in Galilee they that honoured John the Prophet were more than they that honoured Jesus of Nazareth.

But for my part my soul was given up to thanksgiving and to praise of God, because of this new power which He had sent down to men, of forgiving sins. For if it seemed a divine word to say "Let there be light," and there was light, much more divine a word it seemed to say, "Let there be righteousness," and lo, there was righteousness. And when I remembered the saying of the sailor, how that it needed Solomon's ring to find out the heart of flesh in bad men, and when I called to mind how Jesus had found it out, then it seemed to me that a greater than Solomon was among us. I thought also on the words of Nathanael, how that, in the day of Redemption, the Holy One (blessed is He) will bring the Evil Nature and slay him in the presence of the righteous and of the wicked; and my thoughts were swallowed up in wonder.

CHAPTER XIII

THE words of Judas were true, that a great gulf now lay between our Master and the Pharisees; and day by day the gulf grew wider, as I soon perceived. It chanced that Eliezer the son of Arak knew that I was a friend of Jonathan; and desiring to draw me away from Jesus, he wrote a letter to Jonathan begging him to move me that I might return home. This letter of Eliezer therefore Jonathan sent unto me, and it was to the following effect:

"From Eliezer the son of Arak to Jonathan the son of Ezra: salutation and peace. Be it known unto thee, O Jonathan, that this Jesus of Nazareth, concerning whom we once had hopes that he might be a deep well or perchance even an ever-welling spring of the Law, hath proved an empty vessel and a broken cistern. He profaneth the Sabbath and teacheth others to profane it; he eateth without the washing of hands; he teacheth that no man is defiled by that which he toucheth or cateth; in a word, he breaketh the Law and causeth others to profane it. Yet this in part was known unto thee even before, and thou didst deceive thyself, and saidst, 'Perchance he hath a message from God concerning the Sabbath and concerning the Law.' Hear, therefore,

O son of Ezra, what new thing this blind guide hath taken upon himself to do. He not only teacheth all people everywhere to abstain from sacrifice, wresting to his own destruction that hard saying of the Prophet which saith, 'I will have mercy and not sacrifice,' but he also hath dared to make himself as God, forgiving sins. This he hath done publicly in the synagogue, before the face of the congregation.

"Now we would fain deal gently with the young man, because he seemed once to purpose well, and because he hath made unto himself a name for casting out unclean spirits. Moreover he is befriended not only by the rabble that knoweth not the Law, but also by a few of the wise and pious, as, for example, thyself. For this cause we are minded not at once to punish him in accordance with the law for blasphemy, but to make excuses for him by saying that he is beside himself.

"And this indeed seemeth to be not unlikely, for he is not as other men are; for ofttimes he sleepeth not, but watcheth (as I am informed) whole nights together; and albeit he seeth no vision (which sheweth him to be no prophet), yet he carrieth himself in such strange fashion as if he saw visions daily; also he is wroth at small faults and at no faults (as thou thyself knowest), and yet withal easy to forgive great faults. Moreover of late he most strangely forsweareth the company of all the pious and learned, and consorteth publicly with tax-gatherers and sinners; insomuch that, but now, having called one Matthew a tax-gatherer, to be one of his disciples, afterwards, at a feast in the house of this Matthew, amid mirth and wine-bibbing, he took upon himself to forgive the sins of that Barachiah the son of

Zadok, who, as thou knowest, is by all men called the child of Satan.

"Now therefore, for the sake of the young man Jesus himself, it beseemeth thee, O Jonathan, to cause this evil to cease, and to warn his friends, if perchance they may see fit to restrain him. Write therefore, I pray thee, to his mother Mary, and to his brethren (but I grieve that his father no longer liveth to restrain him) that they may come and lay hands upon him: for they will listen to thy voice. We desire also that thou wouldst write to the young man, thy pupil and friend, Joseph the son of Simeon, that he may return to Sepphoris, lest he too fall into the pit of destruction along with this blind guide Jesus. If also thou shouldst inform Joanna, the mother of Joseph, concerning all these things, she would peradventure join her voice to thine, that thy pupil might return. But in any case it were well that the certainty of the madness of this Jesus should be noised abroad among all thy friends and acquaintances, to the intent that we may the more easily restrain him.

"Hearken, I pray thee, unto my words, O Jonathan, for I will not hide the truth from thee, that certain of us judge the young man Jesus of Nazareth more harshly, saying that he is possessed by Beelzebub. Others also say that hands should be laid upon him without delay, and that he should be delivered to Herod. Now if he hearken unto thee and desist from his consorting with sinners, or if his kinsmen lay gentle hands upon him, then we are willing that he should suffer few stripes; but if not, many stripes will be needful. But if he should be delivered to Herod, or if the people should peradventure take up stones to stone him, who knoweth the end thereof? Peace be with thee!"

Together with the letter of Eliezer was a letter from Jonathan, who besought me to send word unto him about the welfare of Jesus; and I could perceive that, albeit the old man was wroth that any should say that Jesus was possessed with an unclean spirit, yet even he inclined his ear to believe that Jesus was beside himself. For after some words touching the health of my mother, the letter ended thus, "Alas, because of the iniquity of this generation! For verily Jesus was fit to be the Redeemer of Israel; but the generation was unfit. He was as the morning star in his joy, and as the sun in the glory of his brightness; but the night cometh apace, and the sun must give place to the darkness. Verily, Jesus was of them that have entered into Paradise, and have tasted of the honey of the highest heaven. But perchance he hath seen things not vouchsafed to men to see, even the mystery of the Chariot; and the vision hath been too much for the eye of man, and with much honey the mind hath been demented."

When I received these letters, I purposed at once to inform Jesus concerning the plots of the Pharisees. But he was not at that time at Capernaum, but at Bethsaida Julias; so I hastened thither. When I was come thither, Jesus was exhorting the people; and there was a great concourse to hear him, so that I could not come nigh unto him for the press. But while I stood afar off, behold, Eliezer the son of Arak advanced towards him through the midst of the press; and all men made way for him. But he, making as though he could not advance further, called to Jesus in a loud voice, so that all men should hear : " Behold, thy mother and thy brethren stand without, desiring to see thee."

Now could I see from Eliezer's countenance and from the manner of his speech, and from the faces of some of the Scribes that were sitting in the principal places, yea, and from the faces of some others that were in the outermost part of the crowd (for they nodded and beckoned each to the other) that here was indeed the very plot of the Pharisees whereof Eliezer had made mention in his letter to Jonathan. For the mother and brethren of Jesus had come with intent to lay hands on him, having been persuaded that he was beside himself. And immediately all that were in the chamber seemed to become aware of the plot. For Jesus ceased from his teaching; and many stood on tiptoe gazing toward that quarter of the crowd where the mother of Jesus was waiting, and then they gazed back on Jesus again, marking how he bore himself. So there arose a marvellous great stillness, while every one waited to hear what Jesus would say: and my heart beat so that I could even hear the beating thereof. But Jesus said, "Who is my mother, and who are my brethren?" Then he looked round about on those of his disciples that sat nigh unto him and he said, "Behold my mother and my brethren. For whosoever shall do the will of God, the same is my brother and my sister and mother."

When he had said these words, then the countenance of Eliezer fell. For he had hoped either to have found occasion against Jesus (as though he paid no reverence to his mother, not rising up or going forth to meet her), or else that the brethren of Jesus should have laid hands on him as he went forth, and so all men should ever after have esteemed him as one beside himself. But the words of Jesus manifested that he ceased not to love and honour his mother, howbeit he loved and honoured others also, even as many as were in the Family of God, unto whom he was as a brother or as a son; neither ought he to have forsaken all the Family of God to please the family of Nazareth; for, had he gone forth to meet them that stood without, he had forsaken and caused to stumble all them that sat within. So they perceived what was in the mind of Jesus; and they magnified him the more.

When the Pharisees perceived that they had not prevailed with the common people, they began to adventure a second plot. For they procured a certain Scribe to accuse Jesus in the synagogue, and to say that he cast out devils through Beelzebub the prince of the devils. The name of the Scribe was Hezekiah the son of Zachariah, from Jerusalem; even the same Hezekiah of whom I spake before, when I spake of the meeting of the Galileans in the valley nigh unto Sepphoris. Howbeit, neither did this plot prevail with the common people. For the same accusation had been brought by the Scribes against John the prophet: but in vain. For the people could in no wise be persuaded that such an one as Jesus was possessed with an unclean spirit, nor that sick men could be healed and devils driven out by Beelzebub.

But that which caused most surprise to many of the disciples was to note how great a wrath was kindled in Jesus by this accusation. It chanced, as I remember, that we were in a small synagogue in the town called Jotapata. He had driven out a devil from a young man, and the devil tare the young man as he passed out of him, so that the young man lay on the ground lifeless. Jesus, as his manner was, took the young man by the hand for to help him to arise; and because there seemed no life in him, he stooped down and embraced him for to lift him up. Now the rest of them that were with Hezekiah held their peace, albeit against their will; so great was their marvel at the deed, and so mighty was the presence of Jesus. Only Hezekiah still hardened his heart. Therefore while Jesus was now lifting up the youth, of a sudden was heard the voice of Hezekiah crying aloud, "Thou castest out devils through Beelzebub the prince of the devils:" and all the people were as men amazed, and stood agape, expecting what Jesus would do.

Jesus himself, at first, seemed like unto one in a dream, turning his eyes from the young man (whose life had now returned to him) to the face of Hezekiah, and from Hezekiah again back to the young man; as though either he himself had not heard aright, or else Hezekiah had not seen clearly how great a work had been wrought for the young man. For belike he could scarce believe that any man in Israel could refrain from rejoicing at the young man's deliverance; nor did it seem possible to him that any among the children of men could suppose that a devil could be cast out save by the finger of God. But when he perceived that the face of Hezekiah was set as a rock against him, and that his eyes were as the eyes of one mocking him; and when he looked round also upon the people, and perceived that some of them were abashed and shaken in their faith because he had as yet made no answer, then indeed his countenance was changed against Hezekiah, and he made answer to him after his folly: that, if it was so indeed, and if Satan was divided against himself, then let all men rejoice, for behold, Satan could not stand. But if not, and if he cast out devils by the hand of God, "Then," said he, "the Kingdom of God hath come upon you unawares."

When he had spoken these words, he stood, as if in pause, and fixed his eyes on the face of Hezekiah. But he looked upon him no more with anger, but with a marvellous pity; and behold, his countenance, which was wont to shine as the sun, became pale and cold to look upon, even as the moon in her brightness, looking down upon a man drowning in deep waters; and he added and said, "All manner of sin and blasphemy shall be forgiven unto men; but the blasphemy against the Holy Spirit shall not be forgiven unto men. And whosoever speaketh a word against the Son of man, it shall be forgiven him: but whosoever speaketh against the Holy Spirit, it shall not be forgiven, neither in this age, nor in the age to come." Never before had we seen Jesus so moved. Hezekiah himself was confounded, and gasped for breath and could not speak, but went out of the synagogue in confusion; neither was there one in the congregation that went out with him.

But when the congregation had departed I went to Nathanael and questioned him concerning this matter.

For even from the first, Nathanael had a discerning spirit, able to discern matters wherein I groped as in darkness; but moreover of late I had noted how he had seemed to grow in wisdom and discernment, so that it was a marvel to see how great a change had come to pass in how short a time: and he was to me, as it were, an interpreter of the words of Jesus. So I asked Nathanael what Jesus meant by the words " blasphemy against the Holy Spirit," and why that sin was above all other sins so that it could not be forgiven.

" For," said I, " Jesus was blasphemed as a gluttonous man and as a wine-bibber, not many days past, in this very place, and I noted well (but thou wast not with us) with what a calmness, yea, even to mirth, Jesus endured the charge. For we chanced to be passing through this very street, and the children were coming forth from the school and sporting after their manner; and Jesus sat him down on the stone yonder and watched them at their sports. And behold, the children had divided themselves into two companies, a small company and a large company; and the small company had pipes and tabors, and were to play thereon; but the others were to conform themselves to the music of their fellows. But when they were now beginning, the larger company could not agree among themselves, and (after the manner of wanton children) they knew not their own minds. So when the pipers piped merry music they would not dance, but cried out for sad music; but when the pipers piped sadly, then they would not beat their breasts, nor make as if they were in the house of mourning, but stopped their ears and called for merry music: whereat the pipers were vexed, and complained of the inconstancy of their fellows. Then do I right well remember how Jesus noted it all, and smiled thereat. And turning to us, he said, still smiling (though with some touch of sadness), that this generation was like unto those children: for he had come piping merry music, and John the Prophet had come piping sad music, but the men of this generation would listen to neither; for they said that John had a devil, and that he himself was a gluttonous man and a winebibber, a friend of publicans and sinners. Now wherefore, thinkest thou, did Jesus endure so lightly to be blasphemed as a gluttonous man and a winebibber, but endured not to hear the words of Hezekiah? And what is this sin against the Holy Spirit?"

While I was saying these words, standing beneath the olive-grove on the side of the hill which looketh on Jotapata, Nathanael sat down upon the grass; and I sat down likewise. Then he said to me, "Not many days gone by, I heard Jesus speak concerning the Holy Spirit; and his words were on this wise. As in each man the man's breath or spirit is the life of the body, so in each man there is a certain holy breath or spirit which is the life of his soul; whence also cometh every good thought and deed unto the man. Moreover thou seest that the air which we breathe, and which is the breath of our bodies, is but a part of that great sea of air which embraceth the whole earth so that there is nothing hidden from the touch thereof; insomuch that the same air or breath which is coming towards us from yonder mountain top, making the terebinth-trees to bow, and which even now rustleth in the olive-trees above us, even this is our breath and our life. Now I have heard Jesus say that there is a likeness between this breath of our bodies and the breath or spirit of our souls. For as the wind bloweth where it listeth, and we hear the sound thereof, but know not whence it cometh nor whither it goeth, even so it is with the spirit of our souls, the spirit of goodness, which is the Holy Spirit of God."

Then I said, "But how shall we obtain this Holy Spirit? Or is it indeed needful that we should obtain it, seeing that we have it already? Or do some have it, but others have it not?" Nathanael answered and said, "All have it. But some have little, and none much; and Jesus hath come that we may have it abundantly. But how we shall obtain it, this I know not now. But this I know, that Jesus hath the Holy Spirit in himself, and that he will impart it to us. For I heard him say that no man can enter into the Kingdom of God unless he is born again of the Holy Spirit."

Then he paused, and said, "Is there not, O Joseph, a certain saying touching the Shekinah, how that it dwelleth not with one man, but with many?" And I replied, "Yea, but with one also; for it is said, 'When *ten* sit and are occupied in words of the Law, the Shekinah is among them, for it is said, God standeth in the *congregation* of the mighty. And whence dwelleth it even with *two*? Because it is said, Then they that feared the Lord spake often *one* to *another*. And whence even with *one*? Because it is said, In all places where I record my name I will come unto *thee* and bless *thee*.'" Nathanael smiled and said,

"Our Master also teacheth that the presence of the Holy Spirit is with two or three, whensoever they are gathered together in his name. But this doctrine he foundeth not on words of Scripture; but methinks he seeth that there is a certain Spirit of Goodness or Kindness which passeth from one man to his neighbour and gathereth strength as it passeth. But when a man is alone and without neighbours, it cannot in this way gather strength. For it is a Spirit of Love. Wherefore, as it seemeth to me, our Master teacheth that the Holy Spirit is present, in some sort, in the intercourse between man and man, whensoever men do aught together as the children of God."

"But yet," said I, "I would fain know why Hezekiah the Scribe was thus rebuked, and why the blasphemy against the Holy Spirit is not forgiven." Then said Nathanael, "All men have within themselves some portion of the Spirit of God; even as we now have some portion of that great wind and breath of heaven which here in Jotapata is rustling in the olive-branches, and yonder at Capernaum is driving the fishing-boats, and out in the Great Sea is speeding the ships of Tarshish on their path. Now if thou closest thy mouth and thy nostrils against the winds of heaven and sayest, 'The air is as poison to me, I will not breathe it,' behold, thou perishest. Even so is it with the Holy Spirit. Every man that cometh into the world, hath in him some portion of the Holy Spirit. For the spirit which is in him breatheth of the Holy Spirit, and dependeth and liveth thereon. But if he shall say knowingly in his heart, 'I will not breathe thereof; I will call good evil, and the Holy Spirit I will call unholy'; then lo, his spirit dieth within him, and he can no more enter into the life of God."

Then I said, "Is not the sin of Hezekiah less than the sin of Barachiah the son of Zadok, who cursed Jesus? And Nathanael replied, "No, for Barachiah cursed Jesus in his anger and in his haste, knowing not the truth: but Hezekiah saith in his heart, 'Lo, the truth is not pleasing unto me, therefore I will not look upon it; nay, it is hateful, therefore I will call it evil.'"

Then I mused for a space, and afterwards I questioned Nathanael yet again and said, "Thou hast said that in the Day of Redemption the Holy One (blessed is He) will slay the Evil Nature of men. Therefore at the great day what thinkest thou of them which have blasphemed the Holy Spirit? Will they also perish together with the Evil Nature? Or will there be yet another age after the age that is to come, so that even the wicked may yet be in the end redeemed? For Jesus said that they should not be forgiven, neither in this age nor in the age to come." But Nathanael could not answer this question; and we feared to ask Jesus concerning the matter.

While we thus spake together, behold, Barabbas stood before us: and he saluted us and besought us that we would sup at his house; for he dwelt at Jotapata. But I asked him for what cause he had been absent from us of late, and where he had been, and what the people of Jotapata said touching the words of Hezekiah the Scribe. Touching the cause of his absence he made no answer; but as concerning the people, he said that the men of Jotapata were of one mind, that Hezekiah had spoken for envy. "Nor is it possible," said he, "that a man should believe that Jesus hath a devil, unless he himself should have a devil. For they which have devils say and do all things without forethought and with distraction, as if divided against themselves; but in Jesus there is the contrary from these: for he doth all things with forethought, yea, and perchance" (these words he uttered with some show of anger) "with more than enough of forethought."

Now Barabbas spake with something of austerity, which was not usual with him. Moreover I marvelled at those words which he had said touching "too much of forethought." Therefore I asked him again where he had been of late, and why he had forsaken the disciples. But he answered with still more of passion than before, "Because I am weary of these idle wanderings about Galilee, which bring forth no fruit. Not to sit on stools at the feet of a Scribe did I and my friends join ourselves to Jesus of Nazareth. Why tarrieth he so long idle? Why is his hand so backward to smite the oppressor?" But I bade him be of good cheer, for the hour was not yet come, and Jesus would know better than we the season fit for our uprising.

But he replied, still in great heat, "Thou wouldst fain know where I have tarried these twenty days. Well, I will tell thee. I have but even now come from Machærus, where I have tarried these two weeks and more, nigh unto the fort called the Black Castle, wherein John the Prophet is imprisoned. With the Prophet himself I had no speech; for he is kept in close durance, insomuch that he pineth, as I hear, for lack of air and freedom. This I heard from one of the guard, who is a kinsman of mine. Moreover my kinsman told me that had it not been for Chuza the Steward, the

Prophet had been slain ten days ago. For the Tetrarch, after supper, being heavy with wine, was moved by the adulteress, even by Herodias, to write letters that John should be beheaded. Howbeit Chuza took order that the letter should be stayed for that time, and won the Tetrarch from his purpose. But what surety have we that the adulterous woman may not win the Tetrarch to write even such another letter to-morrow? And when John shall feel the left hand of the Thracian gripping his hair and the Thracian scimitar (may it be accursed!) hacking at his neck, will he not then cry unto the Lord in his sore agony and say, 'Jesus of Nazareth hath forsaken me: Jesus of Nazareth is guilty of my blood'? For this cause do we Galileans begin no more to trust your Master, because he speaketh many fair words, but we see not from him any doing of deeds."

His words so troubled me that I knew not what to say; Nathanael also was silent. But I besought Barabbas to trust in Jesus because of his mighty works, and because of his Gospel, which surely was a message from God. "Certainly," I began, "Jesus of Nazareth will not suffer the Prophet to die as a dog dieth." But, even while I spake, it came into my mind that the ways of Jesus were not as the ways of other men; neither could I foretell what Jesus would do, or not do, save only I knew that he would do right. So I paused, and added, "or, if otherwise——." But Barabbas, at that word "if," brake away from us, and was departing in fury. Howbeit, remembering himself, he returned and constrained himself, and courteously besought us to tarry with ·him that night. But we could not; for we were to pass on to another town, and not to tarry at Jotapata. So we bade him farewell.

As we journeyed eastward, I looked back now and then to the high rock whereon the tower of Jotapata is built: for it was exceeding high, being indeed one of the fire-stations whence the new moon was wont to be proclaimed. And as the sun was now sinking towards the west behind the rock, the castle seemed to stand up very clear, and easy to be seen against the red sky. But as often as I looked thereat, the words of Barabbas would come again and again into my mind; and there rose up before me the black castle of Machærus and the face of the prophet shut up in chains and darkness, and waiting for a deliverer. Then it seemed to me that the shadows of evil were encompassing our own Master also. For the Pharisees had set their faces against him; and though he had avoided their first snares, yet I knew full well that they were even now making others ready. Yea, Eliezer himself had confessed as much; for he had said in his letter to Jonathan that, if other means failed, it was purposed to deliver Jesus over to Herod. And now behold, the Galileans also were like to sever themselves from Jesus and to desert him. So all things seemed full of danger, and there appeared no path of deliverance.

In my dejection there came one upon another into my mind all the dark sayings of Jesus, and especially the words which he had spoken to us in the house of Matthew the tax-gatherer, that "The days should come when the bridegroom should be taken away from the children of the bridechamber, and then should they fast in those days." So I marvelled and pondered what those words might mean, "the bridegroom should be taken away." But they were too deep for me to understand, and I was as one wading in them and out of my depth; nor could I light upon anything solid in them save only this, that they appeared to prophesy some evil.

CHAPTER XIV

ON the third or fourth day after that we had seen Barabbas, we came to Bethsaida. And behold, as Jesus was exhorting the people, there came into the synagogue two disciples of John the Prophet. And the principal Scribe of the place brought the men in, saying that they had a message from the Prophet to Jesus of Nazareth. Then all men held their peace and expected what the message should be; and I remembered the words of Barabbas concerning John, and my mind presaged that the prophet had sent to bid Jesus release him. But the Scribe (for he knew what the message was, and desired to discredit Jesus) said aloud that the message was a strange one, not fit for the ear of the common multitude; therefore it should be reserved for the ear of Jesus alone. But all the people listened the more intently; and Jesus gave command that the messengers should deliver their message aloud, and they did so. Now the words of the message were these, "John the Prophet hath sent us to thee from the prison of Herod, saying, 'Art thou he that should come, or must we look for another?'"

When we heard these words we all looked that Jesus

should either rebuke the Prophet for his want of faith, or else make some comfortable answer, saying that he would come with speed and deliver the Prophet from his bonds. Howbeit Jesus made no answer, but continued his exhortation; and he drove out certain unclean spirits, and forgave sins. But when he had ended these things, he called to the disciples of John, and he repeated to them those passages of the prophets which describe the signs of Redemption, and in particular the prophecy of Isaiah: how the ears of the deaf shall be unstopped to hear the tidings of Redemption, and the eyes of the blind shall be opened to discern the truth of the Lord; and the lame man shall leap as a hart in the paths of salvation; and the tongue of the dumb shall sing the praises of the Lord. And he said unto the two messengers, "Go and show John the things which ye do hear and see: the blind receive their sight, and the lame walk; the lepers are cleansed, and the deaf hear; the dead are raised up, and the poor have the gospel preached to them." Then he added these words, "Blessed is he who shall not be offended in me."

When the messengers were departed, Jesus spake to the people concerning John, saying that John (howbeit he might have changed and fallen from his first estate, seeming to be, for the time, unstable as a reed or pliant as a courtier) was, none the less, truly a prophet, yea, and the greatest of prophets, inasmuch as he was sent by God as the herald of the Redeemer. Then he added thereto a certain saying which filled us all with amazement: yea, and even now after forty years, though I be enlightened with the Holy Spirit, yet can I not choose but be amazed thereat. For the words were these: "Verily I say unto you, among them that are born of women, there hath not risen a greater than John the Baptist: notwithstanding he that is least in the Kingdom of Heaven is greater than he."

When the congregation brake up, many of the people said among themselves that this was an hard saying. Others asked what Jesus meant by dividing them that were "born of women" from them that are in the Kingdom of Heaven; and whether the former meant the living and the latter meant the dead. Now I understood (for Nathanael had instructed me) that Jesus put a difference between them which are born of flesh and blood, and them which are born of the Spirit; wherefore I partly perceived the meaning of his saying, namely, that the kingdom of the Law and of the Prophets now had an end, and that the kingdom of the Spirit of God was at hand; and that the greatest in the former kingdom was less than the least in the latter. Likewise I understood Jesus to say that the sending of this message and the moving of Jesus to take up the arms of the flesh argued in John a certain nature of flesh; as if he thereby shewed himself to be born not of the New Kingdom, but of the Old Kingdom of flesh and blood, albeit the greatest therein. Yet for all this, that such an one as Jesus of Nazareth, whose gentleness and meekness (albeit mixed at all times with a certain royal carriage and demeanour) for the most part exceeded the meekness of a little child, should notwithstanding seem to rate so low the greatest of all the prophets of Israel, and exalt so high the meanest of all the citizens in the Kingdom that was to come (which also seemed perforce to include a certain magnifying of himself as being chief in that Kingdom); this, I say, for all my poising and pondering, still perplexed and distracted my mind, as a thing new and strange, and (I had almost said) monstrous to human reason.

I desired to question Nathanael the son of Zebedee concerning these things; but I could not. For having noted the face of one of my mother's household in the congregation, and fearing lest he might have some message touching my mother's health, I hasted to seek the man out: and it proved even as I feared, for my mother was indeed sick, and had sent, desiring that I would come to see her. Therefore I went to Jesus at once, and besought him that he would suffer me to go to my mother. As I went to Jesus, I met Eliezer the son of Arak, and would have passed him. But he, noting that I was somewhat moved, stayed me, and having questioned me, he said, "If thou art wise, thou wilt not go to Jesus: for but now, he forbade one of his disciples to bid farewell to his parents, and another he would not so much as suffer to bury the dead body of his father. For he rageth like a young lion taken in the net of the hunter; and whoso leaveth his side, though it be for an hour, seemeth to him a traitor. Be persuaded, therefore, and quit this Jesus of Nazareth, and his rabble of sinners, and come unto the side of the learned, and thou shalt have eminence among us."

Now I could not indeed deny that Jesus had forbidden certain of his disciples to leave him; but he had done it for their advantage, and because he knew that it would have been ill for them to leave him. Therefore

I answered Eliezer with the same proverb which the ruler of the synagogue had said to Jesus, that it was better to be the tail of the lion than the head of the fox; and so I left him. For he spake out of a malignant heart, and not because he loved me. Moreover, I knew that if Jesus should say, Go not, it would be well said; for I trusted him in all things.

I found Jesus surrounded by many disciples, who had been asking him questions concerning John the Prophet, and concerning the manner of his deliverance. For all we at that time were assured in our minds that John would be delivered: for men counted John the son of Zachariah and Jesus of Nazareth as yoke-fellows in Israel, and the safety of one seemed to depend on the safety of the other, and the salvation of Israel on both. And indeed I myself have often marvelled that Jesus was not moved to adventure to deliver John. But, as I judge, he rejected all such motions as temptations of Satan, because he knew that he had not been sent to smite with the sword but only with the breath of his mouth. Wherefore, if he were tempted at all, it was rather, as I suppose, that he should die with John than that he should fight that John might live. And at this time, methinks, it came into his mind that if indeed it was ordained that John the Prophet should be slain, and perchance he himself also, then was it high time that new labourers should be sent into the harvest of the Lord, to take the places of them that were to pass away. Howbeit, concerning these things I can but conjecture; but, as I remember, when I came to Jesus, he was looking at the young corn in the fields around very intently, and as if he espied in the sight more than others could see. Presently he said to them which sat next to him, "Say ye not, There are yet four months and then cometh the harvest? Behold, I say unto you, Lift up your eyes, and look on the fields, for they are white already to harvest. And he that reapeth receiveth wages and gathereth fruit unto life eternal; that both he that soweth and he that reapeth may rejoice together." Then Judas said to them which sat nigh unto him, that these words signified that John should be delivered at once, and that a levy was to be made throughout all Galilee: and he added aloud, looking to Jesus, that, "The reapers were ready," or words to that effect. But Jesus answered and said, "The harvest truly is plenteous, but the labourers are few: pray ye therefore the Lord of the harvest, that he will send forth labourers into his harvest."

Then I spake to Jesus and told him that I desired to go and see my mother. But I thought perchance that he would have restrained me, if it were so indeed that a levy was to be made throughout all Galilee. But he restrained me not, but bade me go in peace and blessed me, and spake comfortable words to me; and wished me to comfort my mother.

On the next day I came to Sepphoris, and behold my mother was grievously sick and nigh unto death. But when I took her by the hand and delivered to her the message of Jesus, saying that he bade her be of good cheer, even in that instant her strength came back to her, and her disease abated; and on the fourth day it departed, so that she rose from her bed. But when the day came that I should depart, so it was that my mother desired me to go first to Tiberias, there to collect certain debts which were owing to her now many days. To this I agreed, nothing loth, for it seemed to me that by passing through Tiberias to Capernaum I might bring unto Jesus the newest tidings touching the doings of Herod, and perchance also touching the state of John the Prophet. For there were certain of mine acquaintance in the house of Chuza, the king's steward, who lived in Tiberias nigh unto the royal palace. So I set out for Tiberias first. But when I reached the city, it being now about the tenth hour of the day, I found the people gathered together in the Greek quarter by twos and by threes in the streets; and in our part of the city, instead of rejoicings (which I had expected, because the Feast of Purim was at this time), there were everywhere signs of lamentation and mourning. So I saluted one of them that passed by, and asked him what these things might mean. But he glanced at my mule (which I had borrowed, for more speed, of a Greek in Sepphoris; for not many in Galilee, except Gentiles, use to ride on mules), and he said, "I perceive that thou art but a sojourner here, else wouldst thou surely have known these tidings which are in the mouths of all the people, since the eighth hour of the day, touching John the Prophet." Then I said, "What tidings?" He answered "That he is dead, slain with the sword; and they say that his head hath been given to Herodias on a charger. But why speak I of things that concern me not?" So saying he looked at me, as I had been a spy (for the spies of Herod were everywhere in Galilee at this time, and most of all in Tiberias); and so he passed on.

Straightway I hasted on to come to the Greek quarter, seeking the house of Chuza. But on my way thither I passed the royal palace; and at the gate thereof were certain of the Thracian guard keeping watch. Now as I passed them, one of the soldiers called to his companion and said, "But wherefore dost thou keep guard to-day?" And the other said, "I keep guard in the place of Thrasymachus who is gone with three centuries to Capernaum." "And wherefore to Capernaum?" said the first. "There is like to be a tumult in the town," replied the sentinel, "because of the beheading of this John in Machærus; and they say that the rabble will set some leader at their head, who is to be arrested." "Nay," said the other, "and sayest thou arrested? I would have no arresting, but make quick despatch with these leaders of the rabble. But hath Herod heard of this leader?" "Not so," said the other, "for he is busy in the south with the army; but our general meaneth to take order that Herod shall never hear of him." With that he laughed, and made a sign to signify beheading, drawing his hand across his throat; then he bade his fellow go carry some message for him, for he should be busy that day; "For," said he, "the cohort hath not been gone one full hour yet, and will not be here again these six hours or more, for they mean not to take him by force publicly, but will arrest the man quietly at nightfall."

When I heard these things, my spirit fainted, and there was no strength in me; but when I came to myself, it seemed best to journey forwards at once to Capernaum if perchance I might prevent the coming of the Thracian guard and give the alarm to Jesus.

So I turned the mule's head straightway toward the city gate, and rode on the way that leadeth to Capernaum. But she was sore wearied by reason of the length of the journey, and could scarce carry me. Howbeit after the space of an hour's riding I came up with the rear of the Thracians: but I perceived that I could not pass them. For a certain merchant riding on a fresh mule had passed out from the city gate before me, and behold, they had stayed him, and suffered him not to pass; but he rode behind with the rear. Now when I saw this, I smote my hands together, for I saw that I could be of no avail to my Master. And by this time the houses of Capernaum, that is to say the quay and the houses near the quay, were in sight, and not far off. For one headland only remained between us and the headland whereon the town standeth; and when the Thracians should have passed round that first headland, there were but six furlongs between them and the market-place of Capernaum. But the sun was now nigh setting and the barbarians began to quicken their pace.

Therefore I cried unto the Lord in sore distress and left my mule and climbed up to a rock whence I could watch what befel, and there I offered up prayers to the All-Powerful, who alone is able to save. Now behold, by this time the Thracians had passed round the first headland, and the last of them were out of my sight, so that I could see nothing but the quay of Capernaum and two or three fishing-boats riding at anchor just off the quay: and there seemed no signs of tumult; for there was no man stirring there. And presently began the helmets of the Thracians to shine again before mine eyes as their front guard drew near unto the town, and still no man perceived them; for the cliff lay between them and the town, and there were still none save two or three sailors on the quay. Then I took off the covering from my head and waved it in the air that the sailors perchance might take note of it: but they took no note.

Now by this time there was but about a space of two furlongs between the front of the column of the Thracians and the quay of Capernaum, and I could hear the captain give the word of command (albeit not in a loud voice) to hasten their march that they might enter the town the more quickly (for darkness was now falling upon the lake); and as the word of command sounded across the water even to my ears in the stillness of the evening, behold, the Thracians hastened their march so that they began to run. Now I held my breath, for I could not so much as pray for very trouble; when lo, a great noise of shouting from the other side of the headland, even from Capernaum; and at the same time a great concourse of people upon the quay, and immediately a long galley appeared, which rowed forth very swiftly toward the eastward side of the lake. Then the barbarians halted, even without the word of command; for they knew that the bird was escaped from the snare of the fowlers: and the noise of their cursing and clamour came up even unto mine ears as I sat upon my place of watching. But I glorified the God of Israel; and gave thanks to Him whose mercy endureth for ever.

CHAPTER XV

WHEN I came into Capernaum, I thought to have heard all men rejoicing for that Jesus had not been taken by the Thracians. But, go where I might, I found it quite contrary; for all men were wroth with him for departing. Barabbas was there, and James the son of Judas of Galilee, and many others of the Galilean sect; but I could not have much speech with them, so hot was their anger against Jesus; but on the morrow, lighting upon my cousin Baruch, I questioned him touching that which had happened, and he said that " the Prophet had turned from him all the hearts of the Galileans because he would not raise up Israel to avenge the death of John."

Then I asked how soon they had received tidings of John's death, and he said "Yesterday a little before sunset." I marvelled how the news should have been brought past the Thracians; for, said I, "they stayed all travellers from Tiberias, neither suffered they any to pass them." But Baruch said that James the son of Judas had contrived that lights should be held up each night from Gamala on the other side of the lake, to the intent that the Galileans in Capernaum might know how John fared; and one light should signify that the Prophet lived, but two lights that he lived not. "And," said

Baruch, "yestereven before the sun went down, many of the Galileans had gathered together by twos or by threes upon the strand to watch for the signal. And first one light appeared, as was usual; and the men said that it was well, for they had one more day wherein to labour for the Prophet's deliverance. But then Barabbas cried out that there were two lights; and at first no man would believe it, for (because the sun had not yet set) the lights were not plain to see. But presently Judas also saw the second light, and then they all saw it. Hereupon arose a loud lamentation, and the news spread at once through all the city, and the women began to wail, and the men rushed forth into the streets, and there was a great gathering. Presently with one consent the multitude ran together to the door of the house where Jesus lodged; and first Barabbas went in to ask Jesus to be leader of the host, but soon he came forth again, saying that Jesus would not. Then went in James the son of Judas, saying that he would beseech Jesus in the name of his father, who had fought and died for Israel. With James there went in also three others of the eldest and most reverend of the Galileans, and they remained in the house longer, so that the people thought they had prevailed upon Jesus; and there was a great expectation. But when the elders came out, they showed by their countenances that they had not prevailed.

Then there was much clamour; and the greater part cried out that they would not depart from before the threshold of Jesus till they had persuaded Jesus to be leader of the host; and some cried out to draw him forth by violence and to make him leader of the host. But immediately the door opened, and Jesus himself came forth. Then they no more talked of violence; but Barabbas and others of the armed men held out their right hands to him, and promised to give up their lives for his sake if he would be their king. Others fell down on their knees before him; and some caught him by the garment to have stayed him. Only James the son of Judas said nothing; "and it seemed to me," said Baruch, "that at the sight of James, Jesus was more moved than by all the rest. Howbeit he halted not, but moved straight down to the beach.

"Then when the people perceived that he would leave them, they cried out even louder than before, and threw dust in the air and poured it upon their heads; and some threw themselves on the ground in his path for to stay him; and some also spared not threatening. But Jesus took no heed thereof, but went still onward with his eyes fast set upon the ground; till one thrust himself before the rest, crying aloud and saying that they would do more for John dead than for Jesus living, and that it was better for a man to lose his life, as John the Prophet had lost it, than to save his life as Jesus desired to save it. Thereat Jesus stayed for an instant, and lifted his eyes from the ground; howbeit not in anger, but rather as he is wont to do (for thou well knowest his manner) whensoever he heareth a Voice of God. But when all the people shouted again, supposing that he had been bent from his purpose, then Jesus beckoned with the hand, and when he had commanded silence, he spake briefly unto them, and said the hour was not yet come; and so he departed.

"Now," said Baruch, "while Jesus was speaking to the people, and even afterwards while he was in the sight of the people, it was a marvellous thing to see how still they were; for he hath a power over the hearts of the people so that when he is present no one dare move his tongue against him. But as soon as the boat had rowed away and they could see him no more, straightway Barabbas and his friends began to curse and swear; and they said that they would never again ask aught of Jesus, nor place any faith in him. James the son of Judas said little, but his mind seemed to be the same. For this cause therefore all the Galileans are incensed against Jesus; insomuch that, whereas they had begun to rate him far above John, they now esteem the memory of John more than the presence of Jesus."

After this, Baruch began to advise me to sever myself from Jesus and to return to my home at Sepphoris, for, said he, "He hath the Pharisees for his enemies; and the richer sort are also estranged from him; and it is commonly reported that Herod the Tetrarch seeketh to slay him with the sword; and now behold, even the Galileans are turned away from him. Now therefore be persuaded, and come back with me to the house of my father Manasseh, and tarry with us for the night, and refresh thyself, and on the morrow set forth for thy home."

But I made him some fair answer and bade him farewell; for I had determined with myself to take ship that same night, to have sailed over to the other side. But on the morrow, I thought it good (albeit perchance I erred therein) to return first to my mother and to relate to her all that had come to pass, and to bid her farewell: for all men now accounted of Jesus as of one that must either fight or perish: for it could not be that he should live and be honoured of men, and yet not avenge the death of John the Prophet. Wherefore, before I joined myself to a cause that seemed so full of peril, I desired to take leave of my mother.

On the fourth day after I was come to Sepphoris, word was brought that Jesus of Nazareth was gathering the people for battle, and that he was making a levy throughout all Galilee, and for this intent had chosen out twelve of his disciples, whom also he called Apostles; and these he had sent out by two and two through the several villages and towns. Jonathan the son of Ezra brought me these tidings; and I was with him next day, walking on the road between Sepphoris and Capernaum, when we met Simon Peter and Andrew.

They told us that they had been sent forth by Jesus to proclaim the Kingdom of Heaven, and to drive out unclean spirits, and to heal diseases. They came without wallet, or food, or money, trusting to the alms of the people. But when we questioned them as to the Kingdom, and whether indeed it was to be achieved by force of arms (as the rumour went), or by signs such as fire from heaven and the like: concerning this they knew nothing. As for the healing of diseases, we saw with our own eyes that they had this power; for they healed certain that were sick in Sepphoris, and even cast out three or four unclean spirits.

When we had bidden farewell to Simon Peter and Andrew (for they were in haste, passing from place to place like messengers of war) then Jonathan turned to me and said, " Whoso pulleth down his old house and doth not first build for himself a new one, is he wise?" I replied, " Nay." Then said Jonathan, " Lo, Jesus of Nazareth pulleth down the house of the Law; tell me therefore, what buildeth he in the place thereof?" I was silent, for I knew not what to answer; but at last I said that Jesus spake of a certain new Spirit which would purify the children of men and enable them to attain righteousness without the Law. But Jonathan said, "Nay but, my son, can a Spirit tell each man of the children of men, from day to day, what meat he shall eat and what he shall not eat; and when to fast and when to feast; and what to do on the Sabbath day, and what not to do? Now if the Spirit shall tell each man different things, shall there not be a confusion as of Babel? But if the same things, then why should not these things be written in a law? Moreover who shall tell which man hath the Spirit and which hath not? For all will say they have it." Then I said that I could not answer those questions, but that I trusted in Jesus of Nazareth as in one sent from God, who could not deceive, neither be deceived, for that his deeds and words were those of a prophet. After this manner I answered; but Jonathan said nothing, but only shook his head a little, as one that doubted more than he hoped.

Now on the third day after this discourse (it being, as I remember, the month called Adar, a little after the Feast of Purim), my mother being now completely recovered of her disease, I determined to return to Jesus. For tidings came in daily that all Galilee was ready to rise up when he gave the sign, and I was unwilling to show myself a laggard if matters should come to smiting with the sword. But every day I heard that Jesus was more and more beloved of the people. For all (save only the Pharisees) were now drawn towards him, in that he seemed to be bent upon avenging John the Prophet. And his fame began to be noised abroad through all the country of Galilee and the parts beyond, insomuch that many that had not heard of him before, began to cast in their minds what he could be. And some said that he was Elias. For the common folk, yea, and the Scribes also, were ever expecting that Elias should be sent down to earth, according to the saying of the prophet Malachi. But others said that he was John the Baptist risen from the dead; and this saying was commonly reported, especially among the Gentiles which border on the land of Galilee and in Decapolis, insomuch that Herod himself heard of the rumour, and feared lest it might be even so. But whatsoever men reported about Jesus, in any case his fame waxed very great at this time. For before John was beheaded, the fame of John prevailed over the fame of Jesus in the minds of many; but now all alike, even the disciples of John, looked to Jesus as the avenger of John and as the only Deliverer; insomuch that, at this time, Jesus had both his own fame and also the fame of John the Prophet.

I found Jesus in a village about seven miles to the north of Galilee. But when I had saluted him, I noted that he was marvellously changed; yet not so that he was austere, nor even very sad; yet still changed withal, albeit I knew not how nor why. But I had expected that he should have rebuked me for that I had been so long absent, neither had I come to him with all speed so as to be present when first he made the levy in Galilee. Howbeit, he reproved me not; but questioned me kindly touching my mother's health, and rejoiced when I gave him a good report: but afterwards he gave himself again to meditation. When I was come forth from his presence, I asked the disciples concerning the state of Galilee, and what number of men were ready to fight on our side, and when the levy should be made, and the hour for battle should be at hand. But the rest were silent, and Judas alone made answer, that concerning these things the disciples knew nothing; yea, and from certain signs he conjectured that even to Jesus himself the hour of uprising was not yet known, no, nor yet the manner of it, nor the means for it.

"But," said I, "did not the people in Galilee receive you when ye went forth to proclaim the Redemption?" "Yes truly did they," said Judas, "but all of the baser sort, and the poor folk which have naught of their own; wherefore they be always ready for warfare." "And what answer made Jesus to your report?" asked I. "Truly a marvellous answer," replied Judas, "for when we said that only the poor and simple folk received us, he rejoiced thereat, and thanked God that it was even so." "Nay," said I, "that were hard to believe." "But yea," said Judas; "for his words were these, that he thanked the Father, because He had hidden these things from the wise and the prudent, and revealed them unto babes." Then I looked at Nathanael to know whether it was even so, and Nathanael nodded his head, as if to say that it was so.

But Judas continued: "This also is not the worst. For he hath not only turned from him the Galileans; but besides, since our flight, whereas there is special need to be busy and striving, behold, these ten days, he museth and meditateth, and ceaseth not. Neither are his musings touching war, nor vengeance, nor military matters; but he broodeth over prophesyings and abstruse matters. And a stranger might go near to think that he had conceived an imagination that, because the Lord hath suffered John the son of Zachariah to die, therefore he must needs die also. But unless he be speedily raised up from this humour of dejection, all is lost."

He said no more at this time, for Jesus came forth into the court-yard where we sat together around the fountain; and straightway we held our peace. Then we fell to discourse of John the son of Zachariah, how great things he had prophesied, and how we had hoped that he should have triumphed with us in the Kingdom of God; and one likened John unto Elias the prophet, saying that he spake in the spirit of Elias, and that many of the common people would have it that this John was indeed Elias risen from the dead. Then another spake of the love in which the disciples of John the son of Zachariah still had their Master, and how, though he were dead, yet did they still cleave to him in their hearts; insomuch that his spirit seemed to rule over them yet more than his living presence. But another said that John the Prophet could not be Elias: for was it possible that the Lord should suffer such an one as Elias to be slain? And to him Nathanael replied that Isaiah the Prophet was sawn asunder, and wherefore not also Elias? Then Thomas, one of the Twelve, lamented for John the son of Zachariah, because he had been thus swallowed up by destruction, neither had he left children to stand in his stead upon the earth; "for they that die, leaving children behind them," said he (quoting a certain proverb of my countrymen) "die not, but only fall asleep: but they that die and leave no children, these die indeed." To this John the son of Zebedee made answer that whoso leaveth behind him children perverse and alien from his own nature, he liveth not, for all his children; but whoso leaveth behind him disciples and followers like unto himself and imbued with his own doctrine, such an one liveth, yea even though he be childless and lie in the grave. Hereat methought Jesus was strangely moved: howbeit he sat still where he was, and spake never a word.

But presently mention was made of Jonah the Prophet, how that he also was an exile and fled from his country, even as our Master had been forced to flee. Then Judas said that Jonah had done ill to flee, for that none could flee from the presence of the All-seeing, the Maker of all things, "for," said he, "the son of man, while he liveth, is like unto a horse tethered by a cord which suffereth him to graze, but resteth still in the hand of his owner." Thereon some one took up the discourse and said, "Nay, but rather the cord is a cord of love, and the owner is not an owner, but a father;" and another disciple quoted the words of the psalmist, "By thee have I been holden up from the womb." Thereat Jesus smiled as if to say that that disciple had spoken well, and he bade John repeat the rest of that same psalm. But when John came, in his repeating, to the words, "O God, Thou hast taught me from my youth: and hitherto have I declared thy wondrous works," then did Jesus seem somewhat moved. But afterwards when John came unto the words, "Thou, which hast shewed me great and sore troubles, shalt give me life again, and shalt bring me up again from the depths of the earth;" then indeed the face of Jesus kindled with a marvellous light, and he bade John cease. But he himself sat, still musing, and his lips moved like unto one repeating the same words over and over again: "Thou shalt bring me up again from the depths of the earth."

It came to pass that, about two or three weeks after these things we came to Nazareth, where Jesus was born. Now Jesus had not gone to the place these many days. Some said that he came thither now for to shew unto his mother and his brethren (for his father had been long since dead) that he was sound in health and not possessed nor distraught. Others said that he desired to cause his brethren to believe in him; for at this time they believed not. But others said that he desired to bid farewell to his mother before he went forth to deliver Israel; and to this most people agreed.

But when we came to Nazareth, we marvelled that there was so little faith in the men of that place. For they thronged us, as in the other towns, and they were fain to look on Jesus, and called him by familar names (some being playmates and schoolfellows, some his kinsfolk, and almost all of the number of his acquaintances); moreover they were eager that he should do some mighty work before their eyes; yet could they not believe that he was a prophet, much less that he was the Redeemer of Israel. Neither would they believe that he could drive out evil spirits or heal diseases.

Hence it came to pass that Jesus could do no mighty work there. And when they brought unto him many that were sick, and possessed with evil spirits, he looked on them, but perceived that they had not faith to be healed. Wherefore he healed none of them; save only that he laid his hands on a few that were sick of slight diseases and healed them, and even these not without labour. For the same things happened as once in another city, where a man was healed that had been afflicted with a deaf and dumb spirit. For there, because of the man's want of understanding and lack of faith, Jesus took him apart from the people (for there was a great stir of traffic and of men coming and going), and made signs to him, at the same time touching his ears and his tongue; and he also spake very loud in the man's ears, not in Greek, but in the language of the Jews (which is used by the poorer people), saying *Ephphatha*. In this way the man was healed, but only with labour and by degrees. And so it was now, but even worse. Wherefore Jesus himself marvelled at their unbelief.

Now the cause of their unbelief was that they knew him from a child. For, said one of them to Jesus himself in my hearing, "Behold, these thirty years we have known thy goings out and thy comings in; we have also sat by thy side in the school, and whatsoever thou didst learn we also learned; thou didst play with us at our games round the well; we have seen thee a-working in thy father's house; our couches and our seats are made by thy hand; and shall we call thee the Redeemer of Israel?" Moreover another bade him come back to the carpenter's shop; and a third cried out that he had changed trades for the worse, for the Redemption of Israel was a dangerous trade. All these were moved by jealousy, and spake out of the malignity of their hearts.

But a certain old Scribe, Josiah the son of Hezekiah, (which also was the chief Scribe of the place, and had known Jesus and loved him of a child) coming forth from his house, met him and fell upon his neck, and blessed him, and embraced him; and then, when he had looked more narrowly at his countenance, he began to mourn over him as if he were his own son, lamenting for that the bloom of beauty had departed from the countenance of Jesus: ".for behold," said he, "sorrow hath driven out the former brightness of thy joy. Thou wast as the dew of the morning, O my lamb, but art become as the parched ground at noontide. Behold, O my lamb, around thy cradle mercy and righteousness joined hands together; and when thou didst sport amid this valley, lo, truth and peace went ever with thee, and thou didst still hold converse with the angels of God? Unfit art thou, O my gentle one, to do battle with the wickedness of wicked men, and with the cunning arts of the adversary. Verily thou wilt be led as a lamb to the slaughter. Hast thou fathomed the depth of the pit of destruction? Or dost thou know by experience the snares of deceit? Return, O thou that art the apple of mine eye, while there is yet time, lest evil befal thee. For I know that danger compasseth thee around, and if thou shalt go hence, thou wilt come back to me no more."

Jesus spake comfortably to the old man and consoled him; and while he consoled him, his face shone with joy and love; insomuch that the old man also rejoiced, saying that Jesus appeared now again as he appeared in the days of his youth. But still he besought Jesus to return and to avoid contention with the Pharisees, saying that "no vessel but peace can hold blessing."

But Jesus answered him kindly and bade him farewell. And so we departed from Nazareth.

When we were now come to the top of the hill which looketh down on Nazareth, we rested a little to recover our breath. Now Jesus was sorrowful because of the unbelief of his kinsfolk and acquaintance, and he was silent (as was his wont when sorrow fell upon him), musing and meditating, and, as it seemed to me, praying; even as one striving to unloose the knot of some hard saying or riddle. For the unbelief of his kinsfolk had filled him with astonishment. While he thus mused, we conversed together, and Judas said that it was an error to have come to Nazareth. "For who knoweth not," said he, "that a prophet hath no honour in his own country? For a prophet known is a prophet despised."

But John the son of Zebedee replied that it was a strange thing that the acquaintance and kinsfolk of Jesus should suppose that they knew the mind and spirit of Jesus because they knew his outward shape and mien and manner of speech: "For his mind and spirit pass knowledge; and the more a man knoweth thereof, the more a man must needs wonder thereat." So spake John; but Judas jested at him, and said that John spake as a babe and as a simple clown, knowing nothing of the world. "Yet," added he, looking up at Jesus, "it is strange methinks that even our Master should also wonder at that which is in no way wonderful." Then John rebuked him and said, "Knowest thou not the saying of our Master, 'They that wonder shall reign, and they that reign shall rest?' Wherefore who knoweth whether it may not be that even our

Master day by day learneth some new revelation from God whereat to wonder? For whoso increaseth not diminisheth."

When I heard these words I looked at Jesus, and behold, it was even as John said. For the sorrow that rested upon his countenance because of the unbelief of his kinsfolk seemed to be passing away, and to be revealing beneath it an exceeding joy, as of one learning some hidden mystery, or hearing some glad tidings. And there came into my mind the words of Barabbas (which were contrary to the words of John), how he said that Jesus did everything with forethought; and behold, both the words of John seemed true and also the words of Barabbas; but the words of John seemed the truer. For though Jesus did naught in haste nor in fear nor perturbation; yet was he not like unto one that seeth all things to come, great and small alike, marked out for him as in a chart, nor like unto him which trusteth in the strength of his own unchangeable will. Nay rather, even as a little child hangeth upon the bosom of his mother and hath no will of his own, even so did Jesus continually look upon earth and heaven and on the deeds and words of men; and, look where he might, he discerned in all things some new knowledge, some revelation concerning the will of the Father in heaven; insomuch that no day passed, yea no hour of the day, but Jesus in this wise held communion with his Father.

By this time Jesus was arisen from his seat, and we ceased conversing together when he drew nigh. But Judas, desirous to say somewhat (so as to hide what he had been saying), pointed down to the white houses of

Nazareth and to the fields and orchards which compass the city round in the bottom of the valley; and he said to Jesus that the place was exceeding beautiful, like unto a handful of pearls in a goblet of emerald. But Jesus looked narrowly at Judas for an instant, and then down at Nazareth, and then at Judas again; and the sounds of the bleating of the goats and the piping of the shepherds came up to our ears, and the laughter of the children as they sported round the well. When Jesus heard these things, he sighed, and cast his eyes down again on Nazareth, even on the place of his nativity; and he looked at it for a long while very lovingly. Then he turned away his head and departed, and he saw it no more.

CHAPTER XVI

Now so it was that, at this time, the more the hearts of the people were drawn toward Jesus (for though the people of Nazareth had rejected him, yet was he much honoured in the rest of Galilee), so much the more did Jesus seem to thrust them away. For he began to teach us at this time that he should give us no new law, but a certain manna or bread from heaven. Now if he had said no more than this, this was not hard to understand; for our Scribes also taught in parables after this fashion : but he added that this manna or bread from heaven should be himself, his flesh and his blood, which should be given for the life of the world. Now albeit I have myself heard the Scribes speak of "the days when Israel shall *eat* the Messiah,"[1] meaning that Israel shall enjoy the presence of the Messiah, yet Jesus seemed to mean somewhat more than this, insomuch that his words were a stumbling-block unto many. And straightway many of them departed from him.

But when I went (according to my wont) to question Nathanael touching these words, he replied that they were hidden from him also. Notwithstanding it seemed to him that at this time our Master was receiving some new

[1] See Note III.

revelation, whereof these words might peradventure be a part. For he said that on the day before, when I had been absent, mention had been made of the coming Passover, and how Jesus would not be present thereat; and from mentioning the sacrifice of the Passover they came to speak of other sacrifices; and one said that Jesus had come to take away sacrifice, for that he had said that God desired mercy, and not sacrifice, and that the right sacrifice was that the whole nation should serve the Lord and do His will. Then another, quoting the Scripture, said, "Nay, but the people may perchance stand in the place of the fuel and the fire: but where is the lamb for the burnt-offering?" Then answered another from the same Scripture, and said, "God will provide himself a lamb for the burnt-offering." And at these words, said John, "the countenance of Jesus changed as if he had heard some new word from God." Hereat I marvelled greatly, and wondered what new thing the Lord was preparing for us and for our Master. And the words of Judas came to my mind that, because John the son of Zachariah had been slain, therefore Jesus had begun to imagine that he also must needs be slain. But it was but for an instant; for I durst not so much as entertain the thought of so great an evil.

But, as I now judge, the Lord Jesus began at this time to see clearly that he must needs die for Israel, even as John the son of Zachariah had died, and that he must needs rise again (according to the Prophets); even as the common people spake, saying that John the Baptist was at this very time risen from the dead. For he perceived that the needs of the world, that is to say the will of the Father, required that he should rise again from the dead. Moreover as John the son of Zachariah had gained strength through death, so that all men still loved and honoured John, and were more ready to die for him dead than living; even so Jesus perceived that he also should have more strength to help us after his death than before his death. But touching the manner of his rising again, and the time of it, and whether he should appear in his own shape (as he did indeed), or in some other shape (as did Elias in the shape of John the Baptist), concerning all this, what was revealed unto him I know not; the Lord only knoweth. But that he should of a certainty rise again from the dead, this was without doubt revealed unto him; and, as I conceive, about this time.

For this cause, because he perceived that by the giving of his body and blood to die for men, his spirit would pass into his disciples (even as the spirit of John the son of Zachariah had passed into the disciples of John), for this cause, I say, he spake at this time (as he did also afterwards), saying that he would give himself to be the food of men, even the Bread of Life. For his spirit was a spirit of sonship to God, and of brotherhood to men; and except the world should receive this spirit into itself, the world could not be quickened, and the nations of the earth could not pass into the family or kingdom of God.

From this time also he began to be very careful, even to disquietude, concerning us his disciples, what should be our estate when he should have departed from us; and he desired to impart to us this Bread of Life that we also in turn might impart it to the multitude. Moreover he would fain exercise us already in imparting this

Bread of Life, yea, before he had passed away; to the end that, by beginning in his presence, we might learn by degrees to be steadfast in the ministering of the Bread even though he were absent from us. And for this he found occasion not many days afterwards. For about the tenth day before the Passover, Jesus being still on the other side of the lake (but I had been sent with Judas on an errand to Capernaum), it came to pass that much people resorted to him; some from Capernaum, and others from the parts round about the village wherein he had lodged. For, because of the Passover, which was at hand, many were going up to Jerusalem. Also of the Galileans some came; howbeit not James nor Barabbas, nor any of them which had most authority with the Galileans. Now Jesus himself ministered unto certain of them the Bread of Life, and forgave sins, and healed the sick. But afterwards, because of the multitude of them which came unto him (for they were more than five thousand) he caused the disciples to divide them into companies and to minister the Bread unto the people. So they ministered as Jesus bade them, and the grace of the Lord was with them; insomuch that Thomas (who had been at the first loth to minister the Bread, as not being worthy) came afterwards to Jesus saying, "Of a truth the crumbs of thy Banquet which are fallen from the table of the guests do suffice unto them that minister: for the Lord hath increased the Bread of Life within us." So mightily did the Bread of our Master increase in the hands of the Twelve. And Matthew said that Jesus had not only spread a table in the wilderness for the hungry, but that he had also fulfilled his saying, "Give and it shall be given unto you. For," said he, "behold, to each of the disciples there cometh back his basketful of the fragments of the Feast." And the like happened on another occasion, when they ministered the Bread unto another very great multitude about four thousand in number.

All this I heard when I returned with Judas from Capernaum, bringing word that the Thracians had left the town. So we returned to Capernaum, and there we kept the Passover; for Jesus would not go up to Jerusalem to keep it, though we were very desirous that he should go up; but he said that his hour had not yet come. But scarcely had we been in Capernaum five or six days, and the Feast of the Passover was still not ended, when we fled (upon some new rumour of danger) from Capernaum again to the eastern side of the lake. Now while we were rowing across, some of us murmured (though not so loud methought that Jesus could hear) concerning our many flights and wanderings, and we wondered why our Master would not suffer the common people to make him king.

In the midst of our disputing Jesus called unto us from the hinder part of the boat and said, "Beware of the leaven of the Pharisees and of the leaven of the Sadducees." Then we looked one at another, for we felt that we were guilty; for in the haste of our embarking, because we had come on board before it was well dawn (for fear of the arrival of the Thracians, which was reported to us) we had forgotten to bring with us any unleavened bread; and the feast of the Passover wanted yet two days before it should have an end, and behold, we were going to a Gentile country where our customs were not regarded, so that we could not easily obtain such bread as was needful. Therefore we confessed to Jesus, and said that indeed we were verily guilty of sore neglect.

But when Jesus heard our words, he rebuked us for our want of understanding; and he asked us whether we did not remember how the disciples had ministered the Bread of Life to the four thousand and to the five thousand; and he made mention of the saying of Thomas, one of the Twelve, how the bread had been multiplied in the hands of the Twelve, and also of the saying of Matthew the son of Levi, how the fragments of the Feast had returned to them that ministered, and had satisfied them. So we perceived that he spake not of the leaven that leaveneth bread of corn, but of the leaven which leaveneth and corrupteth the bread of the soul.

Yet forasmuch as the Pharisees agree not with the Sadducees (neither do they teach the same doctrine, nor observe the same customs) I could not understand what this "leaven of the Pharisees and Sadducees" might be. But when I asked Nathanael thereof, he said that perchance Jesus desired to warn us lest we should be led away in our hearts by the desire of this world, and by the haste to be prosperous. "For," said Nathanael, "the Sadducees love place and wealth and ease, and the Pharisees love power with the people, and the salutations of the rich, and the respect of the poor, and the name and reputation for piety; and these sects do both go straight towards their several ends. But, though several in appearance, their ends are really the same. For both the Pharisees and Sadducees serve themselves, and live for their own pleasure. And methinks our Master feareth lest we too in the same way may follow him not out of love and out of faithfulness, but from a desire to be prosperous."

"But are we not," asked I, "to be prosperous in the end?" "Yes, assuredly in the end," replied Nathanael; "but the end may perchance be somewhat farther off than we suppose, and our course may perchance be somewhat slow. For in all works there are two courses, the course of men and the course of God. Now men work visibly and speedily, and with much stir and noise; but the Father in Heaven worketh for the most part invisibly and slowly, and very gently. Now it may be that the slow ways are best. But in any case I begin to perceive that our Master loveth the slow ways best, according to his saying that the Kingdom of Heaven is like unto the wheat, which is sown and watered and resteth long unseen in the earth, and springeth up at last and by degrees, and putteth forth, first the blade, and then the ear and then the full corn; and all this by slow ways, quietly and gently, while the husbandman riseth and sleepeth and goeth in and out, and taketh no heed how great a work the gentle hand of the Lord is working around him."

Thus spake Nathanael, and I gave heed unto his words; for he seemed day by day to grow in the love and knowledge of our Master, and behold, the knowledge of Jesus seemed to bestow upon him knowledge of all spiritual things, so that he was not like the same Nathanael whom I had first known now a year ago. And the other disciples also were greatly changed from their former selves. For we had now been a full year with the Lord Jesus; and it was the sixteenth year of Tiberius Cæsar.

CHAPTER XVII

BETWEEN the Feast of Passover and the Feast of Weeks I was not much with Jesus; for when I perceived that Jesus was in no instant peril, I returned to Sepphoris for a while, partly by reason of my mother's health, and partly to gather in the harvest. And during this time, when it was perceived that Jesus went not up to the Passover, neither made any levy of the people as had been expected, the Pharisees for a while ceased to lay snares for him: and the common people, though they murmured that he went not up to Jerusalem, nevertheless had him in honour. But the harvest being now over, when I went back to meet Jesus at Capernaum, I found there one of mine acquaintance, a merchant (whom I had known at Alexandria in my uncle's house), a Greek learned in the knowledge of the Greeks. This man was not a proselyte; neither did he in any wise conform himself to the Law of Moses. But he spake of himself, at that time, as a seeker after truth; for he did not join himself to any of the schools of the Gentile philosophers, but chose forth from each whatsoever seemed to him useful or true. He had read our Scriptures, and was greatly given to the study of our psalms and prophecies; and when he had heard me speak of Jesus of Nazareth as being our Messiah, his heart was moved to hear Jesus preach the gospel. So it came to pass, about the first or second Sabbath after the Feast of Weeks, he accompanied me into the synagogue where Jesus was to speak to the people. But as I went, I perceived Abuyah the son of Elishah; and with him were certain of the Sadducees, and some also of the Herodians. And when I saw them, I knew that they had come for no good purpose.

And so it proved. For when we were now assembled in the synagogue, Abuyah came forward and said to Jesus, "Behold, thou art a vessel very full of knowledge, and the people are come together at thy feet for to hear of thee the words of wisdom, according as it is said, 'Powder thyself in the dust of the feet of the wise, and drink their words with thirstiness.' Now therefore, I pray thee, suffer me to ask of thee touching a certain matter." And Jesus said, "Ask." And Abuyah said, "Is it lawful for a man to put away his wife?"

Now when Abuyah spake these words, all the Herodians and Sadducees listened with greedy ears, as though they would devour the words that fell from Jesus, if perchance he should say something against Herod the Tetrarch. For Herod had put away his own wife and had married Herodias, the wife of his brother Herod Philip, which thing was not lawful for him to do. And it was for this cause that Abuyah had asked the question. For the Pharisees considered that in this way they would do one of two things; either they would incense Herod against Jesus (even as they had incensed him against John the son of Zachariah, whose death they had procured), or else they would cause

Jesus to appear unto the people a time-server and a prophet of smooth things, a prophet not to be trusted.

But Jesus knew their devices and said to Abuyah, "What did Moses command you?" And Abuyah said, "Moses suffered a man to write a bill of divorcement and to put his wife away." But Jesus answered and said, "For the hardness of your hearts he wrote you this precept. But from the beginning of the creation God made them male and female. For this cause shall a man leave his father and mother, and cleave to his wife: and they twain shall be one flesh. So then they are no more twain, but one flesh. What therefore God hath joined together let not man put asunder." By these words we understood Jesus both to find fault with them that allowed of divorce for every slight cause (as did certain of the Pharisees); and also to disallow of divorce generally, except (as he afterwards said) for adultery; which alone is, of itself, a divorce. But it was quite after the manner of Jesus to found this doctrine not upon the Law, but upon the nature of things, as it was created in the beginning; teaching that woman was not made as an afterthought, nor as a mere pleasure to the man; but that mankind was made, from the first, male and female. And according to this doctrine did Jesus ever behave towards women, showing unto them not only gentleness and kindness, but also a singular reverence.

After these words Jesus began to exhort the people: and he taught them that God requireth purity in the inner parts, namely, in the soul, saying, Not that which goeth into a man defileth a man, but that which cometh out of a man, evil and impure thoughts and deeds, these, he said, defile a man. Hereat many of the disciples were sore grieved that Jesus should thus openly, as it seemed, trample upon the Law of Moses ; and from this time certain Essenes that had hitherto followed with us, now altogether left Jesus. And one of the younger Scribes, interrupting him, cried aloud," He that despiseth the washing of hands shall be rooted out." But Jesus went on to say, Nay, but every plant that the Father in Heaven had not planted, should be rooted out; and as for the teaching of the Pharisees, he likened it to the tares, the end whereof is to be burned. He also likened them and their pupils to blind men leading other blind men ; who should all together fall into the pit.

Then he drew, as it were, a model of the New Kingdom ; wherein, he said, the only thing needful would be that a man should love God with all the heart, and his neighbours as himself. And when some one asked him who were a man's neighbours, he replied, in parables, that whosoever was sick, or naked, or an-hungered, or in pain or sorrow, whosoever in fine was in need of aught, that man (yea, even though he were a Samaritan), was neighbour unto each citizen in the New Kingdom ; and towards every neighbour the citizens were to do whatsoever they would desire that their neighbours should do unto them.

When the people were come forth out of the synagogue, the Greek merchant walked by my side for a while in silence : but Abuyah, who walked behind us, was plainly heard blaming Jesus as one that brake the Law and taught others to break it. Hearing these words, the merchant nodded over his shoulder, and exclaimed, "Yonder pedant, who with his washings would purify the very sun, is altogether void of understanding; else would he perceive that the philosophy of thy Teacher mounteth up to something far higher than the pulling down of the laws of thy nation." Then he questioned me touching Jesus, and of his former doctrine and manner of life since he had begun to teach; and I replied to all these things and asked of him in turn what he might mean by his words about the philosophy of Jesus. But he seemed rapt for the time in other thoughts, and, instead of answering me, he questioned me further concerning the birth and rearing and childhood of Jesus; and in particular, whether both his parents were of Israel, or whether his mother were not a Greek. But after that I had answered again to all his questioning, when I perceived that he was still musing on his own thoughts, and took no heed of my words, I waxed impatient, and repeated my question somewhat loudly.

Then my friend made answer, howbeit not in the way of a direct reply to my question, but rather as still partly meditating with himself: "Thou describest a gracious, a very gracious nature, ignorant of evil throughout his youth, seeing ever in his mind's eye the Isles of the Blessed, and desiring that same blessedness for all mankind. And lo, whatsoever he desireth that he seeth: for he deceiveth himself, feigning that all things are like unto that beautiful idea which he seeth in his mind." But I said to the merchant, "Nay, friend Xanthias," for that was the man's name, "but when Jesus spake of the Pharisees, did he then seem to thee ignorant of evil?" "Thou didst not give me time," replied the merchant, "to finish my speech: for I was about to say that, as it seemeth to me, thy

teacher is even now awakening to the evil that is in
the world; and, becoming at last undeceived, he seeth
his fair phantasma vanishing away. Thus his gracious
nature, yielding to the over great pressure of the evil
that surroundeth him, is becoming marred and wounded.
Alas for the pitiful change! For behold, his former
life, as thou describest it, was like unto a deer sporting
gladly in the woods, to whom the flowers of the fields
are as friends, and the wind ever bringeth glad tidings.
But to what shall I liken the latter end of his life?
It is like unto the same deer wounded by the hunts-
man, who passeth by the same way, and through the
same woods; but she is glad no longer, for the dart
still cleaveth to her side, and the flowers delight her no
longer, and the breezes are messengers of evil."

I was grieved at his words, and all the more because
they agreed with certain fears in the depth of my own
heart, whereof I had up to this time made no mention
even to Nathanael, no, nor yet unto mine own self. But
I was grieved also because the Greek knew not the true
nature of Jesus. For he spake of him as of one
gracious and lovable, but he knew not the might and
the power of our Master, how he was like unto a rock
immovable, unchangeable; even such another as the
Gentiles fable Atlas to have been, who bore up the
world by the strength of his shoulders. For I knew
that, if heaven and earth had set themselves in league
against Jesus, to make him do aught against the will of
the Father, Jesus would have stood up alone against
earth and heaven, and hell to boot. Moreover, I had
noted how there still came forth from Jesus a new
strength to bear each new burden, and a new knowledge

to discern each new Revelation from the Father, yea, and a new delight to delight therein. For though it were true indeed, as the Greek had said, that Jesus had sometimes marvelled at evil (when it befel him) as though he had been ignorant thereof before, yet was it also true that he seemed to have become greater through the increase of the knowledge of evil. But Xanthias knew naught of this. For he was deceived by the gentleness of Jesus, not perceiving that this same gentleness of Jesus was stronger than the strength of kings. Therefore was I grieved at his words; but I constrained myself and asked him yet again what he might mean by saying that the philosophy of Jesus mounted to somewhat higher than the pulling down of the Law.

Then said the Greek, "Are there then in this country no slaves?" "Thou knowest," I replied, "that there are slaves: howbeit, not many, nor ill used, nor treated like beasts, as the Gentiles treat them." Then said he to me, "And wouldst thou willingly be a slave in this country?" I said, "Nay." "And if thou wert a slave, wouldst thou wish that thy master should retain thee as a slave, or should enfranchise thee?" I replied, "The latter." Then said the Greek with a smile, "But if ye all became followers of Jesus of Nazareth, would ye not perforce confess that all men were your neighbours, yea, even Greeks and Romans; yea, even Samaritans; yea, even your own slaves?" Then was I silent: for I understood now that his meaning was, that the teaching of Jesus would in the end bring to pass the enfranchising of all slaves, and I knew not what to reply.

But he, still smiling, said, "I perceive that thou understandest my meaning. For the teaching of thy Master aimeth at nothing less than the destroying of all manner of slavery. But without slavery the race of man neither hath existed, nor can exist, as thou knowest very well. For without slaves no work could be performed except the tilling of the land, which alone is fit for free men." I said then to him that in Israel there was not the same disliking of handicrafts as among the Greeks and Romans. But he said, "Dost thou suppose that thy Master's philosophy concerneth only thine own people?" "Yea, of a surety," said I; "our own people, and none else; for he himself proclaimeth the Kingdom to no strangers." He replied, "That may be, for a time: but is not the Samaritan thy neighbour?" Then was I again silent. For there came into my mind that ancient prophecy which saith that in the seed of Abraham, that is to say in the Messiah, all the nations of the earth shall be blessed; and I remembered how oft Jesus had of late taught us that the Samaritans were neighbours to the citizens in the Kingdom. But I put the thought away from me; for the truth was at that time hid from our eyes: neither could I at that time perceive how we could be redeemed or delivered, if we were to treat the Romans as neighbours. But while I mused thereon, Xanthias continued his speech concerning Jesus, and he said that Jesus did wisely in that he seemed to encourage marriage, and to prohibit many wives, and to forbid divorce. "For," said he, "herein I incline rather to Aristotle than to Plato, believing that the state is composed of families; and if the family be rotten, the state cannot be sound.

But to hope to destroy slavery is to hope to pull down the pillar whereon the life of all states is based."

Now was my heart hot within me; and I was fain to speak, and to say that Jesus would indeed pull down slavery in Israel, and make our people to be a nation of priests and princes for the world, and would in the end destroy even the Evil Nature of man. But I abstained from speech; for I knew that my words would be foolishness in his ears, and that he could not understand the Redemption unless he understood Jesus himself. Therefore I made him some courteous answer and accompanied him toward the house where he lay.

But he still continued his discourse of the philosophy of Jesus (as he called it), and he likened Jesus unto the Greek Teacher Socrates, in that neither Socrates nor Jesus would receive teaching upon mere authority, nor because this saying or that precept chanced to have been written in books: but Socrates trusted to a certain power of reason or dialectic, and Jesus to a certain power which he called a Spirit: the two being diverse in appearance, but in truth following one and the same method. Thus Xanthias continued his speech of Jesus; but as he bade me farewell near the threshold, it came to pass that Abuyah, who had been walking behind us, came near, still talking with his companions, and saying in a loud voice that Jesus was as the bramble, whereof Jotham maketh mention in the Scriptures. "Wherefore," said he, "meet it is that we cut down this vile thorn-tree, lest there come forth fire from the bramble and consume the olive-tree, and the fig, and all the fruitful trees of the forest."

When Abuyah had passed by, the merchant said

unto me, "Truly I have heard no philosopher whose lectures have so pleased me as the teaching of this thy Teacher; and, though I esteem little of wonders, whereof we have enough and to spare at Alexandria, yet if even the half of that which thou sayest touching the acts of thy Jesus be true, he will deserve worship even better than Æsculapius or Amphiaraus. But as thou knowest, my dear friend, I am one of them which doubt all things; and I incline to the belief that there are no gods, or if there be, that they deal not with human matters. And thereto I incline the more because I see all human things full of misery and oppression. And, unless my fears deceive me, this my belief will be confirmed by the fate of thine own Teacher. For I fear, I greatly fear, lest the friends of Abuyah the Scribe may prevail over the friends of Jesus the philosopher of the New Kingdom and deliverer of the slaves."

So saying he turned himself round to depart. But I was scarce gone ten paces when he called me back, and taking me by the hand very earnestly, "I pray thee," said he, "tell me by what name doth thy Master call himself. A prophet? or a teacher? Or doth he say that he is your Messiah? or a lawgiver like unto Moses?" But I made answer that Jesus called himself by none of these names; but, for the most part, only "Son of man." Hereat Xanthias marvelled and said, "But wherefore useth he this title? For thou, and I, and all men, are not we all sons of men? Doth thy Master therefore fear lest his disciples may perchance forget that he is a man and deem him to be a god? For such a title as this, albeit humble in appearance, seemeth in verity too proud for any save such as aspire to be gods. But perchance your prophets have so used this title that it hath some strange meaning, whereof I know naught." Then I said that the word was indeed used by the prophets: for whensoever the Lord speaketh to Ezekiel as to a mortal creature, the Lord calleth him Son of man, as if to set the mortal infirmities of the prophet over against the divine nature of the Lord; but again the prophet Daniel saith that, in the day of Judgment, there shall appear one like unto the Son of man, sitting on the clouds of heaven, and coming in glory to judge the nations of the earth : wherefore the title seemed to signify the weak nature of man, whether infirm or whether exalted. Howbeit, added I, before Jesus, no prophet spake thus of himself as the Son of man.

Hereat Xanthias marvelled the more, saying that this was indeed a strange title, and such as no philosopher had ever before taken upon himself. Then he mused a while, still holding me by the cloak, and would have questioned me farther; but I could tell him no more. So at the last he let me go, shaking his head, and saying that it was strange, it was passing strange, and that there was more in this than he could understand : and as he turned himself to depart, I heard him repeating again to himself that it was a proud title, a very proud title, and such as no wise and sober philosopher should take. And thus he departed, meditating as he went, and so rapt in his study that he forgot to bid me farewell. But when he was departed, so that I had leisure to think on his wonder and on the cause thereof; then I also began to perceive that there was more than I had as yet understood, in this title of the Son of man.

CHAPTER XVIII

No evil followed on the words which Jesus had spoken concerning divorce; and we remained many days in peace, even till the day of Atonement, which falleth toward the beginning of the autumn in the month called Tisri. But we had friends in Tiberias, who were to send us word by day, or signify to us by lights during the night, if perchance any plot were intended against Jesus.

Now so it was that some of the Galileans did not consent to James the son of Judas, and to Barabbas in forsaking Jesus, neither did they allow the conduct of the Pharisees; but having gathered themselves together they agreed that it was not fit that Israel should so long halt between two opinions; but as it had been in the days of Elias the prophet, so should it be now. "For," said the chief man among them, "Elias gathered the people together and the people promised to be on his side, if he brought down fire from heaven; and he did so. Now perchance this Jesus is even Elias; for many so report of him, and even the Scribes say that Elias must come, and some say that Elias hath come oftentimes before now. But whether he be Elias or no, doubtless, if he be a true prophet, he can work the sign of Elias. For a false prophet can work signs on the earth and in the air, and in the deep; but a sign in heaven or from heaven he cannot work. Therefore meet it is that the Pharisees, instead of setting snares for Jesus, should promise to obey him if he will work a sign in heaven in their presence. My counsel is therefore that we ask Jesus to work a sign in heaven; and if he consent, then that we obey him, even though all the Pharisees speak against him, yea, and though he bid us hold out our throats to be cut by the Romans."

Thus spake the Galileans at their council, not many days after the discourse of Jesus concerning divorce. And the counsel of the Galileans was reported unto the Scribes. But when Abuyah the son of Elishah heard it, he said that this was according to the Scripture and the Traditions, and that it should be so. But Eliezer the son of Arak said that it should not be so; for that it was in no wise certain that a magician could not work a sign in heaven, or at the least, a sign that should appear to be in heaven. But if he could, said Abuyah, then, though the sign should not really be in heaven, yet if it appeared to be therein, all the foolish rabble, even the people of the land, would be drawn after Jesus, and the Pharisees also would be obliged to submit to him. "For," added he, "I have heard of magicians which can make statues walk, and can knead loaves of stones; and of others that can become serpents, and transform themselves into goats, and can open locked gates, and can melt iron in a moment of time; but if they can do things so wonderful, think ye they cannot likewise perform signs which shall appear to be signs in heaven?"

Others also protested to the same effect, and one said that he had been present when a certain magician had been smitten right through his body with the sword, but behold, the sword had passed through him as through smoke, and he had taken no hurt; and another said that he had seen an enchanter at a banquet create all manner of images, and cause dishes to be borne of themselves to wait upon the guests, no bearers being seen. At the last Abuyah himself confessed that he also had once seen a certain magician roll himself on the fire, and yet not burned; and the same man also to fly in the air. "Wherefore," said he, "true it is, as Eliezer saith, that one flying high enough in the air, might seem to fly down from heaven, and so to perform some sign in heaven; and thus might he lead away the common people, which know not the Law." All this I heard from a certain Scribe, a friend of Jonathan the son of Ezra; his name was Eleazar the son of Azariah, and he was present at the meeting of the Scribes.

The same Eleazar also told me that whilst the Scribes were yet debating what they should do, a message was brought, as from one that had spoken with the chosen disciples of Jesus, saying that Jesus would certainly not work a sign in heaven; for that he had refused to do this, though he had been besought by his disciples. When they heard this, they rejoiced greatly; and Eliezer the son of Arak rose up and straightway gave his judgment that they should now change their policy. "For," said he, "the Lord having revealed this new thing unto us, meet it is that we change our path accordingly, neither harden our faces against the will of God. Wherefore my judgment now is, that we ask this Jesus to work a sign in heaven before the face of the whole congregation in the synagogue. For when it shall be perceived that he cannot work a sign in heaven, all men will go from him; for they will know that he is a false prophet." And thereto the rest agreed, and it was so resolved. But I knew not thereof till many days after.

It was the intent of the Scribes to have asked Jesus to work a sign in heaven on the next Sabbath; but in the meantime, lights having been held up by night in Tiberias (on I know not what report or rumour of some danger intended to Jesus by Herod, or some marching forth of the Thracian guard), Jesus gave command to pass over again unto the other side of the lake. We accompanied him, albeit sorely against our will; for there seemed to be no end unto these wanderings or flights; and each new flight was like to turn the hearts of the people more and more from Jesus. Moreover, the manner of Jesus at this time disquieted us, and made some of us to doubt. Not that he seemed to fear; for fear had no part in him, neither did he seem to know what fear meant. But he appeared again (as in former days) like unto one waiting for a message and marvelling somewhat that the message came not.

During these days, and these wanderings to and fro, the words of the prophet Jonah were often in his mouth, and he seemed as if he discerned a certain likeness between that prophet and himself; but what it was we understood not. For sometimes he spake of Nineveh, and how Jonah thought only of his own people, and had no compassion upon that great city of the Gentiles, yea, and fought against the voice of the Lord, who bade him go prophesy unto them; and how he wandered hither and thither, if perchance he could flee from the voice of the Lord. But at other times he spake how Jonah cried unto the Lord even from the belly of hell, and how the Lord inclined His ear unto him, and heard him, and raised him up to prophesy unto the Gentiles; and he quoted oftentimes the words of the prayer of the prophet, "I went down to the bottoms of the mountains; the earth with her bars was about me for ever; yet hast thou brought up my life from corruption, O Lord my God." Likewise he made mention of some sign of Jonah, which he said should be manifested to this generation; but whether he meant that he should be sent far away unto the Gentiles, or that he should be cast into the depths, and delivered again, as Jonah was, this we understood not, and the saying was hidden from us.

Now it came to pass, when we had journeyed now many days on the other side of the lake, we came nigh to the mountain of Hermon. Snows cover the top of this mountain both summer and winter; and when the sun in his strength shineth on the snows thereof, it is as though the glory of the Lord had come down from heaven. Towards this mountain Jesus had set his face as though he had an errand thither from the Lord; and as we journeyed towards it, he gazed often thereon and rejoiced greatly. But it came to pass, as we now drew nigh unto the mountain, we journeyed through a certain village of the country; and because we were in haste and Jesus desired that none should know him, we were to have passed quickly through the village before dawn. For the fame of Jesus, how he could cast out unclean spirits, was spread abroad even in that country. But as we passed through the village, we heard sounds as of one calling after us; and some thought they heard shrieks. Howbeit we turned not back, but journeyed forward the more quickly.

Now a certain woman in this village (a worshipper of idols, after the manner of the people of that land) had a daughter possessed with an unclean spirit, which, whensoever it took her, drove her to all manner of wickedness, even to the attempting of her mother's life. So the woman had resolved in her own mind that when Jesus passed by (for he must needs come through that village), she would beseech Jesus to heal her daughter, and she had told her daughter of her purpose, and likewise all her friends and acquaintance; and she had been advised of the approach of Jesus and was watching for us. Therefore seeing us pass quickly through her village, she adventured to bring out her daughter unto Jesus: but her daughter would not come. For even then, at the hearing of the name of Jesus, the devil took her, and she shrieked aloud and strove against her mother, and would have slain her: but her mother ran forth from the house and followed Jesus, calling and crying aloud and piteously lamenting.

Now to us it seemed a strange thing and an unseemly, that a prophet of Israel should thus be beset and importuned by an heathen woman. So we expected that Jesus should have at once sent the woman away. But Jesus uttered never a word, nor so much as turned his face towards her, but journeyed steadfastly forward. And even as one running a race towards a goal settleth his soul upon the prize that is before him, even so seemed Jesus to settle his soul upon the snows of the mountain of Hermon: for they shone in the light of the rising sun, like unto a dove sent from God, whose breast-feathers are as silver, and whose wings like unto fine gold. But the woman ceased not from her following and lamenting, and poured forth before Jesus all the story of her troubles.

At last we adventured to accost Jesus, and we besought him to send her away. But he answered us, still not turning his face, "I am not sent but unto the lost sheep of the house of Israel." Yet as he spake, he slackened his going, and spake, as it were, like unto one doubting somewhat, and willing to have his words amended. Now came the woman in haste up to him, and threw herself before his feet and said, "Lord, help me." Then Jesus stayed. Yet did he still keep his eyes fixed on that which he saw afar off; and for a brief space he was silent; but then he said, as though he were asking a question of his own soul, "It is not meet to take the children's bread, and to cast it unto the dogs?" But the woman answered, "Truth, O Master, yet the dogs eat of the crumbs which fall from their master's table."

When Jesus heard these words he turned his face straightway from the glory of the mountain and looked down on the woman; and behold, he rejoiced more because of that which he beheld nigh unto him, than because of the glory that was afar off. For the fashion of his countenance was changed so as I cannot describe it. And immediately he stooped down, and took the woman by the hand and raised her up, and said unto her, "O woman, great is thy faith; be it unto thee even as thou wilt."

Now when the woman ran back to her house, she found the child on a bed, struggling, and scarce held of her friends; who stood by, weeping and supposing the child to be possessed, not now with one devil but with many. Then she cried aloud for joy, and told her acquaintance how that Jesus had granted her prayer. And straightway, when the devil heard this saying, even at the mention of the name of Jesus, he tare the child, and departed, leaving her, as it seemed, lifeless. But presently she rose up whole and sound, being delivered from the devil; nor was she ever again afflicted. All this was done by the word of Jesus spoken by the Syrophœnician woman; for he was not present to heal the girl; albeit (as I gathered) the girl had before heard oftentimes of her mother that Jesus was to come to heal her, and how great things he had done for others that were possessed. But when Jesus had heard the words of the Syrophœnician woman, he was no longer minded to journey towards the north, but went back into the village where was the girl afflicted with the unclean spirit. Now the people would fain have constrained him to tarry with them; but he would not, but set his face southward again to go toward the Sea of Galilee. For the faith of the Syrophœnician had strangely moved him, insomuch that he spake as if the Redemption were nearer than it had been before; and, as I judge, he desired to make one more proof of the Pharisees, whether they also would not have faith in him. And straightway he crossed over and came again to Capernaum.

As we rowed across the lake back to Capernaum we rejoiced greatly; for we thought that the time was at hand when the Galileans (for of the intent of the Pharisees we knew naught) would ask Jesus to work a sign in heaven, and Jesus would now grant their request. But when Jesus had done this, we trusted that the whole nation should have believed in him, and that the time should have come that he should redeem Israel. Howbeit certain of the disciples (and more especially Judas of Kerioth) took it ill that Jesus should have listened to the prayer of an heathen woman which was an idolater. For although Esaias saith that the Gentiles are to come to the rising of the Lord, and that the Gentiles shall seek to the Deliverer of Israel, yet had it been always fixed and rooted in our hearts that the deliverance of the Gentiles (if it should come to pass at all) must come by the uprising of the children of Israel, who should be princes and kings, conquering and triumphing over the nations of the earth. And then the Gentiles were to seek to Israel and to become proselytes, entering into the true fold. And this belief Jesus had confirmed in our hearts in that he had bidden us to go not to the Samaritans nor to the Gentiles, but only to the lost sheep of the house of Israel. Which saying Jesus himself now seemed to contradict, having thus healed the Syrophœnician maiden. But whether it had been revealed to our Master, through the words of the Syrophœnician, that the deliverance of the Gentiles should come more speedily than had been supposed, and not by fetching a compass, as it were, round all the borders of Israel, but by a more direct course, concerning this I know nothing: but Quartus judgeth that it was so.

CHAPTER XIX

GORGIAS the son of Philip exceeded the rest of us in his rejoicing at the return of Jesus, and in the largeness of his expectation, saying that it could not be that our Master, when he adventured to work a sign, would suffer himself to be surpassed by any, albeit the most cunning magicians. "Now," said he, "I have heard an Alexandrine say that there are certain magicians which, in the middle of the market-place, in return for a few obols, will drive out demons and diseases, and call up the souls of heroes, and costly banquets, tables, dishes, and dainties, all as though ready for a feast; all which at the magician's wand shall vanish away. If therefore a common magician can do such things for hire, how much more can Jesus do greater things than these for the Redemption of Israel!" Judas also spake after the same manner, and he said that perchance it was well done of Jesus not to work a sign in heaven at first; for had he worked the sign too early, it would have been counted cheap, and would have been despised. "Much wiser," continued he, "to hold the sign back till the people crave for it, and till the Pharisees (supposing forsooth that he cannot do it) venture to promise obedience to Jesus on the condition that he work a sign in heaven. For thus shall they be taken in their own snare." Only John was doubtful, saying to Judas, "Hast thou then forgotten how once in our presence our Master said he should work no sign in heaven?" But Judas replied that our Master had more than once changed his course, suiting it to the needs of the time; "And," said he, "when he shall once perceive that the Redemption of Sion dependeth upon the working of a sign in heaven, then, trust me, the sign will not long be wanting. And so strongly am I assured thereof, that it would even seem to me to be a friendly deed to tell the Pharisees how Jesus hath said that he will never work the sign, and in this way to move them to ask Jesus to work the sign; to the intent that they may dig a pit for Jesus and fall into it themselves."

Now this he spake jesting; but (as I afterwards learned) Judas had indeed moved the Pharisees even, as he said, to ask Jesus to work a sign in heaven. And Judas it was that had sent to Eliezer that message whereof I have before made mention. But these things Judas did, not because he desired (at that time) to harm Jesus, but wishing to help him, and supposing that he should help him by forcing him to do that which, of himself, Jesus would not do. Howbeit of all these things we, at this present, knew nothing; and we took the words of Judas as if spoken in jest. But John shook his head and made no answer.

It was in the winter, in the month called Chisleu, that we returned to Capernaum. But it came to pass, on the first Sabbath day after that we had returned, we went into the synagogue after our custom, and Jesus taught the people; and the hand of the Lord was present among them, and the people were very attentive to hear him. But when he had ended his words there rose up Abuyah the son of Elishah; and he spake after the manner of the Galileans, saying that it was not right that Israel should be any more divided against itself, but that all should confess that Jesus was the Anointed or Christ, if indeed he could shew that he was the Christ. "But the proof," said he, "is, as we all know, the working of a sign in heaven. For signs on earth and in the deep, false prophets can work; but not in heaven. Now, therefore, this is the sum of the matter: thou wouldst have us, the Scribes and teachers of Israel, to believe in thee and to follow thee. Our answer is, Work a sign in heaven such as Elias worked, and straightway we follow thee."

While Abuyah was speaking his last words, a hesitation and a gasping overcame him, so that he was almost speechless. For he was abashed by the aspect of Jesus and by the stillness of the multitude. And, to say the truth, when Abuyah spake those words, "such as Elias worked," we held our breath; expecting when the fire of heaven should come down, as in the days of Elias, and should consume Abuyah, and Eliezer, and all the enemies of Jesus; or else we thought that the earth should have opened and swallowed them up, as the earth swallowed up Korah and his fellows. But when Eliezer had ended all his words, and no gulf yawned nor fire came down from heaven, then indeed our hearts sank within us. But Abuyah and Eliezer began to be of good cheer; for they perceived that they had been well advised, and that Jesus would work no sign in heaven.

When Jesus made answer to Abuyah, the people

listened to him and were silent; but their hearts no longer inclined unto him as before. For indeed his words were not easy to understand. But he bade the Pharisees note the signs of the times, even as they noted the signs of the weather, and therein, he said, they should find proof enough. Moreover he spake those same strange words which he had spoken before to us privately, to wit, that they should have no sign but the sign of the prophet Jonah. Having said these words he departed from the synagogue; and at sunset, finding that the hearts of all men were turned from him, he gave command once again to launch the boat and to pass over unto the other side.

Never before were the minds of the disciples so troubled as now: for we had all been assured, in the very depth of our hearts, that Jesus had even for this cause returned to Capernaum, because he purposed now at last to work a sign in heaven. Neither could we in any way understand why he should thus suffer the slanderers to triumph, delaying so long the Redemption of Sion. Judas especially inflamed our grief, saying that all was now lost, and that one sign in heaven would have been better worth than a thousand discourses about the Kingdom of Heaven.

But suddenly we were silent; for we heard the voice of Jesus speaking; and he told us that he had formerly been tempted in a like fashion, even as the Pharisee had tempted him; for he had been led by the Spirit into a wilderness, and there in some vision the Evil Spirit had placed him upon the battlements of the Holy Temple, bidding him cast himself down as a sign unto the multitudes of them which were walking in the courts of the Temple; and the Evil One had said unto him, "If thou be the Son of God, cast thyself down : for it is written, He shall give His angels charge concerning thee ; and in their hands they shall bear thee up, lest at any time thou dash thy foot against a stone." But Jesus had made answer, saying, "It is written again, Thou shalt not tempt the Lord thy God." Now therefore we all understood (after a dark fashion, and, as it were, obliquely) that Jesus esteemed the temptation to perform a sign in heaven to be a temptation from Satan. But why he so esteemed it, was hid from the most of us, and we feared to ask him thereof.

When Jesus lay down on the sleeping-cushion, I questioned Nathanael why Jesus would work no sign in heaven. "For," said I, "signs on earth and in the bodies of men he daily worketh; as but now, when he raised up the daughter of Jairus (all men supposing her to be dead) : and again, at another time, albeit he neither said nor did aught, a woman was healed, though she did but touch him, and that too in a throng: so powerful was the mere garment of our Master to work healing. And when Jesus perceived the woman (discerning the pressure of her hand, albeit in the midst of the throng), then, as thou rememberest, he was neither wroth nor chid the woman for thus, as it were, stealing a miracle; but bade her go in peace, and be healed of her disease. Wherefore then worketh he no sign in heaven ? Did not Moses and Elias work signs in heaven ? Yet our Master is greater than they." To these words Nathanael made no answer for a while ; but at last he said, "Concerning Moses and Elias, and concerning what they did or did not, I am not able to speak. But as touching Jesus of Nazareth, thus much I know, that he lightly esteemeth all signs, both in heaven and in earth, except they reveal the mercifulness of God. For he teacheth that heaven and earth shall pass away, but his words shall remain for ever. And assuredly he seemeth to me to be greater than Moses and Elias, yea, though he should work no sign at all. For he moveth upon the face of the earth like unto the Son of God, and looketh upon all things that are, as being the servants of his Father. But seeing that they are the servants of his Father, he loveth them; yea, he cherisheth even the flowers of the fields; the sky also, and the winds, and the waters seem to him as the ministers of his Father; and the more he loveth the Father, the more he loveth his Father's servants; neither will he check them nor chide them save according to his Father's will, but submitteth himself unto them even more willingly than others submit themselves. For this cause he endureth to be cold, and an-hungered, and athirst, and homeless; neither doth he chide the frost, nor stamp on the ground to make the wheat spring up for him; nor strike waters from the rock; nor bid the stones come together at his word for to build him an house." "But is not this patience," asked I, "the condition of a slave?" "Yes, truly is it," replied Nathanael, "but what saith our Master? He that is to be greatest among men must be as he that is least; he that is to rule must be as he that ministereth; he that is to be king over all must be as the slave of all. Only it is needful that we serve not unwillingly, but willingly. But whoso serveth the Lord in all things willingly, he is no slave, but a son.

"For this cause, in part methinks, Jesus calleth himself the Son of man; as if to shew that he is willingly subject to all the fleshly weaknesses wherewith the All-Wise hath encompassed the souls of men to the end that they may depend on Him. For he teacheth that he, being the weakness of man, shall be made strength and exalted to the very throne of God, and we with him; so that we shall reign with God, and the Kingdom of God shall also be a Kingdom of man, according as it is said, 'What is man that thou art mindful of him, and the son of man that thou visitest him? Thou madest him to have dominion over the works of thy hands: thou hast put all things in subjection under his feet.'"

"Yea, but," said I, "the Psalmist speaketh only of the things of the earth, to wit, the 'sheep and oxen and the beasts of the field, the fowl of the air, and the fish of the sea, and whatsoever passeth through the paths of the seas.'"

But to this Nathanael made answer, "In the Kingdom of God the Son of man shall be Lord over all things in heaven and earth, not on earth merely; yea, over death itself, and over the Evil Nature in man. For this cause, even as an earnest of that which is to come, our Master checketh and chideth diseases and devils in them which be possessed. For our Master hateth the devils and diseases even as he hateth the sins of men, esteeming them as the work of Satan, and not as the work of his Father. But the course and appointed order of the world he esteemeth as the vesture of God, whereof he would not disturb one single fold."

Now herein Nathanael spake truly. For once only

(as I have heard) did Jesus so much as appear to adventure to alter the course of the world. It was on a winter evening, and the disciples were on the lake; but I was not with them. A great storm had suddenly come down on them (as storms are wont to come down from the mountains round about the lake) and the boat was now well-nigh filled with the waves and like to sink. Then the disciples lifted up their voices for fear, and ran to Jesus as he slept upon the cushion, and besought him, saying, "Master, carest thou not that we perish?" Then he arose in grief for them, as it seemed, that they should, after so cowardly a fashion, tremble before the winds; and he opened his mouth to rebuke them. "And all this while," said Matthew (for he was present), "the winds yet raged, and the waves beat in upon the deck, and in another instant, methought, we had been all dead men. But Jesus, noting this, turned himself from us toward the sea, and then (as if it were revealed to him that he, being the safety of the world, could not be wrecked by any turbulence of winds or waves, and therefore that the storm was to cease), behold, he stretched out his hands to the tempest, praying; and straightway the storm seemed to abate a little; and then, perceiving the will of the Father, he stood up like some great king or emperor, and rebuked the storm, bidding it be still; and immediately there was a great calm."

Now on this only occasion did our Master appear to change the course of the world; and methinks, even here, he did it only in appearance. For he spake as he was moved by the Holy Spirit, it being revealed to him that the storm must needs cease lest the fortunes of the world should be shipwrecked, if the Son of man should perish. But if Xanthias findeth fault with this story, saying that on this only occasion our Master spake after the manner of a Mænad, and not worthily of himself, to this I reply that, if Jesus of Nazareth was the Son of God (as I doubt not), then it was fit that he should feel faith, yea, a singular faith in God his Father. And if Caius Cæsar, the first Emperor, could be assured that he was not to be drowned, saying to the boatmen that they must be of good cheer because they carried Cæsar and his Fortune; how much more might the true Emperor of men be assured that the Fortune of mankind should not be shipwrecked, yea, and rather than this should come to pass, that the storm must cease? For this cause I incline not to the opinion of Xanthias; who saith that Jesus rebuked not the storm, but the disciples, bidding them not be fearful and of little faith. And, though I was not myself present, yet was the matter reported to me afterwards by one that had heard the relation thereof from Matthew the son of Levi, as I said above.

While I spake with Nathanael, there came into my mind certain words of my Greek friend, whom I had met at Capernaum (I mean the Alexandrine merchant), how he had praised Jesus in that he breathed a spirit of soberness and peace, so that, wheresover he might be, he seemed happy and at home; and I told this to Nathanael. But he said, "Thy friend said well; for to Jesus the world is as a great instrument of music giving forth sounds which we hear not, but he both heareth and enjoyeth. And well I remember how once, in the presence of Jesus, there arose a dispute between a musician and another, concerning the sense of hearing and the sense of sight; and the other said, jesting at the musician, 'To believe thee, the sun should have a voice if it is to be perfect.' 'Nay,' said the musician, 'but the sun hath indeed a voice to those which have ears to hearken; for when it riseth in the east, it is not a large round shining shekel, but it is a minister of God and crieth with ten thousand times ten thousand voices, Holy, Holy, Holy is the Lord God Almighty.' And thereat Jesus smiled and said that it was even so, and that in the time to come there would dwell this power of sound not in the lights of heaven alone, but also in the earth, and all that therein is; insomuch that the vine-twigs and grape-clusters should have voices of their own and commune with the children of men."[1]

By this time we had reached the coast, and we went forth from the vessel, and took our way to a little village lying in the road which leadeth unto Cæsarea Philippi. And as Nathanael had been sent on before the rest to prepare lodging for us, I could find no more occasion that day to converse with him. But my mind was still beating on the dark saying of Jesus touching the temptation of Satan, and I still assayed to understand why Jesus would not work a sign in heaven: for the words of Nathanael had not sufficed to make the matter clear unto me.

Only concerning the sign in heaven, thus much was revealed unto me, that I myself was not drawn unto Jesus by his signs and wonders, but by reason of my love for him and trust in him; and the same was true also of the other disciples. Moreover Jesus desired that men should be drawn unto him in this way, by love and

[1] See Note I.

trust, and by feeling that he was needful to them, and not by being astonished at signs and wonders. Further I questioned myself and said, "If Jesus had caused the sun to stop still, would Abuyah the son of Elishah, and Eliezer the son of Arak, and the chief ruler of the synagogue straightway have loved Jesus and trusted in him, as Jesus desireth his disciples to love and trust in him?" Now I knew that they might have obeyed him and followed him, but they could not have loved him. For Jesus was light: but they loved darkness. Wherefore Jesus could not redeem them nor deliver them, even though he had worked a sign in heaven. For he could not deliver them which loved him not; no, not though he had worked ten thousand signs in heaven.

CHAPTER XX

As soon as day dawned on the morrow, we left the village where we had lain that night, and journeyed northward ; and Jesus set his face once more toward Mount Hermon. We were all very silent, more than was our custom ; for we were downcast and dejected by reason of our often fleeing from before the face of our enemies, and because of the delay of the day of Redemption. And though we still loved Jesus and trusted him after a manner, yet we knew not what to think concerning the things that he had done of late. As we journeyed, Jesus spake much concerning faith, and how, without faith, no one could truly believe in him. From time to time he looked at us, as we went by his side ; and he seemed as if he were measuring our thoughts by our faces, and reckoning up the sum of our strength : and now he seemed desirous to speak, and now to delay speaking ; watching over us as if some great burden were at hand, and as though he feared lest the burden should be more than we could bear.

But as concerning faith he said some things hard to understand ; to wit, that if a man had not faith, there should be taken from him even that which he seemed to have ; and yet, at the same time, he said that no man could have faith in him nor come to him unless he were drawn by the Father. Moreover he said that whoso had faith as a grain of mustard-seed, should be able to overthrow trees or mountains. Likewise he added that, if two or three would agree together touching anything that they would ask of the Father in heaven, it should be done for them.

Now as touching the overthrowing of mountains or destruction of trees, some have supposed that Jesus really wrought such wonders as these; and I have heard that stories of this kind are currently reported in the Church. But Jesus did never any such thing. But in our language an "uprooter of mountains" was a name given to any Rabbi that had power by his words to remove great difficulties out of the path of the righteous, and to make smooth the rough places in the ways of the Law. And after the like manner, as I suppose, are to be interpreted the words of Jesus touching the answer to prayer. For it entered not into his mind that his disciples should ask for earthly things as their hearts' desire; but they were to ask for heavenly things, and earthly things should be added to them, sufficient for their needs. Howbeit Quartus explaineth this saying somewhat otherwise, as I shall set forth further on.

As we journeyed, Jesus would not that any should know him: and few took heed of us; for instead of a great multitude, none now went with him, save the Twelve, and three or four others beside myself. But passing by a certain house wherein dwelt one of our countrymen (though we were by this time far beyond the bounds of Galilee) Jesus entered in asking for water; for the weather was exceeding sultry. And so it was that in the house the good folk were making ready to circumcise a child; and (after the manner of the people in Galilee) an empty chair had been set for the prophet Elias, as being the prophet of the covenant of circumcision. But some one of our company (Judas of Kerioth, as I remember) not knowing wherefore the chair was thus set, asked the cause thereof. So the good man of the house said that it was set for Elias the prophet, "who hath ofttimes appeared," said he, "in the guise of a merchant, to one or other of the Scribes in old times; and, three days before the Messiah come, he needs must appear for to anoint the Messiah: but I have heard it said of many, these ten days, that he hath appeared indeed as a prophet, on the other side of the lake, for to avenge the death of John the son of Zachariah."

When he said these words, we looked each at other but held our peace: and Jesus, after he had courteously thanked the man, came forth and addressed himself again to the journey; but, methought, even more sadly and sorrowfully than before. But still his discourse (as oft as he said anything) was on faith; and presently he began to say in a low voice a certain psalm (which was both at this time and during many days afterwards upon his lips); and in the psalm are these words, first of supplication and then of praise: "Deliver my soul from the sword, my darling from the power of the dog, save me from the lion's mouth, thou hast heard me also from among the horns of the unicorns. I will declare thy Name unto my brethren; in the midst of the congregation will I praise thee." Now when he spake these words touching the "congregation," and also the following words, "my praise is of thee in the great congregation," then so it was that Judas, who had been scarce able, these many days, to restrain himself because of his anger at the tarrying of Jesus, spake aloud and very vehemently, saying that, but one or two months ago, there was indeed a congregation, and a great congregation, which also had been ready with one consent to have risen up against the Romans; "but now," said Judas, "we be scarce a score in all."

Hereat Jesus stayed, and turned round and looked at Judas, methought, to have rebuked him; but when his eyes fell upon our "little flock," as he was wont to call us at this time, not a score in all (for herein had Judas spoken truly), then it seemed as if his thoughts for us drove out the thought of Judas: and he paused as if he would have questioned us: "Do ye also say as Judas saith?" But then he turned again and went before us, beckoning to us to follow a little behind; and so he continued his journey, steadfastly looking toward the north, where the Mount Hermon rose up before us all glorious to behold. But so far as I could gather from some words that I heard, he still spake to himself concerning the "congregation:" and once I thought I heard him praying for us with great passion, and beseeching God that he would bring us out of the horrible pit, out of the mire and clay, and set our feet upon the rock.

When I spake with one of the disciples concerning that which was to come, and how the Kingdom was to be established, now that all Israel was against us, he would fain have kept silence; and when I urged him, he said, "What know I? Sometimes I am lifted up in my soul, and I know and am sure that the Kingdom shall come; but at other times I know not what to think, nor can I understand why Jesus would work no sign in heaven. But then again I say unto myself that whether he be the Redeemer of Israel or no, he is of a surety the Redeemer of my soul. For in his presence I find life: but to be absent from him is death. The sum is, that I trust in him to-day, for I know not what else to do: but as for the morrow and what it may bring forth, behold, all things are uncertain and unshapen in my mind." The like also said others of the disciples, albeit not in such plain terms, for almost all spake unwillingly. Yet could I not but perceive that the most part had been sorely shaken in their faith, because Jesus had denied to work a sign in heaven: and it was even as Jesus had warned us; the leaven of the Pharisees and of the Sadducees had entered into our souls. Wherefore, although we all still called our Master, as before, the Christ or Anointed, and the Redeemer, or at the least, the Prophet, yet inwardly we were wavering in our hearts; and a breath would have moved us this way or that way, towards belief or towards unbelief. For indeed we were being driven down, as it were, from our former faith, whereby we had believed in Jesus as a worker of wonders or fulfiller of prophecy; and we were falling (as it seemed, but in truth we were rising) to another and a new belief in Jesus as a man, full of tenderness, and suffering, and patience, and withal of a goodness that could not be deceived nor disappointed; and this perchance was the very thing whereat Jesus aimed, to wit, that we should believe in him as the Son of man, conquering through weakness. For our former belief was as the mire or shifting sand, because it could give no firm footing: but our new belief in the Son of man was to be as the rock whereon we and all others were to stand immovable for ever. But we, at this present, being, as it were, still on the sand, and not yet aware of the Rock, how nigh it was at hand, we, I say, knowing in our minds that we wavered, were notwithstanding desirous to keep our wavering secret; insomuch that we spake little on this matter one to another, yea, we would scarce confess it each man to himself: so greatly did we tremble at the very thought of severing ourselves from Jesus. Yet, for all our dissembling, Jesus knew our thoughts; even as though he had been seated in our hearts.

By this time the aspect of the country shewed that we were leaving the region of the lake. For the thickets of oleander, which but yesterday we had seen blossoming thickly with red blossoms, were here, in these northern and higher parts, still green and in bud. Now also the snows of Hermon seemed very nigh, even over our heads; and we were not far from the town called Cæsarea Philippi. The grass was everywhere green under our feet as though the land knew not drought; and trees of diverse foliage shaded us overhead; and as we drew nigh to the town, we heard the sound of many rushing waters.

Yet though all things shewed thus fair around us, our hearts were sad, yea, all the sadder for the beauty of the place, which seemed to rejoice while we sorrowed. Jesus himself looked not now (as he was wont to do) on the glories of the mountainous country, but rather on our faces; neither did he take note of the cedars, and the olives, and the groves of oak-trees; nor of the great plains of green grass; nor even of the Mount Hermon, the top whereof, all covered with snow, waxed daily larger and yet larger as we journeyed still northward. Ever and anon he turned to us as if he would have said some new thing to us; but as often, he turned again, as if still perceiving that the hour was not yet come.

We were now nigh to the outskirts of the town called Cæsarea, even at the place where the fountain of the Jordan floweth forth; and here Jesus bade us sit down. If we had had leisure to admire, there was much cause for admiration. Before us, just above the spring, was a cavern wherein the inhabitants worshipped a certain false god of the Greeks, which haunteth thickets and forests, and he is called Pan: whence also the town in former times had been called Paneas. Higher up, on the summit of the cliff, stood a temple of marble, white and fair to look on, built by Herod in honour of Augustus Cæsar. Below, from the foot of the same rock, there flowed forth, under cover of poplars and oleanders, many little rills of pure clear water, which, meeting together, made a rushing stream, the noise whereof was exceedingly pleasant. This stream it is which passeth through the lake called Merom, and, flowing southward, becometh our river of Jordan.

But for all these sights we had at that time no leisure; or if we noted them, they brought no delight to our eyes, being unto us but as signs and tokens that we were exiles. Our great river Jordan, the river of Joshua and of Gideon, a river of mighty works and wonders of the Lord, how exceeding small did it appear, even as a mere rivulet, in this land of the Gentiles where it first arose! The cavern of Pan also and the temple of Augustus filled us with sad thoughts, to think how all the world was covered with the worship of false gods as with a net; so that, save in one little corner of Syria, the true God was not known. The name of Augustus also, yea, and the very names of the town whereon we looked, Paneas and Cæsarea Philippi, these all but spake aloud, testifying unto us how great was the power not only of the Greek worship, but also of the Roman kingdom, inasmuch as our own princes built these temples and towns, and called them by the names our conquerors. Wherefore it was not possible that a son of Israel, fresh from Galilee, should look on such sights as these and not feel downcast.

Jesus stood a while, steadfastly beholding the temple; then he sat down amid the rest of us. Our speech among ourselves had, even before, become less and less while we waited for that which was to come from Jesus: for we had all perceived these many hours that he purposed to say unto us some new and strange thing. But now, because we knew that the time was at hand, none dared so much as to open his mouth; and a deep silence and a great fear fell on us; and we saw the lips of Jesus moving as if in prayer. But when Jesus at last opened his mouth to speak, he said nothing at first such as we had expected and dreaded. For he neither rebuked us nor prophesied evil, but only asked us touching himself (calling himself by that familiar title whereof I have made mention above) what the common people considered him to be, saying, "Whom do men say that I the Son of man am?" Straightway all the disciples began severally to make answer, saying that most men in that region deemed him to be Elias risen from the dead; but that others supposed him to be the prophet concerning whom Moses had prophesied, and others again called him one of the prophets. These several answers we made to Jesus readily and promptly, for our hearts were lightened because we supposed that this was the question that he had had so long in mind, for which we had all been waiting. But Jesus, as I noted, listened to our speech as a mother listeneth to the prattle of her children. For his lips still moved as if in prayer, and his eyes were fixed upon the temple on the rock before him; and his mind was not with us nor with our words, but with something that still was to come from the depths of the future.

And lo, while we were still reporting this and that, touching the opinions of the common people, Jesus turned himself round and set his eyes full upon us who were sitting before him, but most directly (as it seemed to me) upon Peter, who was face to face with him: and he opened his mouth and said, "But whom say ye that I am?" As he spake these words, he looked at us for an instant as if he could read our inmost hearts, and as if he knew that we could not and would not deceive him. Then he turned from us again, as though to leave us to our own thoughts, because he would not constrain us nor draw forth from us any word that was not our own: and so he remained, gazing steadfastly on the rock and waiting for our answer, for as long, I suppose, as one would take to count ten very slowly.

I have read in a certain story of enchantments how a prince was caused by a magician to plunge his head into a vessel of water and to hold his breath, and behold, while he was holding his breath beneath the water, he seemed to himself to have travelled long journeys and to have been shipwrecked and to have had many other adventures, and to have married a wife and reared up children, and to have passed through a life of many years even till he had reached old age, and all this within the compass of a single breath. Even so was it with us while Jesus was waiting our answer. For we seemed in that moment to be summing up all our past life and all the life that lay before us, in order to answer this question of Jesus aright. For we dared not lie to him nor flatter him; yea, rather we would have displeased him sooner than have flattered him. Such a constraint lay upon us to speak the truth at all times in his presence; and especially now. But what the truth might be we knew not, and searched through all the past and groped in the future, if perchance we might light upon it.

A few Sabbaths, before, we should have been very ready with an answer; for then all men said that Jesus was the Redeemer, the Christ; and we had often said the same thing. But now many stumblingblocks lay in our path. The Scribes and the pious and the learned, all, save a very few, had rejected Jesus. The patriots had joined themselves to him for a long time, but they too had cast him off; yea, and even the rest of the men of Galilee had been led away with them. The poor, as well as the rich, were now against us. In fine, none were now on our side except a few of the lowest of the people, sinners and tax-gatherers and the like. Besides all this, John himself, a prophet, and one whom Jesus had called the greatest of the prophets, even he seemed to have wavered in his faith in Jesus; and when he had besought help in prison, Jesus had helped him not. Yea, and Jesus himself of late seemed to have cast off faith in himself. For when he had been challenged to work a sign in heaven, which seemed an easy thing for a prophet to do, he had refused to do it. Also, he had fled from the face of Herod and from the Pharisees, and seemed to have become a wanderer rather than a deliverer. Else, why were we, children of Abraham and inheritors of the Land of Promise, sitting there like exiles, looking on the temples of false gods in a foreign land? Even in the words wherein he had questioned us, Jesus had spoken of himself as the Son of man. Might it not be indeed that he was, and knew that he was, naught more than one of the common sons of man? When had he called himself the Redeemer? Never.

We seemed in that instant to have been brought by the hand of the Lord into a place where two roads met, and we had to choose one of the two. And if we went by the one, behold we had against us not only Rome and Greece and the whole inhabited world, but also the princes of our own people, and the priests and the patriots, and the traditions also of our forefathers handed down through many hundreds of years, and the Law given unto us by God for which many generations of our countrymen had fought and died; yea, even Moses himself seemed to be as an adversary if we went by that road. But on the other road no one stood against us; only we saw not Jesus there. So the conclusion seemed to be that we had in that instant to choose between Jesus and all the world.

And, as I judge, even for this cause did the Lord lead us into the wilderness together with our Master in sorrow and in exile, to the intent that there, being apart from the world, we might weigh, as it were in a balance, on the one side all the world, and on the other side the Son of man; a man of sufferings and sorrows, a man of wanderings and exiles, acquainted with rejections and contempts; and then that, having weighed the two, we might prefer the Son of man, because of a certain voice in our hearts which cried within us, "Whom have we in heaven but thee? And there is none on earth that we desire in comparison of thee." And this, as I judge, was the faith that Jesus desired of us: and to this faith was the Lord leading our hearts, while Jesus was patiently waiting for our answer. But though it needeth many words to show even a very little of the searchings of our hearts in that sore extremity, yet the time thereof was short, not more (as I said before) than while a man could count nine or ten very slowly.

Then Peter rose up. If it were possible to judge from their countenances, some of the other disciples also were very nigh unto speaking; for their features were as it were in a flux, dissolving in passion, and speech seemed welling upward through them, and the lips of John the son of Zebedee were trembling as if upon the brink of utterance. Notwithstanding it was reserved for Simon Peter to set forth in words and to shape by the force of his soul the thoughts of John and all the rest. He therefore rose up and spake as I never heard man speak before, neither think I ever to hear man speak again, saying, "Thou art the Christ, the Son of the living God."

Twice or thrice at least, before this time, I had heard words like unto these; when either the disciples or the multitude, marvelling at his mighty works, had hailed Jesus as the Son of God. Also many thousands of times have I heard the like confession made in the accustomed worship of the Church. But never till this day, nor ever after, did I hear the words uttered in the same way. For there seemed to come forth from the mouth of Simon Peter no mere airy syllables, unsubstantial beatings of the wind, but a certain solid truth, able as it were to be seen and touched, and not to be destroyed by force of man. What made the difference I know not: nor know I how to explain the difference, except it came from Jesus himself. For indeed it seemed to me that power passed from Jesus into Peter and gave unto him a strength more than his own, and not human. Yea, again and again, pondering that saying of Simon Peter in my mind, I have thought of the words of Nathanael, how he said that Jesus gave a voice to all visible things even though they be voiceless by nature; and, in the same way, it might have been said also that Jesus had power to give a kind of light to sounds : such brightness did he seem to cast upon the words of Simon Peter, insomuch that the words, though old, seemed new, yea quite new, and never heard before. For the tongue and the voice seemed the tongue and the voice of Peter, but the spirit and the light thereof seemed to proceed from Jesus; so that one scarce knew whether it were truer to say that it was Jesus speaking through Peter, or that it was Peter speaking in the spirit of Jesus.

But when Jesus heard the words of Peter, he turned and looked upon all the disciples and upon Peter, and he rejoiced with an exceeding joy, as if in that utterance of faith the first seed had been sown which was to grow up into the Tree of Life; or as if he had seen before his very eyes the laying of the foundations of a great temple, not like unto the marble temple of Augustus built upon the visible rock, but a temple of human souls compacted together by no hands of man, but by the Spirit of God, and destructible by no power in earth or hell. Howbeit he called it not Temple, but rather (using the word which our fathers had used in old days concerning Israel) Congregation. For oftentimes he had instructed us to believe that the gathering together of the disciples made a temple, wheresoever it might be, even at the ends of the earth: but the Temple could not of itself make disciples: yea, though the Temple itself were destroyed yet he said that God would raise up even in two or three days a new temple not made by hands. So Jesus made answer unto Peter calling him by his two names, first by the name which he had from his father (which name he had as being "born of woman") and then by that name of Peter which he bore in the Kingdom, which name Jesus himself gave unto him: and he signified that Simon the son of Jonah, being changed by faith into Peter (which name meaneth a stone or rock), presented and manifested forth that very Rock upon which the Congregation should be built; and these were his very words: "Blessed art thou, Simon son of Jonah: for flesh and blood hath not revealed it unto thee, but my Father which is in heaven. And I say also unto thee, Thou art Peter, and upon this rock I will build my Congregation; and the gates of hell shall not prevail against it."

Then, as if he already saw the Temple of the New Congregation standing on the Rock, he added yet another blessing upon Simon Peter and his faith, making mention of the key of the New Temple, and promising that he would give this key to Peter, because they which have faith, those alone can forgive : and forgiveness is the key which openeth the Congregation to all the world. Now it is a common prayer with the scholars of the Scribes that "We may not make defiled the pure, nor make pure the defiled ; that we may not bind the loosed, nor loose the bound." But Jesus promised unto Peter something better than this, to wit, that the faith which Peter had this day manifested (that is, the faith of the New Congregation) should have power to loose them that else had been bound ; and that forgiveness below should go hand in hand with forgiveness above ; saying that he would give unto Peter the keys of the kingdom of heaven : and he added, "Whatsoever thou shalt bind on earth shall be bound in heaven, and whatsoever thou shalt loose on earth shall be loosed in heaven."

When he had spoken these words, he arose and went into Cæsarea, where we were to tarry that night. We followed him, marvelling much at his words, and especially because of this promise touching binding and loosing. For we did not understand how we could receive such a power ; and even though we should receive it, we did not perceive how it would avail us to conquer the Romans nor how it could hasten the Redemption of Sion. Notwithstanding, we rejoiced even more than we marvelled ; partly because we dimly understood that the Lord had this day wrought some great work for us ; partly because we felt ourselves to be more settled and confirmed in our allegiance to our Master; but most of all because we perceived that Jesus rejoiced with an exceeding joy, and we could not but rejoice with him.

Only Judas said that he liked not that Jesus should speak of a Congregation and not of a Nation or People. "For," said he, "a Congregation goeth not forth to battle, nor taketh cities, nor setteth up empires and kingdom : but this is the work of a People. Wherefore my mind misgiveth me lest our Master, becoming desperate of his first purpose of setting up a kingdom, should now determine within himself to found a sect such as the sect of the Essenes or Pharisees. For he was not wont before to speak of a Congregation, but he ever spake of a Kingdom of God, or a Kingdom of heaven." But one made answer and said that it was written, "Let the Congregation of saints praise him ; let the saints be joyful with glory; let the praises of God be in their mouth, and a two-edged sword in their hands, to be avenged of the heathen :" wherefore, said he, the meaning of our Master perchance is, that in the time to come, Israel shall be both a nation of conquerors and a congregation of saints. And to this we all agreed.

CHAPTER XXI

From that day forth we noted but seldom in our Master's countenance that look of expectancy which had sometimes perplexed us before. For now, and for many days after, he spake and acted like one that seeth things to come as clear as things past. On the morrow after the blessing of Simon Peter, he called us together, and told us that we must go up to Jerusalem at the next Passover. If we were joyful before, much more did we rejoice now; and Judas smote his hands together for very gladness, esteeming Jerusalem already captured. For he supposed that Jesus could not march up to Jerusalem so as not to raise up the Romans against him, "and when they come against us in battle," he said, "then Jesus will perforce put forth his power against them, and will utterly destroy them."

These words said Judas (but not so loud that Jesus could hear them) during the first stir that followed the saying of Jesus about going up to Jerusalem. But Jesus opened his mouth to speak again, and behold, he prophesied things that passed all understanding; namely, that he should be rejected by the rulers of the people, and delivered over to them, and put to death with insult. But then he added that although this must needs come to pass, yet in a few days afterwards, yea no more than one or two, it should be with him as with Jonah, whose prayer was heard even from the belly of hell, and according to the words of the prophet Hosea, who wrote this saying, "Come and let us return unto the Lord, for he hath torn and he will heal us: he hath smitten and he will bind us up. After two days will he restore us to life; in the third day he will raise us up, and we shall live in his sight."

We stood silent around him, all agape with wonder, and scarce believing our ears. But he spake quietly and cheerfully, like unto one describing what had already been accomplished, or as if he perceived that the thing was as much according to nature as that a stone should fall downwards or a spark fly upwards. For not long afterwards he spake as if this were an ordinance of God, that "Whoso saveth his life shall lose it; but whoso loseth it shall save it:" desiring, as I suppose, to teach us that in death, no less than in life, there prevailed that great Law of God which was ever in his mouth, "Give, and it shall be given unto you:" meaning that whoso gave up his life unto the Father should receive it again abundantly, both now and ever.

Notwithstanding, at this time our ears were deaf and our hearts were hardened against all such words as these, and we feared to ask him concerning them. Only Peter, mindful how Jesus had of late blessed him, and therefore venturing somewhat more than the rest, would fain expostulate. So after he had besought Jesus not to vex the hearts of us his loving followers by prophesying evil things, he spake concerning the death of Jesus, saying, "Be it far from thee, O

Master; this shall not happen to thee." Then Jesus looked wrathfully upon Simon Peter, even as he had looked before upon Jonathan the son of Ezra, and he rebuked Peter as if he had been the Adversary himself tempting him; and he said, "Get thee behind me, Satan; thou art a stumblingblock unto me; for thou savourest not the things that be of God, but those that be of men." Yet was there no hate in his countenance, though he used the name of Satan; but there was grief, and trouble, and many signs of inward perturbation; as if Peter had assailed him where he was weakest, appealing to him in the name of the disciples whom he must needs forsake. Yea, the tears seemed nigh at hand even in the moment of the bitterest rebuking.

After this, Jesus began to speak to us of the journey to Jerusalem, how full of peril, and how desperate it was like to be. For he said that whosoever followed him must be prepared to risk all for his sake. Yea, even as men condemned to die might go forth to their doom with the ropes round their necks or the crosses on their shoulders, even so must we go up to Jerusalem, all prepared for death, if we were fain to go with him. And this he said many times, saying that none might follow him except they would take up the cross; and during all the time of our going up to Jerusalem, the cross was, as it were, the only watch-word that he would appoint for them that went with him: insomuch that some, mocking, called it a journey of the cross, or a journey of the halter. But he added that, if we had courage to go with him, a reward was in store for us: "Whosoever will save his life shall lose it:

and whosoever will lose his life for my sake shall find it. For what is a man profited if he shall gain the whole world and lose his own soul? Or what shall a man give in exchange for his soul? For the Son of man shall come in the glory of his Father with his angels; and then shall he reward every man according to his works."

Now at these last words Judas turned away in anger, saying in a low voice, "He speaketh only of what is after the grave." But Jesus straightway added, "Verily I say unto you, there be some standing here which shall not taste of death till they see the Son of man coming in his Kingdom." At these words we all rejoiced again, and Judas with the rest, for, said he, "These words are no dark saying, but such as babes can understand." So we went out from the presence of Jesus marvelling indeed, but rejoicing even more than we marvelled.

Now when we were come forth, and were alone apart from Jesus, we disputed among ourselves what his words might mean. But Judas said (after his wont) that whatsoever was obscure should be interpreted by that part which was clearer. Now Jesus had declared that he would come and reward his followers and take unto himself his Kingdom even in the lifetime of some that were standing by. But as for the rest, concerning the losing of life and finding of it, and as for what Jesus had said concerning his own dying and rising again, it was clear, said Judas, that the words were used poetically and in a figure, as if one should speak of sinking into the pit of the darkness of ruin and then of being raised up therefrom, as it had been described also by Jonah, and as Hosea the prophet had spoken.

But then Thomas said, "Yet methinks, since all men must die, therefore also the Redeemer of Israel must perforce come to the grave at some time; and then what shall befall the disciples that shall remain in the flesh?" To this some one made reply that Jesus would assuredly not depart from life till he had established the kingdom and trampled all our enemies under his feet. Another said that, if Jesus indeed died as a captive according to his own words, then his death would be like unto that of Samson, who destroyed many thousands of the Gentiles in his own destruction. But still Thomas persevered that, whensoever the time came that Jesus should depart from the flesh, then all the brightness of joy would depart from the disciples for ever.

Then John answered and said that Thomas had well spoken, only that the Lord would provide against so great an evil; and he added, "Let us not suppose that the gates of death can separate us from the love of the Lord, neither let our imagination assure us that the grave is a strong place against the hand of the Almighty. For by the Word of God we were framed; and by the Word of God we were born; and by the Word of God we live; and by the Word of God we die; and by the Word of God we are to give account before the King of kings. Wherefore if even we are in the hand of the Lord though we lie in the grave, how much more is the Redeemer of Israel, who is in the bosom of the Father? Wherefore my counsel is that we trust in the Lord, and that we rejoice because we see our Master rejoicing."

To this we all agreed. Howbeit, when we tried to

understand the meaning of the words of Jesus, the judgment of Judas seemed good to the most part of us. And so it was that when we rejoiced, we rejoiced with John; but when we reasoned we reasoned with Judas. But of this we were all with one consent persuaded, that it could not be that the Lord would permit such an one as Jesus of Nazareth to die a common death; but either he would not die at all, or if he were taken from us, it must be after the manner of Elias, exalted to heaven in a chariot of fire.

But Jesus desired to offer up prayers to the Lord upon Mount Hermon before he set his face to go southward to Jerusalem. For he had long been journeying towards it, and it seemed to be unto him as a goal and limit of his wanderings. Moreover at all times Jesus loved to be alone on the tops of mountains, not as though he counted high places to be more holy than others, but because all visible things testified to him of the Father, and when he looked forth upon the world at sunrise from the summit of a mountain, then the Angels of God which rule over the light and the sky and the earth and the air, seemed to speak unto him with a louder and a fuller voice. Moreover though he spake not of the moon and stars in parables (but only of the flowers of the field and the seed and the smaller things of earth), yet did he oft consider the heavens and the lights therein which are the works of the fingers of God; and for this cause he would sometimes spend a whole night upon a mountain-top alone, meditating on the works of God. So it came to pass that on the morrow after these things we went with Jesus even to the foot of Mount Hermon. There we tarried during the night in a village just below the mountain; but Jesus left us and went up the mountain alone, save that he took with him Simon Peter, and John, and James the brother of John.

Now as for what happened on the mountain, I myself was not present; but the three disciples told us afterwards things that made us to marvel. At first indeed they saw nothing more than common, nor indeed took heed of aught which they saw; for they were wearied with the labour of the long journey, going for many hours up hill, and besides they were faint with hunger; insomuch that, when they were come to that part of the mountain where the snow lieth continually, they were borne down with sleep. Hereat Jesus bade them stay where they were, and pray; but he himself went forward higher up the mountain, as it were a distance of three bowshot; yet not so far but they could hear his voice; for the air was exceeding still, and all sounds came with a marvellous clearness to their ears even from very far off. Now it came to pass that when the three disciples were alone, they strove to pray, sometimes standing up, but at other times kneeling or lying flat upon their faces. Howbeit their eyes were still weighed down and heavy with sleep; but even as they began to slumber, behold, the voice of Jesus, like unto the voice of an angel, fell upon their ears magnifying and praising God. So the night passed, while they lay there betwixt sleeping and waking; sometimes hearing the voice of Jesus and praying with him; anon falling into slumber and dreaming strange dreams and seeing visions; and (betwixt dreaming and waking) scarce able to know what they saw, nor what they heard, nor even whether they slept or waked. But at the last the Lord sent upon them a deep sleep ; and how long they slept they knew not, but suddenly with one consent awaking, they perceived that they were on holy ground, and that the presence of the Lord was around them, and the voice of the Lord sounding in their ears. Yet for the instant they knew not what work the Lord had in hand ; only they felt that He was very nigh.

But when they came to themselves, they heard the voice of Jesus speaking words as if conversing with men present and face to face. Then for a brief space the disciples lay even where they had been sleeping, still and astonied, supposing that it was a dream and that the voice should have speedily ceased. But it ceased not, but continued. And they heard Jesus plainly speaking both to Moses and to Elias concerning that which was to come to pass in Jerusalem ; which, he said, would not be an error, nor a misadventure, but the very fulfilment of the Law and the Prophets, and the fore-ordained will of the Father. (Also Quartus saith (but this I heard not myself from any of the three) that Jesus testified unto Moses, saying that he came not to destroy sacrifice but to fulfil sacrifice.)

But when the disciples perceived that it was no dream, they with one consent started up; and behold, the sun was just risen, and Hermon was all a-fire with the glory of the Lord, and the ice and the snow all around shone like unto burning gold and silver and sapphire, only far brighter, even as the brightness of the Throne of the Majesty on High. But Jesus stood on a rock above them ; and when they looked on him, behold, his garments were exceeding white, whiter than snow, and his face was transfigured as the face of an archangel, and his shape was all glorious to behold, shining with a wondrous light; and his eyes were set like unto one looking on the forms of departing friends. For Moses and Elias were now passed away and were no more to be seen.

But Simon Peter, being nigh distraught at the glory of the sight, and scarce knowing whether he were asleep or awake, cried out to Jesus in a loud voice that they would remain on that mountain-top for ever; and he said, "Master, it is good for us to be here; and let us make three tabernacles, one for thee, and one for Moses, and one for Elias." But Jesus took no heed of his words, but kept still gazing upon Moses and Elias. And while they still looked, the Lord sent down on them a cloud, and compassed them round with darkness; and they feared exceedingly when they entered into the cloud; and there came a voice as of thunder out of the cloud, saying that Jesus was the son of God. Then fell the disciples on their faces, and offered up prayers unto the Lord. But presently, when they arose, the cloud had passed away, and Jesus alone was standing by their side.

When Jesus came down from the mountain, all we that were waiting for him in the village below perceived that he had had a vision; for there was still an unwonted brightness on his countenance. Likewise also the people which were with us (for there was a great multitude) marvelled at the brightness of his countenance; and running to Jesus, they saluted him as a prophet. Some also began to beseech him to heal a certain boy which was possessed with an evil spirit. For so it was that, while Jesus was upon the mountain, certain of the Pharisees that dwelt in that village (for there was a

T

synagogue there, and many Jews dwelt round about that country) came to us bringing one possessed with an unclean spirit and bidding us cast him out. So we adventured to drive him out. But we could not do it. Therefore the Pharisees strove against us and declared that we were vagabonds and deceivers, and that our Master was like unto us; and of the multitude part sided with us and part with the Pharisees, insomuch that there was a great uproar and noise of contention. All these things had come to pass while Jesus was coming down from the mountain; but when we saw Jesus near at hand, straightway on both sides we all ceased from our contention.

Now when Jesus understood the cause of the contention, and that the Pharisees were striving against us because we had not been able to drive out the unclean spirit, he looked around both upon us and our adversaries: and behold, we were all heated with disputing, and angered by reproachings, and there was no faith in us. Therefore he was sorely grieved, and he sighed bitterly, and said, "O faithless and perverse generation, how long shall I be with you, how long shall I suffer you?" Then he turned to the father of the child (for the man was standing nigh, piteously bewailing his child) and he said, "Bring thy son hither to me." So they brought him.

But Jesus, looking upon the boy and upon the father and upon the Pharisees, and upon all them which were standing nigh, perceived straightway that there was no faith as yet that the boy should be cured. Therefore he asked the father certain questions touching the boy, and the man replied that the boy had been possessed even from a child; "and oftentimes," continued he, weeping as he spake, "it hath cast him into the fire, and into the waters to destroy him; but if thou canst do anything, have compassion on us and help us." When Jesus perceived that the man had not yet faith (but only desire bordering upon faith), he said unto him, repeating the man's words, "*If* thou canst; *if* thou canst. Nay, but believe. All things are possible to him that believeth." And straightway the man cried out for anguish of soul, and said with tears, "Lord, I believe; help thou mine unbelief." Then the face of Jesus was glad, and immediately he rebuked the unclean spirit; and it came forth tearing the boy and leaving him as one dead, insomuch that many said "he is dead." But Jesus took him by the hand and lifted him up, and he arose.

Hereupon the multitude departed, praising God for His goodness; but when we were come to the house, we asked him why we had not been able to cast out the unclean spirit. Jesus answered that it was because of our want of faith; and he repeated the words which he had before spoken, that whosoever had but faith, even as a grain of mustard-seed, should be able to uproot mountains. But such spirits as these, he said, could not be driven out save by much prayer. He did not further rebuke us for our ill success: but our want of faith seemed to engender in him a certain disquietude for our sakes, perchance because he perceived that we were as yet too weak to stand by ourselves; and this, though the hour was nigh when his hand could no longer hold us upright. Howbeit he said no more at that season, but only gave command that we should straightway set out for Capernaum.

CHAPTER XXII

As we passed through the country to Capernaum, we began to tell the people everywhere that Jesus had now determined to go up to Jerusalem at the head of his followers, and that the time of Redemption was at hand. But Jesus forbade us; for he would not that any man should know that he was passing through. Howbeit, even though we were silent, the rumour of his journey was everywhere noised abroad, so that he could not be hid. Many therefore left their ploughs, and their fishing-boats, and their trades, and followed with us: or, if they followed not, they appointed to be with us at the next Passover when we went up to the Holy City. For it was already the month called Adar, so that it wanted no more than four or five weeks to the Passover.

Now certain youths and striplings followed us, not deliberately, nor with forethought, but because they were ever unstable and ever seeking after new things. Them therefore Jesus warned to go back to their homes, telling them that they had not counted the cost of the journey. Others were fain to have come with us; but their friends sought by all means to prevent them, telling them what cruelties the Romans had wrought upon their fathers and kinsfolk in former times; how some had been sold for slaves, some slain with the sword, some crucified; and with many tears sisters besought their brothers, and mothers their children, not to go up to Jerusalem, nor to bring them down with sorrow to the grave. Now Jesus did not call upon such as these to come to him; but if they were minded to come, he bade them remember that they must above all things trust in him and love him; yea, he said that they must love him better than houses, or lands, or kinsfolk.

Hence also it came to pass that in a certain village he spake words which have been a stumblingblock to many. For so it was that a certain young man of that village had come forth to meet Jesus; and after he had saluted him, the young man had promised to follow in his army, and to serve him even to the death. Howbeit he besought Jesus that he would suffer him first to go and bid farewell to his father and mother. Now Jesus looked on him, and perceived that he was as a reed that bendeth with the wind. So he said unto him that he must not go: "For," said he, "he that putteth his hand to the plough and looketh back, is not fit for the Kingdom of God." Thereupon the face of the young man fell and he became very sad; yet he obeyed Jesus, for that day, and followed him; but on the morrow he secretly departed for to bid his parents farewell, meaning shortly to return to Jesus. So when Jesus passed through the village wherein the young man abode, behold, the young man was even then coming forth from the door of his home. But his mother ran behind him, and caught him by the cloak, and embracing him besought him again and again not to go with Jesus. Thus she constrained him. But Jesus, looking back on the youth, said, "Verily he that hateth not his father and his mother cannot be my disciple."

Already, even at the beginning of our march, when we first departed from Hermon, there had arisen a questioning among us, who should have the chief places in the New Kingdom. For now, within one month, we looked to see the Romans cast out of Jerusalem, the Holy City and Temple purified, and the throne of the Redeemer established. This done, it seemed to us that Syria would be portioned out to several princes or governors; Galilee to one, Samaria to another, Peræa to a third; after the manner of the Romans, whose custom it is to divide their dominions among many princes. So we disputed among ourselves who should have the best provinces. Judas, as being ever foremost in all actions, claimed a principal share; but the others also were not backward. Thus we disputed as we walked behind Jesus, being now nigh to Capernaum; and so it was that, in the heat of our disputing, we knew not that Jesus was standing still, waiting till we should overtake him. Therefore we walked on, still disputing, with clamour and much anger, till, lo, Jesus was in the midst of us. He looked sorrowfully on us, but said nothing for that time, and we were all straightway silent.

But in the evening, when we were all together in the house, Jesus called us to him, holding a little child by the hand; and when we were gathered round him, he set the little one in the midst of us, and said that we had forgotten his former saying, how that no man could enter the Kingdom unless he became as a little child. Then he added these words, "Whosoever shall humble himself as this little child, the same is greatest in the Kingdom of Heaven." Then said Judas, " Whoso hath wrought much, shall he not receive much ? and whoso hath wrought little, shall he not receive little ? And is not the Master of the work faithful, who will pay us the wage of our work ? "

For an instant Jesus was silent, looking at Judas as though perchance he had not heard his words aright. Then he answered that in the New Kingdom there was no difference of reward ; for the least were to be as the greatest. At the same time he placed his hand on the head of the little one and said, "Whoso shall receive one such little child in my name receiveth me, and whosoever shall receive me receiveth not me, but Him that sent me." He also spake a certain parable to us, as if to shew that the reward in the kingdom is not by way of price but rather by way of a free gift, coming from the Father, as cometh the rain from heaven, and sufficing for all them which receive it ; even as the lord of an estate, out of the kindness of his heart, might give unto all his labourers the same wage (and that sufficing for their needs), even though some of the labourers might perchance be hired later than the rest.

Judas had withdrawn himself before Jesus began this parable. For he was greatly abashed, though Jesus had not rebuked him by name. But Jesus seemed saddened by our disputing, and by our hardness of heart in that we understood him not. Notwithstanding he was still cheerful and gentle according to his wont. For albeit he saw close before his feet the darkness of the valley of death, yet, above and beyond the valley of death was the hill of life, which (at that time) he seemed to see and to describe, even as if he had traversed and measured it out with a measuring reed. Notwithstanding for our sakes he seemed sometimes to be in meditation and sorrow, as though, when he had reached Paradise, he should look back upon us left behind and alone.

When we went forth from before the face of Jesus, we found Judas chafing much at his repulse (for so he termed it), and asking how it was possible that in any kingdom there should be no degrees of rank or honour? For some, he said, must needs be near the throne, others far off; and some courtiers; but others tillers of the land and artificers. To us there seemed much reason in the sayings of Judas, though we liked not that he should pay so little deference to our Master. John also himself confessed that he understood not how it should be otherwise than Judas had said. "Notwithstanding," said he, "if Jesus should see fit not to give us power and wealth in the New Kingdom, we must none the less be content, and not lust after the table of kings; for our table is greater than their table, and our crown greater than their crown, and faithful is our taskmaster who will pay us the wage of our work."

The words of John did not please the most of the disciples; who said that it would not be fit that Jesus should give power and wealth to other servants and courtiers, and should neglect them that had borne the burden of the first persecutions, who were now to bear the brunt of the conflict at Jerusalem. So they went away still disputing among themselves. Then, when we were alone, I asked Nathanael whether he thought that Jesus had any certain plans how to take Jerusalem or how to drive out the Romans. But Nathanael answered that it seemed to him that Jesus had no such certain plans. Then said I, "Wherefore then goeth he up to Jerusalem?" "Because," replied Nathanael, "thus much hath been revealed to him that he must needs go up to Jerusalem, there to be glorified and lifted up. But as to the manner and time thereof, he saith nothing. Yea, and I have heard him speak as if he himself knew not these things, but they are known to the Father alone."

At this time Jesus began to speak more often than before of a certain day of wrath in store for Israel; and, as David on Araunah's threshing-floor saw the sword between heaven and earth, even so did Jesus discern a sword of the Lord; howbeit not stayed, as David saw it, but uplifted and in act to strike. Sometimes he spake as if he himself were to wield this flaming sword; but evermore, beyond the fire and the sword, he discerned the glory of the Kingdom of God; and he spake as if the Kingdom could not come except the fire should first be kindled, and he must needs kindle it himself. Therefore once, when Jonathan the son of Ezra said to him that he was accused of his enemies the Pharisees as if he would fain set all Israel on fire, he replied, "The nearer to me the nearer to the fire; but the further from me, the further from the Kingdom."[1]

Seeing this flaming sword ever before him, Jesus none the less continued to speak of his death. This perplexed

[1] See Note I.

us not a little. For at one time he would say that his enemies would be slain with the sword; or destroyed as tares are destroyed with fire; and yet, on the other hand, he repeated again and again that he should die at the hands of his enemies in Jerusalem. Howbeit of the evil prophecy we his disciples took small heed, but gave our minds to the prophecies of good things. For he spake much of being "perfected," and of being "glorified," and how he should be "lifted up" or "raised up" in Jerusalem. Moreover, Jesus was wont to use the word "dead" of them that were in the deep waters of sin; as when he said that "The dead should bury their own dead;" and again, when he said that "The son of man hath power to quicken the dead." Oftentimes also he spake in the same way of raising up the dead, as when he told the disciples of John the son of Zachariah that "the dead are raised up." Hence it came to pass that, if we heeded at all his words touching his death, we were assured that he meant to say only this, that he should be for some days struggling with Satan, and not at once overcoming, but as it were in darkness and in the shadow and depth of death; but that in two or three days he should be raised up and triumph over Satan.

In this belief we were much confirmed by our Master's constancy and stoutness of heart. For on the second day after we had returned to Capernaum, Eliezer the son of Arak, with others of the Pharisees, came to Jesus where he was seated in the midst of his disciples, and making as if they were reconciled to Jesus, they bade him flee from Galilee lest Herod should slay him. But this they did, not out of love to Jesus, but hoping to rid the city of him, and partly desiring to discredit him with the disciples, as if Jesus once more would go into exile for to avoid strife. But Jesus made an exceeding bold answer, and said that the Pharisees were to tell that fox (for so he called Herod) that he would go on his way to Jerusalem not through fear of him, nor in haste, like unto a fugitive, but healing and teaching as he went, both to-day and to-morrow; and on the third day (for the journey was a journey of three days for a strong man, according to the common saying) he said that he should be perfected, even in Jerusalem. Moreover, when Eliezer, nothing abashed, dissembled still further, and bade Jesus take heed lest he should perish even as the Galileans, whom Pilate had slain, Jesus answered that to be slain did not argue that the men slain were sinners above the rest; and then he added that another sword (which they saw not) was near at hand to smite them also themselves, if they repented not.

This gladdened our hearts and made us eager for the journey: and when on the morrow we went up from Capernaum, journeying towards Samaria, there was not one in our band that was fainthearted nor desirous to return. Now at that time there were about three hundred following Jesus. But the greater part of our friends, as we understood, were not to go with us, but to meet us at the going in to Jerusalem, or at some place nigh unto Jerusalem.

When we were come to a certain village in the road (the name of the village is Beth-Gader) where a man journeying towards Jerusalem from Samaria leaveth the Lake of Gennesareth behind him and seeth it no more, then it came to pass that our Master turned him round to look his last upon Capernaum, and Bethsaida, and Chorazin, and upon all the cities of the Lake, wherein he had taught and wrought. And he stood and gazed a long time, and cried out that it should be ill for those cities in the day of Judgment; for if the mighty deeds that had been wrought there, had been wrought in Tyre and Sidon, they would have repented a long while ago in sackcloth and ashes. But when he saw Capernaum, and the fields thereof, and the gardens which compass it round, all bright with the greenness of spring, and the lake, still and peaceful, whereon were fishing-boats and ships innumerable, then he lifted up his voice and prophesied evil against the place, saying, "Thou also, Capernaum, which art exalted to heaven, shalt be brought down to hell; for if the mighty works which have been done in thee had been done in Sodom, it would have remained unto this day." Then spake he to us, saying, that it should be more tolerable for the land of Sodom in the Day of Judgment than for that city. When he had said these words, he turned his back upon Capernaum and upon all the country of the lake; and he departed and saw it no more.

CHAPTER XXIII

WHEN we were now drawing nigh to the borders of Samaria, it being (as I remember) about the ninth hour in the second day of our journey, behold, a tumult arose in the front of the band, and shouts as of men contending together. Then those of us that had swords drew them; for we thought surely the hour was now come for battle. But Jesus bade us put up our swords; and going forward he saw a multitude of Samaritans gathered together to oppose us, neither would they suffer us to pass through their country; and they reviled us and began to cast stones at us. When he saw this, Jesus neither reproached them nor persuaded them to let us pass, but straightway commanded that our band should go back a distance of many furlongs on the road whereby we had come, and then to turn eastward; so that we might pass through the country beyond Jordan, thus avoiding Samaria. This seemed to the most part of us a grievous thing and scarce tolerable, that the army of the Redeemer of Sion should be thus turned out of the path by a Samaritan rabble. Therefore we besought Jesus with many entreaties, and some even with tears, that he would suffer us to force a passage; but he would not hear. At the last, when he had now begun to go back, James and John, being filled with wrath because the Redeemer of Israel was thus despised, prayed Jesus that, if he would not suffer them to smite with the sword he would, at the least, suffer them to call upon the Lord that He might send down fire upon our enemies. Hereat we all were in suspense, and hearkened eagerly to what Jesus would say; for in our hearts we had long supposed that Jesus purposed in this way to destroy the bands of the Romans, even as the prophet Elias had destroyed the captains and footmen of Ahaziah. But Jesus looked steadfastly upon James and John and said unto them, "Ye know not what manner of spirit ye are of. For the Son of man is not come to destroy men's lives, but to save them." Then he went back by the way whereby he had come; and we followed him, sorely grieving. Some of us also murmured (and Judas most of all), saying that it was a strange thing that our Master should have threatened to cast the Pharisees into the valley of Hinnom, and notwithstanding would not force a passage through the Cuthite strip (for by this name we termed Samaria), nor call down fire on a rabble of unbelievers. Moreover Judas spared not to say that Jesus must be made perforce to shew forth some mighty work against the enemy, or else the Redemption of Sion would not come to pass. And the heart of Judas began from this time to be turned away from Jesus even more than before; and Jesus also, as it seemed to me, began to perceive that Judas was estranged from him. For whensoever his eyes rested upon Judas, then the face of Jesus was as if God had hidden His countenance for a season.

After this we went over Jordan and journeyed through

the country that lieth eastward of Jordan, which is called Peræa. Here we tarried some days, even till the beginning of Nisan, which is the month of the Passover : and, about this time, were completed two full years during which we had followed Jesus of Nazareth. Now the people and the land of Peræa are not like unto the people and the land of Galilee. For in Galilee the fields are small, and they till corn and vines and olives; and the men are exceeding stubborn and resolute, neither very rich, nor very poor. But in Peræa they have great pastures, and some are rich in flocks and herds, while others have scarce bread to eat; moreover the men are of an unstable disposition, fond also of wealth, and given to ease, and not so steadfast as the men of Galilee.

Therefore it came to pass that in this country and at this season, our Master testified most of all against covetousness, and lifted up his voice against them which had their good things in this world and wanted nothing more. At this time also he spake many parables, which it needeth not to set forth at full length, for that they are well known among the saints. But among other parables, as I remember, he spake one against a certain rich and foolish farmer (the like of whom we saw many in that country) who thought not of others but of himself only, and had promised unto himself many years of plenty and ease, but was cut off by God that night; also another parable against a rich man that suffered the poor to lie at his gate untended; but afterwards the poor man was comforted, but the rich man punished in hell.

About this time also began Jesus to speak less of the

Kingdom of God and more of a certain Eternal Life, which, as he said, the righteous and none other should attain. Some would have it that he changed his words, only for fear of the Romans, lest they should suspect his often mention of the Kingdom of God, and lay hands upon him as one aiming to be king; and these men said that Eternal Life signified the Kingdom of God, though in different words. And perchance it did signify the same thing: howbeit Jesus changed not his words for fear, but partly, as I judge, because the covetousness of the people weighed upon him, and because he perceived them to be wholly given up to the lusts of the flesh, insomuch that they were even as dead, and content to lie in the valley of the shadow of death.

For ever as Jesus drew nearer to Jerusalem, the sins of the people seemed to weigh heavier upon his soul, and death and destruction seemed to grow larger in his eyes; insomuch that now he desired to exhort the people not so much to enter into the Kingdom, as rather to flee from death unto life. Yea, so exceedingly did he fear the power of Satan to slay the souls of men, that about this time, when a certain disciple desired to have left him for a season to bury his father, Jesus would have the young man still continue with him, saying that the dead should bury their own dead. Howbeit, though we understood this afterwards, we perceived it not at the time; but whensoever Jesus spake of Eternal Life, then we would interpret the words still to signify the setting up of his Kingdom in Jerusalem.

Notwithstanding, while Jesus spake day by day more earnestly touching them which would not come into the Kingdom of God, and concerning those whose hearts were satisfied with the good things of this world so that they thought they needed nothing, he none the less was tender and gentle to all sinners, and to the afflicted, and to young children, after his wont; yea, and perchance, even exceeding his wont. For albeit he saw daily more and more of the evil nature of men, yet was he not embittered thereby; but whensoever his burden became heavier to bear, then, as it seemed to me, his gentleness appeared greater likewise. Of which gentleness I will here set down one among many instances. When we were come into a certain village, at the end of a day's journey, the hour being now late (for the sun had already set), behold, at the going into the village, stood many women with children in their arms; and they besought Jesus to bless them. Then we (who went before Jesus and the rest to prepare a lodging for him) bade the women take away the children and to bring them on the morrow; for we had walked a long journey and were weary and had fasted long; and, said we, it was not seemly at that hour to trouble the Master. But he was sore displeased at us, and took up the little children in his arms and blessed them and said, "Suffer little children to come unto me, and forbid them not, for of such is the Kingdom of Heaven." He also repeated his former saying, that none should inherit the Kingdom unless they became as little children. These words seemed to some of us well fit for peaceful times and for quiet talk and meditation in Galilee, but not fit now when the hour had come to enter the Kingdom, as we supposed, by smiting with the sword. Howbeit to Jesus these words seemed always fit and seasonable; so gentle was he and so loving, even to the last.

It came to pass that in the throng, listening to these words of Jesus, there was a certain young man whose name was Tobias the son of Zechariah. He also came that same night to the inn, to hearken to the teaching of Jesus: and he said unto certain of his friends in my hearing that he was willing to do anything that Jesus should say, even to the giving of half his wealth: moreover he made many professions as if on the morrow he would join himself unto Jesus and go forth with us to Jerusalem. Howbeit on the morrow, when we assembled early according to our wont to set forth, the young man Tobias was not with us. But we (for it was usual with us to hear many promises and to see few fulfilments) began our journey without him. But we had not gone more than six or seven furlongs when the young man came in haste running after us, and when he had come near to Jesus, he saluted him and knelt before him. For his heart had been inflamed with admiration of the doctrine which Jesus taught concerning the Kingdom of God; howbeit he trusted not in our Master as the Redeemer of Israel, but he loved him as a very pious Scribe, teaching things lovable and excellent. Therefore, willing to gain the favour of Jesus and yet being unwilling to journey forth with Jesus, he was fain to gain our Master's favour and also satisfy his own conscience, if it might be, by doing some other good work in lieu of doing that which he had promised to do. So he called Jesus "Good Teacher," and said unto him, "What shall I do that I may inherit eternal life?"

Now Jesus perceived that the young man was deceiving himself; for he supposed himself to be righteous, but he was not; moreover he trusted in his wealth and thought to buy the mercies of God with a price. Therefore Jesus took compassion on him; and looking upon him, he loved him, and would fain have opened his eyes that he might know himself and be less content with himself. So he desired to shew him that he was wrapped up in the love of his possessions. Therefore first of all Jesus answered as a teacher (forasmuch as the young man also had called him a teacher), and he bade the young man obey the Law. But Tobias, like unto a pupil reproaching a teacher for that the task appointed is too easy, replied that he had observed the Law from his childhood upward. Then Jesus, knowing what would come to pass, made mention of the watch-word of our desperate journey, calling it the journey of the cross (or halter, as some people termed it); and he said to the young man, "One thing thou lackest: go thy way, sell whatsoever thou hast, and give to the poor, and thou shalt have treasure in heaven; and come, take up the cross and follow me." Then the countenance of the young man fell, for he had not supposed that the teacher would appoint so great a task; for he had great possessions. So he rose up from his knees, and departed, grieving much, and he went back by the way he had come.

Jesus looked after him as he went; even as a physician regardeth the patient which struggleth against the knife of healing. And he stood still, and marvelled much because of the power of the things of this world over the mind of man, and yet more because of the power of the Lord to deliver the souls of men from the things of this world. For when he considered the weakness of men and the strength of this world, then it seemed to him (as he was wont to say) a harder and a greater work to redeem a rich man's soul than to uproot a tree or a mountain, or what else may be wrought by art of magic. So he turned to us and said, "Children, how hardly shall they that have riches enter into the Kingdom of Heaven. It is easier for a camel to go through the eye of a needle, than for a rich man to enter into the Kingdom of God." Hereat we were astonished out of measure, saying among ourselves, "Who then can be saved?" But Jesus looked upon us and said, "With men it is impossible, but not with God: for with God all things are possible."

Afterwards as we walked behind him, we discoursed further among ourselves concerning these words, and Judas said, "How then? Are we never to be rich!" But another said, "He meaneth that none that are rich can enter into the Kingdom; howbeit when we have attained to the Kingdom, then shall we be rich, though we be poor now; but the rich shall be shut out." But Nathanael said to me privately he thought Jesus meant otherwise; as if he divided the children of men into two parts, the one part having their hopes and treasures in heaven and the other part having their hopes and treasures on earth (according as he had himself commanded us to have our treasure in heaven, saying that where our treasure is, there would our heart be also): now if a man have his treasure in heaven, then though he have five hundred talents on earth, yet they harm him not, for he useth them to good end: but whoso hath his treasure on earth, though he have but five hundred pence on earth, yet they harm him, clogging his soul, and hindering him from looking upwards, because he useth his little wealth to the ends of his own pleasure. "For," said Nathanael, "as often as Jesus speaketh of wealth, he meaneth ever some spiritual meaning, as when he speaketh of bread and corn and wine, and the like."

I doubt not that Nathanael interpreted aright the words of Jesus. Howbeit also true it is that very few whom the world calleth rich, entered either then or afterwards into the Kingdom of God. Therefore I judge that Jesus meant also perchance to warn us how dangerous a thing it is for a man to have more wealth than is needful for simple wants. For the experience of the saints hath been, everywhere and at all times, that fewer men come into the Church with five hundred talents than with five hundred pence.

But after we had discoursed a long time concerning the matter, Judas moved Peter to question Jesus, and to ask whether indeed it was true, that the disciples should never be rewarded with wealth. So Peter went to Jesus and said, "Lo, we have left all and followed thee." He said no more, but Jesus perceived what was in his heart; and he answered and said to us all, "Verily I say unto you, there is no man that hath left house, or brethren, or sisters, or father, or mother, or wife, or children, or lands, for my sake and the Gospel's, but he shall receive an hundredfold now in this time, houses and brethren and sisters and mothers and children and lands, with persecutions: and in the world to come eternal life." Then he ceased; but when we thought that he had made an end and we were departing, he added, "But many that are first shall be last, and the last first."

These latter words of Jesus troubled us not a little.

For of late since we had left Capernaum, many new disciples had joined themselves to us, and Jesus had suffered them gladly; and now we thought that his intent was that, in the kingdom of Jerusalem, they, even these new disciples, should have equal reward with us, who had followed him through all his wanderings. Moreover we were vexed because in the beginning of our consorting with Jesus he had set much store upon us his followers, saying unto us, "Whosoever is not with me is against me," as much as to say that only we, which followed with him, were his friends, but all else were his enemies; but now he seemed to set store upon all them that were not siding with his enemies. For of late when John the son of Zebedee saw a certain man adventuring to cast out evil spirits in the name of Jesus, and yet he followed not with us, John would have forbidden him. But Jesus said "Forbid him not: for whosoever is not against me is with me." These words were contrary to the words which he had spoken before, insomuch that we knew not what to think.

But as concerning the first words of Jesus, namely, that all our goods, whatsoever we had left for the sake of Jesus, should be multiplied an hundredfold, and that too even in this life, we rejoiced exceedingly. For some that had left small fields, began to reckon that they should have great estates; others that had left houses or boats, counted up whole villages and navies that should be theirs when Jesus should be king in Jerusalem. Moreover a certain Scribe, who followed with us, said "This saying of Jesus is also in accordance with the sayings of the Wise; for it is said all things are done according to exact retribution, whether in way of punishment or reward. Even as Samson (who followed after the desire of his eyes) was blinded by the Philistines; and Absolom (who boasted of his hair) was hanged upon the tree by his hair, so that he died. Moreover also Ham the father of Canaan (who sinned by seeing and by telling, that is with the eyes and with the teeth) was therefore made a slave; as Moses also enacted that whatsoever slave was sinned against by his master in the matter of teeth or eyes, so as to suffer loss thereof, he should be made no longer a slave but free. For this is according to the law of retributions; for with what measure a man measureth, THEY measure to him."

"Nevertheless," said Matthew the Publican, "I would fain know how, when we attain to the Kingdom, the mothers of the faithful should be multiplied an hundredfold." But some one said, in answer to Matthew, that perchance the meaning of that hard saying was, that as many as were in the Kingdom should be as one family; so that all men, esteeming one another as brethren, should look upon the mothers of their brethren as being their own mothers. Howbeit most of us agreed to the words of Judas, who said that we should take our stand upon the clear sayings of Jesus and leave the dark sayings: now Jesus had said that our houses and lands should be multiplied an hundredfold, and that saying ought to suffice for us.

Thus for that season we gave not much heed to the deep saying of Jesus: but afterwards when I wrote concerning it to Quartus the Alexandrine, of whom I spake before, he explained it after a different fashion. For he said that Jesus had in his mind a law of retribution indeed, but not such a law of retribution as that whereof the Scribes spake, but a far deeper one, a certain retribution of the soul. "For," said he, "the meaning of Jesus is (as I understand it) that whatsoever the mind of man giveth to God, this returneth from God to the mind of man again with increase, in like manner as there returneth from the earth to man whatsoever fruit or produce man trusteth to the earth. For God giveth to man many good gifts, such as food, and houses, and lands, and wealth, and friends, and kinsfolk; and these all are as seed. Now if a man keep these good gifts to himself, and use them for his own pleasure, he is like unto a husbandman that should keep his seeds in a vessel, or closet, feasting himself with the sight thereof, and not venturing to trust them to the earth; wherefore they grow not nor return him fruits of increase. But whoso trusteth all these seeds to God, and useth them according to His will, behold, unto him there ariseth a harvest in heaven.

"For whosoever useth food aright, there springeth up for him cheerfulness and thankfulness and temperance and self-restraint; and whoso useth aright lands and houses and wealth, there springeth up for him liberality and generosity and magnanimity; again, whosoever casteth the seed of friendship into the lap of the divine goodness, behold there springeth up for him a tree of living friendship that knoweth not death. And in the same way, whosoever consecrateth unto God the love of mother and father, he receiveth a new power of love multiplied an hundredfold, and a new feeling of fatherhood, whereby he is drawn nearer unto the Eternal Father. For assuredly, whensoever Jesus speaketh of the increase of houses, and lands, and money, and the like, for them that enter into the Kingdom; he hath not in his mind shekels, and vines of Eschol or Engedi, but he ever seeth a certain spiritual coinage and a spiritual vineyard of the Lord."

After this manner wrote Quartus unto me; making mention at the same time of the words of Jesus, how he had said that whosoever should receive a righteous man, *i.e.* an observer of the law, in the name of a righteous man, should receive a righteous man's reward; and whosoever should receive a prophet in the name of a prophet, should receive a prophet's reward. "Now by these words," said Quartus, "Jesus signifieth not that a man shall have more or less of shekels, or more or less of food, or raiment, or happiness, for that he receiveth a prophet or a righteous man; but his meaning is this: that whoso by force of fellow-feeling and by the links of faith shall be bound to a righteous man, or shall be bound to a prophet in his heart, he shall become one with the righteous man or one with the prophet, so that he shall receive the like reward with the righteous man or with the prophet, to wit, increase of righteousness, or increase of the knowledge of God's will."

Whether Quartus, or he that made answer to Matthew, be the better interpreter of these words of Jesus, I know not even now: howbeit at that time we gave not much thought to these words, nor to aught else of the doctrine of Jesus. For whatsoever we had learned or whatsoever we thought that we had learned aforetime, while we were in Galilee, concerning the forgiveness of sins, and the not resisting evil, and the becoming as little children, behold, all these lessons now began to seem to us dim and far off, and fit rather for the schools of children than for the stir of the lives of men : because we were now going up to Jerusalem, and because the Day of Decision seemed nigh at hand. For each morning, when we arose, we said unto one another, " Perchance the Romans may this day attack us," and each day, when we lay down to take rest, we reckoned the time and said, " There wanteth now one day less to the day of the Passover : and on that day, if not before, Jesus must of a surety redeem Israel with the strong hand."

CHAPTER XXIV

On the last day of the month Adar, as I remember, we left the young man Tobias behind us: and about three or four days afterwards, to wit on the third or fourth day of the month Nisan (which is the month of the Passover), we came down to the valley of Jordan over against Jericho. Now therefore there wanted but ten days to the fourteenth day of the month, which is the great day of the Passover. As the time drew nigh for our entering into Jerusalem, Judas began to complain very bitterly that Jesus neither strengthened nor encouraged his followers like a wise leader, but kept back some from following, and others, which followed, he made to be of a faint heart. Especially he reproached Jesus for that he did not set forth the Kingdom in clear words; "For," said he, "two or three words would suffice, if Jesus would but tell us plainly the when and the where thereof; but now he speaketh darkly, saying at one time, that it is at hand; at another time, that it is among us; anon, that it is still distant; then, that we must strive to enter into it. Wherefore, to what is this Kingdom of God like? Even to a mist, which taketh many different shapes, because it hath no substance."

Now Jesus seemed to me to perceive what was in the

mind of Judas, and to be grieved thereat; but he took no note thereof in our presence, although Judas had been these many days turning his heart from our Master and inclining himself to leave him. For indeed he had by this time begun to repent that he had ever joined himself to Jesus. Notwithstanding even now, at certain seasons, while Jesus was speaking, Judas was drawn towards him as in old times; but, as it were, perforce, and in spite of himself. Hence it came to pass that he was sorely distracted in his mind, being tossed now this way, now that, like unto a troubled sea. For sometimes, upon no apparent cause, he would break out into protestations of love for Jesus; but at other times, when he thought no one was at hand (yea, and even in our hearing when the passion was on him) he would rage and fume that he had ever left Kerioth for to join such a leader as this, declaring that Jesus would ruin all them that followed him, and saying that he could well-nigh hate him as a blind leader of the blind.

Oftentimes hath it been marvelled how it should come to pass that Jesus should have chosen Judas to be one of his apostles; for he knew what was in men. Why therefore did our Master choose for an apostle one that should afterwards betray him? But the answer which Quartus giveth is this, that, at the first, perchance Jesus did not know that Judas would betray him; yea, and had not Judas hardened himself against Jesus, he might have become a chosen vessel of the Lord.

For, at the first, Judas was no traitor, nor like unto one that should be a traitor; but of a sanguine complexion and disposition, cheerful even to mirthfulness, and frank on a first acquaintance; not given to musing nor premeditating; but active and strenuous, and withal a lover of Israel: albeit perchance somewhat too ambitious and less ready in friendship than in counsel. From a child his mind was ever given to great purposes; and towards these ends he bent all his faculties: for he was of a deep understanding, skilled in the ways of men, and of a discerning spirit, quick to perceive what means were fit to accomplish his ends. But the mischief was that the power to understand was quicker in him than the power to love; for his understanding moved as a flame of fire, but his heart was very cold.

When he first became acquainted with our Master, he straightway clave unto him as unto a great leader of the people, who was like to redeem Sion. Howbeit his heart went not out to Jesus as the heart of John the son of Zebedee, and as the heart of Simon the son of Jonah. For I remember once, when I questioned Simon Peter for what cause he first joined himself to Jesus, Peter said, "Because he had been drawn unto Jesus he knew not how, and by the hand of the Lord"; but Judas said, "Nay, but thou speakest as a sheep or a goat, in whom there is feeling but no understanding: but I applied myself to him with deliberation, as deeming him to be the fittest instrument to do good unto Sion."

Now perchance because Judas gave not so much of his heart unto our Master, for this cause he received not so much back again; wherefore he grew not in spirit like the rest, but went backward rather than forward. And when he found that Jesus of Nazareth was not to be used as an instrument, no not even to do good to Sion; then he began to repent that he had joined himself unto him. Afterwards, when Jesus first took upon him to forgive sins, this was, as it were, the turning-point in the course of Judas. For he was sore disturbed at that time, insomuch that he carried his searchings of heart written even upon his countenance. For he was much moved to have poured himself out before Jesus of Nazareth, beseeching him to take away the coldness of heart, and to give him a heart of flesh. Howbeit Satan hindered it, taking advantage of his pride; for the man was always very proud, and had hitherto been foremost among the apostles; nor could he brook now to step down from his high place and to make himself even as one of the sinners. Wherefore he opened himself not to Jesus, but hardened himself against the voice of the Lord within him.

Yet methinks the conflict was no light one in his heart; and even to the last, he could scarce refrain from giving himself up to Jesus. And, as it seemed to me, for this cause Jesus called him to be one of the Twelve, perceiving how great gifts the Lord had bestowed upon him, and also hoping, by this means, perchance, to have cast out the jealousy and the pride from his heart, and in the end, to have drawn him wholly towards himself. For if Judas could have felt that he was altogether trusted, even as the chief of all the apostles, then belike he would have cast away the pride whereon he clothed himself, and would have opened his heart to our Master; and then verily he would have been a light in Israel, not less than the greatest of the apostles. But it was not so to be; for it was otherwise willed by the Inscrutable.

So it came to pass that, from the time when he was

rebuked by Jesus, as I have related above (though in truth the rebuke was not more for Judas than for the rest of the disciples), Judas withdrew himself more and more from Jesus and from the other disciples; neither would he speak freely nor ask questions as before, but he moved the other disciples to question Jesus in his stead. Yet notwithstanding when Jesus exhorted or rebuked us, Judas would ever take the rebuke unto himself above all, and say that Jesus pointed at him, though he did not mention him by name. Then would he fume and rage and depart in anger, and avoid the rest for many hours together. But when he came among the disciples, he would sow strife among us with speech of passion and jealousy; so that he was, as it were, a thorn in the side of the Master.

All this Jesus perceived, and grieved thereat. Yet he said nothing. And, as it seemed to me, his grief for Judas was swallowed up in another and a larger grief; which I understood not then, but now I understand in part. For Jesus at this time began to see more and more clearly that all or almost all in Israel should reject him; and that his disciples should prove faithless, at least for a time; and that he should bring troubles and sorrows and wars upon the earth, as well as joy and peace; and that the day of Deliverance and Redemption was further off than had been supposed. Howbeit, for all this, he turned not to the right hand nor to the left from the going up to Jerusalem: for he knew that the Lord God had an errand for him there; and that his death was to be for the life of men: and that the Lord would in the end give him the victory over all his enemies.

On the fourth day of the month Nisan, being (as I said above) the tenth day before the Passover, we set forth again on our journey to Jerusalem, and much people went with us. And when we came down from the mountains to Jordan, even to the fords of the river, then some expected that Jesus should have stretched out his hand and dried up the river, even as a certain Egyptian false prophet had lately promised to do; and likewise Elias in old times had dried up Jordan, and it had been also dried up at the word of the priests when Joshua passed over. (For both now, and before, and for a long time after, the minds of all in Israel were ready to expect any sign howsoever strange and monstrous, and to follow any that would profess to work such signs; insomuch that, about ten years ago, even on the very day that the Holy Temple was burned with fire by the Romans, even on that last day (as I have heard) a certain false Christ led some six thousand of my countrymen into one of the courtyards of the Temple, expecting a sign from heaven. So strong was faith in Israel; if it be faith indeed, to trust in any that profess to work signs and wonders.) Howbeit Jesus wrought neither this nor any other sign at this season, and we all passed over, even as the other pilgrims, by the fords; but with not a little difficulty and even some peril, for the river was marvellously swollen. Hereat some of the common people that were with us began to murmur, wondering when the time should come that Jesus should put away delays, and work such works as they expected from a Messiah.

When we came unto Gilgal we rested; but Judas made some pretext that he should go on to Jericho before us to prepare the way for Jesus; and, as I afterwards learned, he went to the house of a certain Scribe in Jericho one of his acquaintance, and a principal man among the Pharisees of that city, and he conversed with him a long time. The name of the Scribe was Azariah the son of Simon.

Now while we rested at Gilgal, we looked gladly upon Jericho, gazing at the forest of palm-trees which lay between us and the city. Much did we admire also the four towers of the city, which rose up straight to heaven on the other side of the forest, and the walls high and newly built; surrounded on all sides by thickets of balsam, and gardens of roses, and full of all delights. For the place knoweth not drought, by reason of the perpetual waters; but it is a paradise all the year round. Beyond Jericho, on the other side, we could see, rising up as it were over against us, the mountains that lead up to Jerusalem; insomuch that it was a saying with them of the Holy City that the sounds of the sacred music and the smell of the incense go down even to the men of Jericho. But the ascent is steep and the way bleak and barren, through cliffs and rocks on the right hand and on the left; where no trees are, nor any water; but robbers and murderers lurk at all times in the caves on the sides of the mountains, for to come down unawares upon the pilgrims and travellers which pass by that way. Then said Peter unto John, "Without doubt the Romans will not suffer us to go up; but they will fall upon us by the way. And should not the people be advised thereof, that they may stand upon their guard?" But John said nothing; notwithstanding, he seemed troubled

x

that Jesus took no order for what was to come to pass upon our journey.

When we came unto Jericho, behold, the people had been advised of our coming, and on both sides of the road there was gathered together a great multitude to see Jesus as he passed; and the common people hailed him at this time by the name that was dearest unto the patriots of our nation, calling him a deliverer after the manner of David, and saying, "Hosanna, son of David." But Azariah the son of Simon, who was of the acquaintance of Judas, was come forth also; and he saluted Jesus and besought him to eat bread in his house. Howbeit Jesus would not eat bread in the house of Azariah. For as he passed through the midst of the people, he had espied a certain man, by name Zacchæus, looking down upon him from a sycamore-tree, into the which he had climbed up, out of the fervency of his desire to see Jesus : and straightway he had called unto the man, and bidden him come down, saying that he must eat bread in the man's house. Now the man was a tax-gatherer, as might have been seen by his dress and tablets, and indeed the crowd shouted aloud that he was a tax-gatherer, when they saw that Jesus had chosen him to eat bread in his house ; and they were sore displeased at Jesus. Notwithstanding Jesus was constant in his purpose not to eat bread in the house of Azariah the Rabbi, but in the house of Zacchæus the publican. So Azariah dissembled his anger and came to the feast in the house of Zacchæus, and certain other Pharisees with him. Howbeit they themselves feasted not with the common people and the tax-gatherers; but they conversed with Jesus and asked him questions.

Now it came to pass, during the feast, that the heart of Zacchæus the tax-gatherer was turned unto Jesus (even as the heart of Barachiah the son of Zadok had been turned to Jesus in the house of Matthew the publican, as I related above) : and he stood up and repented aloud of his evil deeds, and promised to make restitution, and that also not twofold but fourfold, saying moreover that he would give the half of his goods to the poor. And Jesus rejoiced at his words and said, "This day is salvation come unto this house, forasmuch as he also is a son of Abraham."

Now while Jesus was saying these words, I took note that Judas was making signs unto Azariah; and Jesus had scarce made an end of speaking when Azariah (upon a set plan, as I conjecture, devised with Judas) said to him, "Thou sayest that the Kingdom of Heaven is at hand : tell us therefore when cometh it, and at what hour? So shall we be prepared and ready when it cometh." But Jesus made answer to him and said, "The Kingdom of Heaven cometh not with observation. Neither shall they say, Lo here ! or, Lo there ! For behold" (and saying these words he pointed to Zacchæus) "the Kingdom of Heaven is within you." At these words the face of Azariah was clouded with anger; for he had not attained that which he desired : and we also were somewhat sorry, for we had hoped that we should have heard some new thing. But Judas straightway went out of the chamber, not able to contain himself for displeasure.

When the guests and the Pharisees were gone forth, and we were alone with Jesus, we would have questioned him still further concerning this matter; but we were afraid. Howbeit many of the common people, yea and some also of ourselves, expected that on the morrow Jesus should have made an assault on the barracks of the guard in Jericho and on the king's palace; or, at the least, that he should have suffered us to burn down the house of customs. But Jesus did none of these things: but on the morrow we set forth again to go up to Jerusalem. It was now the sixth day of the month Nisan, and the eighth day before the day of the Passover.

After we had journeyed for about an hour, the way being exceeding steep, and the sun (although it was not long risen) beating with an exceeding heat upon us, by reason of the rocks and cliffs around us and before us; it came to pass that we sat down to rest. And Jesus looked down upon Jericho, and on the palm-trees thereof and on the balsam-groves, and on all the gardens of the place, and then he turned and looked to the right hand upon the country where Jordan floweth into the Dead Sea, and he opened his mouth and taught us concerning the Kingdom of God. For he said that, as in old time the cities of Sodom and Gomorrah had been swallowed up in that same sea of destruction which we saw before our eyes, even so should it be hereafter: and the Kingdom of Heaven should come in a flash, even as the lightning which lighteneth out of the one part under heaven and shineth unto the other part under heaven. But first he said that trouble should come upon the disciples; for the Son of man should be rejected, and the days should come when we should desire to see one of the days of the Son of man, and should not see it. Most of all he lamented that in the darkness of that time there should be division in

Israel, yea in every household and in every corner of Israel: "I tell you in that night there shall be two men in one bed; the one shall be taken and the other left. Two women shall be grinding together; the one shall be taken and the other left. Two men shall be in the field; the one shall be taken and the other left."

Now this seemed quite contrary to the word which Jesus had spoken yesterday. For then Jesus had said that the Kingdom of God was within us; but now he said that it should come like the lightning. Howbeit, these latter words made us rejoice; for now again we were lifted up in our hearts, supposing that Jesus would work some sudden sign, to destroy our enemies in a moment of time. And Judas was now no longer able to constrain himself (for he had been sore displeased, even before, that the question of Azariah had not been answered by Jesus): therefore, when Jesus had made an end of speaking these words, how that "the one shall be taken and the other left," supposing that now at last he should obtain to know that secret which he had so long desired to know, he leapt up in the vehemence of his desire, and cried aloud to Jesus, "Where, O Master?" But Jesus paused and looked steadfastly at him and said, "Wheresoever the body is, thither will the eagles be gathered together." Saying these words, Jesus arose and turned his face from the Dead Sea and from the pleasant places of Jericho, and bent himself again to ascend the mountainous way which leadeth up to Bethany and thence to Jerusalem. But Judas remained behind standing in the same place, and there I saw him still standing and musing, long after the rest of the disciples had followed Jesus up the mountainous way.

When Judas at last overtook us, he complained much that Jesus knew in himself what was to come to pass, and yet hid it from his followers. "For," said he, "we risk our lives for him, yet he trusteth us not." Now we were displeased at the words of Judas; for we were assured that Jesus did all things for the best. Notwithstanding we were somewhat moved because Jesus thought not fit to tell us beforehand that which was to befall us in Jerusalem and on our journey to Jerusalem. And so it was that, while we were disputing, there was a great clamour in the front of our band, and a cry went up that the Romans were upon us; and straightway there was much stir of men putting themselves in order of defence (those at least that had arms), and certain of the women cried out for fear. And Peter said it was not unlikely that the Romans should fall upon us here; for this was the very place where they had laid ambush for Athronges and slain him; moreover one came running past us saying that he had seen the glittering of their helmets, and that they were lying in wait for us at the corner of the road. Howbeit the report was false; for there were no Romans, but some one had been deceived by the shining of the sun against the rocks, and so had caused all this stir.

Now Jesus was grieved when he saw that some of the disciples were afraid; and he rebuked us, bidding us not to fear destruction of body, but only destruction of soul. He himself also shewed no sign of fear, so that we marvelled at his steadfastness and stoutness of heart. Nevertheless Judas said that it would have been better if Jesus, being a prophet, had forewarned the multitude and had said unto them, "The Romans will not fall upon us save at Bethany, or so many furlongs on this side of Bethany; or, they will not fall upon us to-day, but to-morrow at the seventh hour, naming the place and time exactly:" and this, said Judas, would have been far better than that our band should thus be thrown into a confusion upon a mere rumour.

We said nothing against Judas; for we knew not what to say: neither do I perfectly know even to this day. But Quartus saith that "Jesus knew not all these things exactly, but only generally, and as it were on a large scale; as if a pilot, piloting a vessel into an haven, should know the winds, and the currents, and the shoals, and the aspect and form of the coast, but not all the pebbles upon the strand, nor even the very moment that the ship should come into the harbour. For by certain signs of the times," said Quartus, "Jesus discerned of that which was to come, even as a wise mariner foretelleth the weather by the clouds, and winds, and the other signs in the heavens. Neither was Jesus like unto a magician or common enchanter, who pretendeth to change the course of things by his enchantment; but he was even as a Son of God, who can read what is in the book of the future, yea, and can shape the future, because he doeth all things in accordance with the invisible laws of God."

Thus far Quartus; but concerning these things I know not, neither pronounce judgment. But let us return to our journey. Soon after these things, going to John the son of Zebedee, I found him conversing with his mother; and he received me with a constrained countenance not according to his custom. Presently I perceived that his mother desired him to do a certain thing, which he was loth to do. It seemed that Judas had been speaking to her, saying that it was fit that strife should be quenched among the disciples by determining once and for all who should have the first places in the Kingdom; for, said he, until this be settled, there must still be quarrelling among the disciples. For Simon Peter, forsooth, had supposed himself to be chief, because Jesus had blessed him and given unto him a title; but the sons of Zebedee had done no less deeds, and shewn no less zeal, than Peter; and they, as well as Peter, had received a title, having been called Sons of Thunder; wherefore then (said Judas) should they not claim the first places? For himself, he said, he had no thoughts about such high matters; for Jesus loved him not as the rest. Howbeit, he desired that the expedition should not fail owing to the strife among the disciples. Now Jesus had promised that if two or three of his disciples agreed touching anything they should ask, it should be done for them. Therefore he bade the mother of John go with her two sons to Jesus and ask of him a certain favour; and if Jesus granted it, then she was to ask that her two sons might be next to Jesus in the place of honour in the New Kingdom.

When James and John had been at last persuaded by their mother, they made their petition unto Jesus. But Jesus refused it, saying that to sit on his right hand and on his left hand was not his to give, save to those for whom it had been prepared by the Father. For he would do nothing unjustly, nor out of respect for persons; but here, as in all things, he desired to conform himself to the unseen ordinances of the Father. And herein Jesus shewed himself very different from that which he was supposed to be by Jonathan the son of Ezra. For

Jonathan supposed that he was misled by his desires, and that whatsoever things seemed to Jesus desirable, these Jesus fancied to be true: but it was not so; for no one ever saw, more clearly than Jesus, that which must needs be. Only he rebelled not against it, but willingly submitted himself to it and embraced it, as being the will of the Father, and therefore very good. For this cause both now and at other times, he spake of all his words and works as being prepared for him; saying that he could neither do nor say anything of himself, but only that which the Father had prepared. Also I marked, both at this time and often before and after, how Jesus joined together in himself virtues that mix not well together in the minds of most. For with most men a nature that judgeth well and wisely is somewhat cold; and they which love warmly, love neither wisely nor well, but are fond. But with Jesus it was not so: for the more he loved men, the more he loved justice and truth; because, as I suppose, his love of men on earth sprang out of his love of Him in heaven whose name is Truth and Justice.

On this same day Jesus spake much concerning that which was to come; and all his words tended to sadness. For he lamented over the divisions among his disciples, and the divisions that should be in the world, saying that it was as if he had not come to bring peace but a sword; yea, and that he had verily come to kindle a fire upon the earth. Moreover of the day of Redemption he spake as though it were a great way off, and the disciples would need to wait long for it, and to watch, and to pray, and to resist many temptations. Howbeit in every parable he spake confidently of a certain day of Decision or Judgment, when the good should be separated from the evil, and the evil should be cast into the fire, but the good should be preserved for everlasting life.

These things he said to all the disciples; but when the Twelve, and we that were always with him, were come to him in the inn where he rested during the heat of the noontide, he spake privately to us concerning our disputings and contentions among ourselves. For he had noted how sorely the rest of the apostles were displeased at John and James; and also at other times he had perceived that we were jealous one of another. Wherefore he besought us (and as it seemed to me there were even tears in his eyes) to be at peace among ourselves. Moreover he spake about himself, saying that he had a cup of sorrow to drink and a baptism of suffering to be baptized withal, and that he had come to give his life a ransom for the multitude. Therefore if any man among us desired to be chief of all and foremost of all, he desired that man to be foremost in serving, and in ministering, and in suffering; even as he also came to be a sufferer and a minister for the multitude.

Then he besought us with great passion and fervency to suffer nothing to come between us and our entrance into the Kingdom, saying that it were better for us to cut off our right hand or pluck out our right eye and so to enter into life, rather than to enter with two eyes and hands into darkness, into the valley of Hinnom, where the worm ceaseth not and the fire is not quenched. Finally, he lamented over the world, how that it was not fit to be a sacrifice to the Father because it was not salted; and he called us the salt of the world: "But if," said he, "the salt hath lost its savour, wherewith shall the salting be performed?"

Now some of his words were hidden from us, but these last were easy to understand. And we were ashamed of our disputings, and because we were not like unto our Master in singleness of heart. Judas also himself seemed to be moved somewhat at the time: yet, soon after, he spake again as before, saying that it was impossible to obey Jesus, because Jesus said at one time one thing and at another time another; "Wherefore," added Judas, "inasmuch as our Master will neither plan nor perform aught to do good unto himself, methinks it is meet that we his disciples should strive to do him good, even though it be against his own will."

CHAPTER XXV

AFTER Jesus had made an end of this exhortation, he set forth on his journey to go towards Bethany, which lay still far up above us. There was in his countenance even such a brightness as we had noted when he came down from the mountain with Peter and James and John. Whereat we marvelled, because he that had but now spoken to us with such a passion of sorrow concerning a cup of suffering and death, seemed to go towards suffering and death like unto one triumphing in glory. Howbeit we feared to ask him further concerning these things; but we followed after him, questioning among ourselves.

Now Judas ceased not cavilling at the exhortation of Jesus, saying that it was not fit that a leader should make himself like a child, nor that whoso would fain be greatest should make himself least; "For," said Judas, "a leader must lead, not follow; and he must command, not obey; and he must have the forethought of a man to arrange all things orderly, not the afterthought of a child to adventure all things at hazard. Now Jesus, in his former days, when he was like himself, ever took upon himself the part of leader, yea, even a leader greater than Moses; for he was wont to speak in our ears such words as these, It was said to them of old time, Do this, but *I* say unto you, Do that; and again, Come unto *me*, and *I* will give you rest; Take *my* yoke upon you, and the like. Were not these words the words of a leader? But now what saith he? Even such words as these : 'I am not a leader, but a follower'; 'I am not as the greatest, but as the least'; 'I am not a conqueror, but as one to be vanquished, yea and already vanquished, even as a lamb led to the slaughter.' Nor doth he give command beforehand, nor warn us how to meet the enemy, nor where to expect the onset. But behold it wanteth but a week or less, and there cometh the Passover; and nothing is settled. Verily we are as sheep without a shepherd."

Thus spake Judas in the bitterness of his heart, more freely than he had ever spoken before (at least in our presence), and we marvelled at the bitterness of his speech. But Peter rebuked him and said, "Say not such words as these, O Judas, for of a surety Jesus is our leader even unto death; but his ways are not as our ways, and we must have faith in him. Howbeit concerning what is to come to pass on the day after the morrow, somewhat, as I know, is already settled; for he purposeth to enter the Holy City publicly, even before the face of all that dwell in Jerusalem. Now when that cometh to pass, then doubtless he will be moved to perform some mighty work. I say not that he will smite with the sword; for he ever shrinketh from the sword. But perchance he will pray unto the Lord, and the earth will open for our enemies, even as it opened for the children of Korah, or fire will go forth from the presence of our Master himself, and he will consume his enemies with the fervency of his breath. For the mercies of the Lord are manifold, and very many are His paths for the destruction of the wicked."

When Judas heard mention of the going of Jesus into Jerusalem, he held his peace, thinking (as I perceived from his words afterwards) that this was perchance a sign that Jesus was minded to become a leader indeed. But another, taking up the word spoken by Simon Peter touching the fire from the presence of Jesus, said, "And perchance this fire is even what our Master signifieth, when he saith that the adversaries shall be cast into the fire." But another said, "Nay, but it is written, the punishment of malefactors shall be fire and worms. Also it is written in the prophet Isaiah that, when all things are made anew, in that day the righteous shall go up to Jerusalem to worship the Lord, 'and they shall go forth and look upon the carcases of the men that have transgressed against me; for their worm shall not die, neither shall their fire be quenched.' Therefore it is most certain that, when Jerusalem shall be purified, the adversaries shall be cast forth into the valley of Hinnom, even to the fire and worms; and they shall be an abhorring to all flesh."

To this the most part agreed. Only Nathanael seemed doubtful; but he said nothing in the hearing of the rest. But when I questioned him concerning the meaning of the words of Jesus, he answered that he knew not for certain what they meant; only he felt assured that Jesus had in his mind not a visible but some kind of invisible fire, which preyeth upon wickedness, even as the fire whereon we look preyeth upon fuel. This seemed to me at that time a hard saying, but now I consent unto it.

And to the same effect spake Quartus afterwards, saying, "To Jesus the invisible things were visible, even as those things which are seen with the eyes; yea, they were more visible. Therefore when he looked upon the hearts of men and discerned in them jealousy or malignity or hypocrisy, behold, such men seemed to him as men that are suffering from a sore disease, which disease must be burned away with the fires of God. For as the all-encompassing sunlight bringeth life to them which are whole, but fiery heats to them in whose veins the fever rageth, even so the fire of God (which compasseth all invisible things, so that naught can escape from the flame thereof) purifieth that which will be purified, but consumeth that which is corrupt, according as it is written, 'The jealousy of the Lord burneth like fire for ever.'"

Now Xanthias, the Greek merchant of Alexandria, was wont to say that Jesus would have done well to make distinction between the fire of God and the fires of men; lest his disciples should be led astray by his words, and lest they should suppose that Jesus was speaking of earthly destruction. But if Xanthias had lived unto these days, and had seen how, after the death of our Master, the most part of our nation were given up to darkness and madness, and their city and temple were burned with fire, and they themselves were consumed by hundreds and by thousands, then, as it seemeth to me, he would have perceived that the fire whereof Jesus spake consumeth alike things visible and invisible, and on earth as well as not on earth. Howbeit at this season we understood none of these things, and almost all thought that the Romans and other Gentiles in

Jerusalem, and whosoever of our own nation stood up against our Master, should be slain and cast out into the valley of Hinnom to be consumed by fire and worms.

But while we thus disputed among ourselves, behold, we were now come nigh unto the village called Bethany; which lieth high up on the mountain called the Mount of Olives, and looketh, from above, upon the road that goeth down to Jericho. And from Bethany to Jerusalem is but sixteen furlongs or less. Here therefore our journey was at an end; for our Master was to tarry at Bethany, in the house of Mary and Martha, for that night and during the morrow also; for the Sabbath was at hand. But of the rest of our band, some few remained with us; others went forward a little space to Bethphage, which was about a Sabbath day's journey; others, and these the greater part, hasted to pass into Jerusalem before the Sabbath should have begun; for there wanted but one hour of sunset.

During all that night Jesus said not much to us. Only, while speaking to the women after supper, he discoursed concerning the need of patience, and how the disciples in the New Kingdom must be like unto wise virgins going unto a wedding, which take not only lighted lamps, but also good store of oil that they may keep their lamps alight; but the foolish, which take no oil, have not their lamps alight when the bridegroom arriveth suddenly: wherefore they come too late for the feast and are shut out. Thereby, said Peter, Jesus seemed to mean that he was to leave us for a time and to return suddenly; and whoso was not prepared to meet him should be shut out from the Kingdom. Some other parables Jesus spake to the same effect.

Now concerning these parables Quartus judgeth that Jesus spake in them of his resurrection. "For," said he, "the meaning of Jesus was, that if the disciples had not prayed unto the Lord, and watched and waited after his death (but contrariwise had given themselves over to idleness and folly, as men desperate), then Jesus would never have appeared to them; and they would have been shut out from the Kingdom." Others interpret the words, as if Jesus spake of some other coming, which may not perchance be fulfilled in our days. But I incline rather to think that our Master prophesied partly concerning some future coming which is not yet fulfilled; and partly concerning his resurrection and manifestation to us his disciples, soon to be fulfilled; but partly also concerning our nation: how that, after his death, some few should be ready to receive him, but the greater part should be unready; and as for these, darkness should fall upon their hearts, and then the door should be shut, and they should grope around the door, but find no entrance. Which things have indeed come to pass. For at the first, Israel was desirous to enter into the Kingdom, but now the veil is upon their hearts, so that they can no longer have light to enter into the Kingdom, no, not though they desire it.

The morrow, as I have said, was the Sabbath; and all the day, Jesus sat still in the house talking with the women, especially with Mary and Martha the sisters of our host; neither did he go forth all that day, save that he went to the village of Bethphage to see some sick folk. But in the evening he spake to us very kindly, yea, very tenderly, even more than his wont. And though he said not many words, yet all his words were concerning us, not concerning himself; or, if he spake of himself, it was for our sakes, as if he were striving to look into the darkness of that which was to come, so that he might discern what perils awaited us, for to warn us thereof.

As we walked towards Bethphage, it came to pass that Philip said to Jesus (thinking to please him), that certain Greeks which were in Jerusalem desired to see him. Now so it was, that when Philip spake these words, we chanced to be passing through the fields of corn; and the corn was now strong and in ear, for the spring was well advanced. But Jesus stopped at that word Greeks, and looked down at the corn; and then he said that the hour was verily come when he should be glorified: "For," said he, "except a corn of wheat fall into the ground, it abideth alone: but if it die, it bringeth forth much fruit." Then he went on to say that, after his death, we need not fear lest we should be left desolate, for a Spirit should strengthen us; and of this Spirit he spake, at one time as coming from himself, but at another time as coming from his Father; moreover it should come to us, he said, by a certain ordinance, which could not be altered. For just as the ear of wheat cometh not unless the corn of wheat first die, even so his Spirit should not come, except he also should first depart from us.

Hereat Judas brake out in hot anger, "Wherefore, then, go we up to Jerusalem, if our going is to be for naught, and if thou art to depart from us, and if we are to be left as sheep without a shepherd?" Jesus rebuked him not, neither answered as we had expected; but said that it could not be that a prophet should perish out of

Jerusalem. Hereat one said, "Nay but, O Master, the prophet John perished not in Jerusalem." But to this Jesus made no answer; but only spake a few words touching the difference between the simplicity of the Galileans and the subtlety of the men of Jerusalem; and he condemned the Scribes of Jerusalem and the priests of the temple, for that they made darkness instead of light, causing all Israel, and even the Galileans, to transgress. He also spake as if Satan reigned in the Holy City, and as if he were shortly going down to do battle there with Satan in Jerusalem. So he seemed to signify that Jerusalem was as it were a field of battle, whereon it was meet and right that a true prophet should die. After this he added, that if he were lifted up in the sight of all men, he should draw all men unto him. This joining together of words diverse in nature, of perishing and lifting up, and of departing and drawing all men unto him, filled us with perplexity; insomuch that Judas said in a low voice that the words of Jesus were like unto oil and vinegar, which cannot be mixed. The rest of us also showed, as I suppose, by our countenances that we understood him not; for he looked kindly on us, and rebuked us not, but said that he had yet many things to say unto us, but we could not bear them now. He also added at another time, this promise, that a Spirit of Truth should come, which should guide us into all the truth.

Now so it was that, while Jesus was saying these words, we were now drawing nigh unto Bethphage, and we spake concerning the going into Jerusalem on the morrow. And it came to pass that Matthew, looking upon an ass (which was standing in the village at the back of a house where two ways met), made mention of a certain prophecy which saith that the Messiah shall come into Jerusalem, not as an Egyptian nor as an Assyrian (for they ride in chariots or on horses), but as one of the princes of our nation, who used to ride on asses; and the words were these, "Rejoice greatly, O daughter of Sion; shout, O daughter of Jerusalem; behold, thy king cometh unto thee. He is meek and having salvation, lowly and riding upon an ass, and a colt, the foal of an ass." Now Jesus overheard these words, but said nothing; yet, as it seemed to me, he took note thereof.

When we returned to the house, Jesus gave command for the morrow, that we should rise early to go down into Jerusalem with him, and that certain of the disciples should go before the rest into Jerusalem, even to our friends and companions there, for to instruct them concerning the time of the going down of Jesus, that they might come forth to meet us. Hereat we rejoiced greatly: and all the teaching of Jesus concerning his death and departure, and concerning the days of trouble and of parting, quite vanished away; and even Judas was glad. And now our minds began to be set once more, and even more than before, upon the Kingdom, and upon our places in the Kingdom. So when we lay down on the supper couches, our tongues still harped thereon; and our disputings were so loud that Jesus could not but hear them. Then was he sore displeased that we should thus think of ourselves when he was to depart from us; and he opened his mouth to speak. But he spake not; for it was as if no words could avail to pierce the hardness of our hearts. Howbeit, when supper was ended and I was gone forth from the chamber, then, as it was reported to me by some (but others say that it happened on another evening), he arose from the table, and girded himself as a servant, and would wash the feet of all the disciples; and when they would have resisted, he constrained them; but when he had made an end, he said, "I have given you an example that ye should do as I have done to you."

After this manner therefore that Sabbath ended; but throughout the whole of the Sabbath and all the evening after, yea and on the morrow, and during all the days before his suffering, Jesus, as it now appeareth unto me, was wholly bent upon serving us, and upon helping us, thinking ever of our needs and our weaknesses, and how we should fare without him, and how he could strengthen us so that we might be ready when he suddenly came back to us. For our sakes also, as I judge, he made entry after that public and solemn fashion into Jerusalem, to the intent that no man might hereafter reproach any of us and say, "Thy master was no Messiah; for he dared not show himself as Messiah before the face of the people; neither did he claim allegiance, but only professed himself a servant; nor did he manifest bravery, but hid himself from his enemies even to the last."

For this cause do I in no wise assent to the saying of Xanthias, that the going in of Jesus into Jerusalem was not worthy of him. For, as I judge, he did it for our sakes, and not for his own; yea, and for the sake of the whole world; that it might be on record for ever how that the Son of man, though he were the humblest of men, did nevertheless claim for himself the allegiance of all them that were in the city, yea, and of all that were in the inhabited world; as if he were at once the king and the servant of mankind.

But as touching that other saying (not of Xanthias, but of the Scribe Hezekiah) that, "If Jesus had been a prophet indeed, he should have prophesied unto his disciples the whole manner of his death, and the manner of his resurrection, and the manner of the giving of the Holy Spirit," concerning this I say nothing, as one doubtful and waiting for the truth. But Quartus is perchance herein too bold (though he speak out of his great love for the Lord Jesus) in saying that our Master "knew not little matters that were to come, but only great matters. And so he knew that the fire of heaven would fall on Jerusalem, but when it would fall, this was hidden from him. Likewise, he knew that he must die; for unless he died his Spirit would not come; but when the Spirit should come, this too was hidden from him.

"Yea and even as touching his own death and rising again; that he should go unto the Father he knew, and that he should come again he knew; but on what day he should come again, and at what hour he should manifest himself to his disciples, this he knew not. And even for this cause, perchance," saith Quartus (who was not present in Jerusalem when the Lord suffered and rose again), "he was so earnest with you that ye should give your minds to watching and praying in the hour when he should be taken from you; to the intent that, when he came suddenly back to you from the grave (manifesting himself to you in the night, whether in the first watch, or at midnight, or at cockcrow, or whensoever it might be) he might not find you given over to surfeit and drunkenness, and to the thoughts and cares of this present world; and so your hearts should be closed against the sight of him, and he should not be able to reveal himself unto you. For if, when Jesus died, ye had given yourselves over to despair and recklessness, then though Jesus himself had stood before you, coming from his grave, yet would ye none the more have seen him."

Against these words of Quartus there standeth, as it were, in opposition, a certain prophecy of Jesus, wherein he was wont to declare to us that he should be raised from the dead in three days, limiting the time exactly. And true it is that Jesus made often mention of certain words of the prophet Hosea which speak thus about being revived in three days: "Come and let us return unto the Lord: for he hath torn and he will heal us; he hath smitten, and he will bind us up. After two days will he revive us: in the third day he will raise us up, and we shall live in his sight." Now because of this prophecy, which was very often in the mouth of Jesus, it hath been supposed by many that Jesus knew for certain that he should die on the day of the Passover, and that he should lie in the grave two days, and be raised up on the third day.

But to this Quartus yieldeth not. For he saith that the words "two days" and "three days" were used by the prophet Hosea to signify only "a short time," even as the Romans also, and men of other nations, speak of "the day after the morrow," or "in a day or two," when they mean "a short time hence"; or even as the Hebrew tongue, speaking of past time, useth "the third day" to signify "some time ago." Moreover Quartus urgeth that, if Jesus had known of the day and hour, he would assuredly not have harrowed our souls with a needless sorrow, but would have told them to us; and he thinketh that Jesus spake concerning his coming from the grave, when he said that the day of the coming of the Son of man was not known to any, neither to the angels, nor even to the Son himself, but only to the Father.

"Therefore in my judgment," saith Quartus, "when Jesus spake about the fire which should consume his enemies, and concerning his death and lifting up or glorifying, and concerning his departing and coming again, and concerning the giving of the Holy Spirit, he knew indeed that all these things must needs come to pass, because they were according to the pattern and ordinance of things invisible; but when, and where, and how they should come to pass, he knew not. Neither did he hide that which he knew, cloaking it from you his disciples, for to keep you in ignorance and in suspense; but he spake as he knew, and all that he knew, so far as ye could understand it."

Thus wrote Quartus to me; and sometimes I incline to his words, but at other times I do not. Howbeit, to whichsoever opinion I incline, it mattereth little; for whether Jesus knew little or much of that which was to come (and he himself told us that he knew not all), my love for him is the same: save that sometimes it seemeth to me as if he were almost more lovable and more divine, going forth into the darkness of death in trust and faith, and knowing not everything that was to betide him, than if he had had the descents and ascents and all the paths of Hades marked out for him exactly beforehand as in a chart.

CHAPTER XXVI

On the morrow (which was the first day of the week), some of us rose earlier than the rest, and went down to Jerusalem to carry word to the other disciples and to such as were friendly among the Galileans (for many of them favoured us at this time, and a great number of them had come up to the Feast) that they might come forth from the city to meet Jesus and to welcome him. But the rest of us stayed with Jesus in Bethany. About the second hour of the day, when we were now about to set forth, Jesus sent Matthew the tax-gatherer, and another, to the village over against us, bidding them bring the ass whereof we had taken note yesterday; and if any man said aught, Matthew was to make answer that "the Master hath need of him." When the ass was brought, Jesus mounted thereon, and we set forth at once; and it was now about the third hour of the day.

When Bethany was by this time out of our sight, as we went by the road that lieth between the Tombs of the Prophets and the Mount of Offence, suddenly we heard a shouting as of a mixed multitude, and presently we discerned a great crowd of the disciples coming over the brow of the hill towards us, with many hundreds of the Galileans, all waving palm-branches in their hands, and hailing Jesus as the son of David. Now Jesus was riding before our band, upon the ass; but when the two bands met, there was a great shouting for joy; and the former band turned round and went on as vanguard, but our band marched on behind. Presently, as we drew near to the descent of the Mount of Olives, when we began to descry that quarter of the Holy City which men called the City of David, the shouting became louder, and so it continued, even there where the road descendeth so that the Holy City is no longer seen.

But when at last we attained unto the summit of the Mount Olivet, so that the whole of the city was seen at once spread out before our eyes, with all the roofs, and towers, and pinnacles thereof, and the gilded battlements of the temple, shining like fire in the sun, then indeed the splendour of the sight so lifted up our hearts that we were even beside ourselves for admiration; and looking unto Jesus as the King of all this glory, we cried even louder than before unto him as our King and Conqueror, like unto David of old. But Jesus neither now nor at any time during the entering into Jerusalem seemed at all lifted up by our salutations and praises; nor yet, on the other hand, was he of a gloomy or sad countenance as though he foreboded evil and ruin. Rather he was as one waiting and expecting, looking perchance for some sign of the will of the Lord, in case it might yet please Him to turn the hearts of the Pharisees, that they might be converted and live. Therefore also when he looked on the glory of Jerusalem below his feet, he was neither astonished at the beauty thereof, nor did he (at least at this time) weep or lament over it : but he gazed at it, as it were in suspense and questioning his own spirit ; if perchance it might be the Lord's pleasure to manifest Himself to the daughter of Sion, and to stay His hand from destroying the beautiful city ; or whether that could not be, but evil must take his course.

But we, at this time, perceived naught of that which was in our Master's mind ; but we lifted up our voices and shouted amain, hailing him as Son of David, and crying, "Hosanna to the Son of David! Blessed is He that cometh in the name of the Lord! Blessed is the kingdom that cometh of our father David!" Some also cast their palm-branches down in the road before him, and others strewed their garments in the path to do him honour. After this fashion therefore, shouting, and singing, and praising God, the whole multitude of us came down from the mountain into the valley below.

When we drew nigh unto the gate of the city, we saw that only some few of the citizens were come forth to welcome us. For the most part feared Jesus, lest he should bring down the wrath of the Romans upon the Holy City ; neither knew they him as the Galileans knew him. But instead of the citizens, there stood a great throng of children gathered together before the gate ; and when they heard the voices of the disciples and the voices of the Galileans, immediately they also took up the cry, and sang "Hosanna, Hosanna," in a clear shrill voice, after the manner of children, so that their song sounded forth quite distinctly, and above all the noise and shouting of the multitude. Now of the Pharisees, none had gone forth from the city to welcome Jesus ; but certain of the younger among them, desirous to look on the coming in of Jesus, as on a show in a theatre (and perchance willing, by the manifesting of their contempt of him, to overawe and to control the multitude of pilgrims), were come as far as the gate; and there they stood, over against the children, waiting the coming of Jesus, and with many gestures and beckonings signifying their displeasure. When therefore they heard the sound of the singing, they straightway rebuked the children, and would have them to hold their peace: but when the children would not, then turned the Pharisees in sore displeasure to Jesus, and bade him constrain them. .

Now Jesus all this while had seemed rapt in other matters; even as if he heard not the shouting nor the singing, neither understood the meaning thereof; but as if he heard other voices which we could not hear, and which, even for him, were not easy to understand. And when he drew nigh unto the gate of the city, and beheld the Pharisees, how they stood all together, and made no sign of welcome; then he looked up (methinks as I now remember it) with a wistful countenance to the gate, as though he partly expected that the very stones should cry out from the wall (according to the saying of the prophet Habakkuk), as if bearing witness against the unbelief of the Pharisees. Even thus looked Jesus, as he drew nigh to the gate, and there seemed as it were a shadow of doubt and expectancy upon his face; and just then it was that the Pharisees thrust themselves in his way and bade him stop the brawling of the children, for so they termed it.

Now for an instant Jesus seemed scarce to understand the intent of the Pharisees, nor even the meaning of their words. But when he perceived it, and when he turned his face toward the children (who all this time ceased not from their singing, but cried Hosanna, Hosanna, even louder than before), then his mind seemed to come back to earth, and his countenance became clearer, and he smiled for joy; for methought in the voices of those simple children he acknowledged the very voice of the Father in Heaven speaking by His little ones on earth, and showing unto him how that there must be no sign of fire from Heaven, nor no mighty work of any visible sort; but only strength through weakness, and wisdom through simplicity, and the Kingdom of God through little children, according to the eternal ordinance.

This behaviour of Jesus, though we understood it not then, yet was it partly interpreted to us, even at that time, by the answer which he made unto the Pharisees, saying unto them, "Verily I say unto you, if these should hold their peace, the very stones should cry out." Moreover, afterwards, when they would have had him rebuke them in the Temple, and when they said unto him, "Hearest thou what these say?" then Jesus spake unto them yet more clearly, and said, "Yea, have ye never read, 'Out of the mouths of babes and sucklings Thou hast perfected praise'?"

When we came to the foot of Mount Moriah, we arrayed ourselves to enter into the temple, and we went in by the gate called Shushan. But lo, the courts of the temple and all the ways which lead into the courts were crowded with oxen and doves, and drovers and money-changers; and it was more like unto a market-place or shambles than to a temple of the Lord:

even as I had beheld it two years before, when I came to offer sacrifice during my mother's sickness, yea, and worse also. For during the week before the Passover, almost the whole of the Jewish nation was wont to assemble in Jerusalem for to offer sacrifice, even as many (so it hath been reported to me, but it is well nigh past belief) as three hundred myriads; wherefore, though there should be but one lamb slain for a score of pilgrims, yet the number of beasts to be sacrificed at one time must needs be many thousands, not less than one hundred and fifty thousand. When Jesus looked around on all this stir and traffic, he was sore displeased, and his anger was very hot, yea, such as I had seldom noted the like in him before; and he bade the merchants and money-changers take their wares hence. But when they would not, he made unto himself a scourge of cords and drove them before him; and the disciples and the people did the same, and overthrew the tables of the money-changers, and thrust out them which sold doves. And Jesus said unto the Pharisees, "It is written, My house shall be called the House of Prayer; but ye have made it a den of thieves."

When Jesus spake these words, the Pharisees were exceeding wrath, and certain of their servants ran forward as if they would have laid hands on Jesus. Howbeit, Hezekiah the Scribe (the same of whom I have often made mention above) checked them, lest there should have been a tumult of the people. But it was plain to all men that they would fain have destroyed Jesus, only they feared the people. Therefore Jesus made no long stay for that day in the temple, but gave commandment to return to Bethany (for he would not tarry in Jerusalem by night lest the chief priests and Pharisees should lay hands upon him); and certain of the disciples accompanied us to the gate of the city, but not many.

While we were going through the streets of the city toward the gate, we conversed concerning that which had happened, and especially concerning the driving out of the merchants and the money-lenders; and most said that it was well done, for the presence of them that bought and sold defiled the House of the Lord. But a certain Greek, of Philip's acquaintance (one of them that had desired Philip that they might see Jesus), said that it was not well done of our Master, thus with his own hand to drive out them that bought and sold: "For," said he, "it is not the part of a philosopher to use violence, nor to be moved by passion to anything that is against seemliness and dignity, nor to take upon himself the part of a common door-keeper." Not much was said in answer at that time, for other thoughts possessed our minds; only John said that our Master did well to be angry, because he saw his Father's House defiled. Nevertheless oftentimes, since that day, the words of the Greek have come into my mind, and also other like words of Xanthias, how that "towards the end of his life, Jesus of Nazareth was driven out of the bounds of his patience by the persecution of enemies; so that he became bitter and somewhat austere."

But my judgment is not so. For to me it seemeth that all through those days of tarrying in Jerusalem and in Bethany, our Master was neither bitter nor austere. But he had ever before his eyes the thought of us his disciples; and he was ever musing on our desolation, (which should fall upon us when he should be parted from us), and how we should fare, contending without him against the Pharisees and against all other evil. Therefore he desired to leave it, as it were, on record, that the worst kind of sacrilege is the sacrilege of them which handle sacred things without the feeling thereof. And, as he had entered into Jerusalem like one having authority, so he desired perchance (for our sakes) to manifest himself, in the temple also, as one to whom obedience was due. Again, whereas Xanthias saith that Jesus, ever before in Galilee, taught us to endure evil, and not to put down evil by force, as now in Jerusalem; "The former rule," saith Quartus, "applieth only to the brethren that live in the midst of them that know not the truth. But wheresoever a nation or a congregation, shall recognise a certain law" (as our nation did in the worship of the temple), "there perchance the breaking of the law is not to be suffered, and the law is to be maintained, even by force. For it is one thing to avenge oneself, but another to avenge a law." After this manner wrote Quartus; but, in any case, Xanthias was assuredly wrong in saying that Jesus was "embittered by persecution;" unless it be bitter to call Satan Satan. For he was gentle and tender and very loving even to the last.

Howbeit at this time our thoughts were full of other matters, so that we were the less bent on defending our Master against the friend of Philip. For we were something downcast, and Judas even more than the rest, because nothing had come of our entering into Jerusalem; but, as Judas phrased it, all our great purposes had ended in naught. "For," said Judas, "the Lord hath given occasions, but we have used them not. For first, when we entered in at this same gate this morning, then I looked that Jesus should have given the word to disarm the guard that kept watch therein. But afterwards, when we had entered into the city and all the citizens were gathered to us, then at least I hoped to have heard him give commandment to assail the Fort of Antonia; or else I expected that he would have worked some sign in heaven, to have turned every one to our side, and so to have driven out the Gentiles without shedding of blood. But now we have gained nothing. Nay, we have lost everything. For we shall not again gather the multitude thus round us. And as for the Pharisees, he hath now so angered them that, even were he to work an hundred signs in heaven, I doubt they would not now accept him." Hereupon John said that we must have patience and trust in Jesus; but Judas made answer that the time had passed for patience, and that other courses must be tried.

For the space of two days, namely, the second day of the week, and likewise the third day, Jesus resorted to the temple daily, and taught the people there: but the more he saw of the temple, and of the priests therein, and likewise of the Pharisees and Sadducees (who disputed with him daily in the temple), so much the more his heart loathed the abominations which he discerned, insomuch that he seemed like unto one contending against Satan himself, enthroned in the Holy Place; and his words against the Pharisees in those days were as if he desired that they should be engraven in fiery letters upon the hearts of all that heard him, for ever. So hot was the vehemency of his passion against them; yet not against them, but against the Satan in their hearts, who through them reigned over Israel. For whatsoever Jesus had noted of evil in the teaching of the Scribes in Galilee, and whatsoever of blindness and narrowness, yea, and of persecution and malignity; all this, and much more did he note in the Scribes of Jerusalem; insomuch that the Holy City and the temple itself now seemed to him to have become a very source of evil, poisoning the waters of life for the whole of the people.

At the first, the Pharisees began to lay snares to take him at an advantage before the face of all the people; but he answered them according to their folly, proving to all the people that they knew not the foundations of truth. When they asked him by what authority he did that which he did, he would not tell them; but they must first tell him whether the baptism of John were from heaven or no; which question they feared to answer. As to the giving of tribute, he said that the denarius (which had on it the image of Cæsar) spake, of itself, that they that used it should give Cæsar his due. But when he gave back unto the Pharisee the denarius, saying these words, "Render therefore to Cæsar the things which are Cæsar's," then he paused for an instant, and afterwards added, "and to God the things that are God's." This he said, not as though some things belonged to Cæsar and not to God; but as though each man, in giving unto Cæsar his dues, must bear in mind that he was thereby giving to God his dues also; for a time might come when it might be a defrauding of God to give Cæsar tribute; but, at that time, to have refused tribute to

Cæsar, would have been to refuse God His dues. So he bade them obey the signs of the times, yet so as never to defraud God; nor would he lay down any rule, as they had desired, but pointed to the foundations of righteousness, which lie in the heart and not in the hands. The like also he did in saying that the love of God and of man was the chief commandment of the Law. But concerning the Sadducees and their doctrine, that there is no resurrection, he said that the second life differeth from the first as much as angels differ from men; so that the bands whereby we are bound together here, will not be the same as will bind us together there. Howbeit he said not that there should be no bands hereafter, nor that these present bands should vanish; but only that they should be different, and not carnal, but spiritual. Moreover he questioned the Pharisees concerning their expectations of the Messiah and their interpretations of the Scriptures; and they could not make answer to his questions.

But all these were only as the beginnings of the conflict. For presently the Pharisees began to wax more vehement in their disputations and to reveal their hatred of him more clearly. And when Jesus looked upon their faces, he discerned his own death instant therein. So he turned and spake to the people in parables, likening Israel to an estate let out to greedy husbandmen, which killed the servants of their lord, and last of all slew his son also, when he came to receive of the fruits of the land. Again, he likened the Kingdom of Heaven to a wedding feast, and the Pharisees to murderous people, subjects of a king; who would not come to the wedding of the king's son, but slew his servants that invited them. Then one in the crowd, a Galilean by birth, and a man of loose life, cried aloud, "That is well said, O prophet; for we, that are poor, shall enter into the Kingdom; but the rich shall not enter." But Jesus straightway continued his parable and described an unworthy guest, admitted indeed to the feast, but soon cast out, because he had come in not having on a wedding garment.

Thus all the day was spent in contention; but in the evening, at Bethany, Jesus spake unto us very tenderly concerning the Holy Spirit (the mention whereof was at this time daily more and more upon his lips), and how this Spirit should abide with us for ever and be always our guide and helper. Moreover he encouraged us to be of good cheer, saying that, though the world were against us, yet he had overcome the world : and that he could give us a peace that should last for ever. Likewise he began at this time to say more oft and more clearly (for he had said the like before once or twice in dark sayings) that, besides his little flock (for so he was wont lovingly to call us), there should be yet other flocks gathered unto him, and there should be one fold, and one shepherd. Now of all this we understood not much at that season; for our hearts were not yet opened to it. Howbeit his words were sweet to the ear, yea, and they reached to our very souls; insomuch that we were drawn unto him even more than before, and loved him with an exceeding love: but still it was hidden from us that our Master was shortly to depart.

But as concerning the Pharisees, Jesus told us that the wrath of the Lord must needs fall upon them. And he likened them unto a fig-tree which (after the manner of fig-trees) should, by course of nature, put forth fruit first and leaves afterwards; but this fig-tree, he said, putteth forth leaves but no fruits. Therefore the Lord, seeking fruit, goeth unto the tree, rising up early in the morning; and he looketh on it, and behold there are leaves, but no fruits. Then was the Lord wroth, and breathed upon the tree, and said unto it, "No man eat fruit of thee hereafter for ever:" and lo, when He returned and came by the same path again in the evening, the tree had withered away. When we heard these things, straightway there came into our minds another parable which our Master had spoken in former times concerning a barren tree; how the owner thereof cometh to the gardener and saith, "Lo, these two years I come seeking fruit and find none. Cut it down." But the gardener besought the Lord that it might not be cut down till another year should pass, if perchance it might in the meantime bear fruit. Thence we perceived, comparing the two parables together, that Jesus discerned the wrath of God now nearer at hand. For before, there was mention of hope and of a respite of two years; but now there was to be no hope and no respite.

But most strange it was to us to note how the worship and splendour of the temple, caused him no pleasure, but rather displeasure. Yet so it was. For on the second day of the week, when he was going forth from the city in the evening, a certain citizen of Jerusalem besought the disciples that they would shew him the buildings of the temple; "For," said he, "it were a shame that Jesus of Nazareth should have been now two whole days in Jerusalem and not to have seen these sights." But when the disciples moved him to see these things, he seemed like unto one constraining himself to look upon them that he might do us a pleasure : and when he had looked round upon them all, then he was silent for a while, and we perceived that they pleased him not. At last he opened his mouth and said unto us, "See ye not all these things ? verily I say unto you there shall not be left here one stone upon another that shall not be thrown down."

But when another spake of the many years during which the temple had been a-building, Jesus answered that, even though the temple were destroyed to-day, the Lord could raise up the true temple in three days. Now whether by "three days," he meant three days exactly, or "two or three days," according to the common phrase, concerning this matter, it has been disputed sufficiently above. But when he spake of the true temple, assuredly he meant, not the temple of Herod, but that invisible temple set upon a rock, whereof he had before spoken to Simon Peter ; and this temple seemed to him at all times one with himself: therefore said he that the true temple would be raised up, meaning the Son of man, and, in himself, the Church or Congregation of mankind.

But all this was hid from us at that time, save that we understood Jesus to set no store by the temple of Herod, in that he discerned the fire of God's wrath impending over it. And to us, as I remember, yea even to us that had daily converse with Jesus, it seemed strange that he should so set at naught that same temple which he had himself cleansed. For throughout all the land of Israel, the temple, being but one (and not many, as in Gentile countries), and very full of most ancient memories, because it presented and signified to us the former temple of Solomon and the tabernacle of Moses, this temple, I say, albeit Herod the Idumæan had built it, nevertheless seemed to us, in Israel, very holy, and well nigh one with Israel itself. And for this cause Xanthias blameth the saying of Jesus touching the temple, how that it should be thrown down: for saith Xanthias, the casting down of the temple must needs have seemed to the common folk in Israel all one with the casting down of Israel itself even as the Romans took it ill when, in after days, Gaius Cæsar desired of his gods that the Roman people might have had but one neck that he might have destroyed it at a blow. Wherefore Xanthias findeth fault with this saying of Jesus, as not politic, nor discreet.

But, in my judgment, Jesus spake herein not truthfully only, but also expediently; yea and expediently for all time; bearing witness, as it were, even now to all the churches, lest perchance the service of the Lord become the service of Satan: as it was in the temple of Herod. For all things therein seemed unto him to savour of hypocrisy, being done to obtain praise and admiration of men, but not to lift up the heart unto the Lord; so that the very splendour and brightness hid, instead of revealing, Him whose name is the Truth. Therefore when he was led to the treasury and bidden to mark how great gifts the rich men cast therein, he stood awhile watching; then turning round to us, he pointed to a certain poor widow (who had cast in no more than two mites, or a farthing), and he said, "This poor widow hath cast in more than all they which have cast into the treasury." Many other like words he said at this time: and, in fine, he ceased after the first day to speak concerning the purifying of the temple, nor would he any more call it his Father's house; for he perceived that it was become a den of thieves and that the purifying must be by fire. But that which most of all made us at that time to marvel, was, that he spake of the Chief Priests and Pharisees as murderers. But hereby he meant, as I judge, not only that they desired to slay him, but also that they were slaying the souls of all Israel by giving unto the people a doctrine and a worship, that were as poison to the hearts of mankind. Wherefore, as a man might discern with the eye the spots of blood upon the hand of a murderer, even so (but with much more clearness) did our Master discern the blood of Israel upon the souls of the Priests and Scribes in the temple; insomuch that the temple itself appeared even as a great slaughter-house, and the worshippers as murdered men, and the priests as butchers girt for the slaughter of Truth.

Therefore on the last day, even on the third day of the week, when the sun was nigh setting, and the time was now at hand that Jesus should depart from the temple, and he knew he should enter it no more; behold, he stood up in the presence of all the people, and poured forth denunciation against the Pharisees as being verily the children of Satan. Some of them he charged with love of gain; and he bade the multitude especially to beware of those Scribes who devour widows' houses and wring forth gifts for the synagogues, and for a pretence make long prayers. These, he said, should receive even greater condemnation than the rest.

But even against them that cared not for money, yea even against all the Pharisees, he brought grievous accusations.

For he said they had quenched the spirit of life within their hearts, so that Satan had taken possession of them and used them as his tools. For this cause they could not distinguish between small things and great, between the purifying of the outside and the inside, between that which sanctifieth and that which is sanctified; and they esteemed the tithing of mint and anise and cummin of more avail than mercy, judgment, and truth. Also he said they had made the interpretation of the Law into a gainful profession, doing whatsoever they did for to be honoured and admired of men. Therefore he spared not to call them, not only fools and blind, but also hypocrites. For he said that they knew in their own hearts that they had no sight and no knowledge, yet they professed to see and to know; and they had cast out their own consciences, yet would they fain appear able to judge between right and wrong. Thus they presented one appearance to men, which look only on the outside; but another appearance to God, who discerneth the inside; and therefore he called them actors in masks, or hypocrites; he likened them also unto whited sepulchres, hiding death within them. For they hated the Spirit of life, and they lived by rules and precepts which work death; and they would neither enter into life themselves, nor suffer the people of the land to enter in; and they feared and hated prophets and prophecies, and would fain destroy them; and they had hated John the prophet while he lived, and now they hated Jesus, even to the death: and this, while they professed to repent of the persecutions of the prophets by our forefathers, and to build monuments to their memory, saying, "If we had been in the days of our fathers, we would not have been partakers with them in the blood of the prophets."

After this, he turned round, to go forth for the last time from the temple. But as he came to the steps, he looked back upon all the Pharisees, and upon all their friends (who stood all gathered together behind him, watching him depart), and he pronounced a curse upon them; as though it needs must be that they must yet continue their course; and Satan must accomplish his purpose in them, and must be revealed in all his wickedness working through the Pharisees his bondsmen; and the judgment of the Lord must needs fall upon these servants of Satan: "Fill ye up the measure of your fathers. Ye serpents, ye generation of vipers, how can ye escape the damnation of hell? Wherefore behold, I send unto you prophets and wise men and scribes: and some of them ye shall kill and crucify: and some of them shall ye scourge in your synagogues and persecute from city to city. That upon you may come all the righteous blood shed upon the earth, from the blood of righteous Abel unto the blood of Zachariah son of Barachiah, whom ye slew between the temple and the altar. Verily I say unto you, all these things shall come upon this generation."

CHAPTER XXVII

WHEN Jesus had made an end of denouncing the Pharisees, many of the young men with them and their servants were desirous to have laid hands on him; and they came near as if for that intent, but the older sort checked them. Yet was their wrath clearly to be read in their faces: and when I came out of the temple, being a little space behind the rest, Hezekiah the Scribe overtook me and said, "Young man, I warn thee that thou mayest with speed sever thyself from this blind shepherd: for lo, he hath to-day provoked war, and war shall fall upon him; for unless he perish we shall perish." But I made answer, that I should follow Jesus constantly even to the end. Then he spake again of the evil which, he said, had befallen that rash young man Barabbas; how that he had been taken ten days ago by the Romans on the road that goeth down to Jericho, while he was riding at the head of a band of Galileans that were raising sedition: and, said Hezekiah to me, "Thy friend of Jotapata is to be crucified, as I hear, two or three days hence. Take heed therefore unto thine own steps, lest thou also fall into the same destruction." I made him no further answer, but departed, sorrowing not a little for the sake of Barabbas : for I had not before heard how great an evil had befallen him.

When I overtook the rest, I heard the disciples conversing earnestly one with another ; and the Greek, even the friend of Philip, bade us take note that we were beset with spies and watched; for "When ye issued from the temple," said he, " I perceived that the servants of the chief priests and the Pharisees watched you whithersoever ye turned ; and, meseemeth, it is their intent to lay hands on your Master this night. But I marvel why your Master so inveighed against the Pharisees, transgressing the bounds of seemliness and decorum, at least in my judgment." So spake he, after his Greek fashion ; but Judas also spake to the same effect, and said that we had come up to Jerusalem to destroy enemies, and lo, we had destroyed none, but made many.

The rest knew not what answer to make to these words; neither did I myself at that time. Howbeit, now I know well that Jesus came not to prophesy smooth things, but to teach us the truth. Therefore was it most needful that he should speak the truth, and nothing less than the truth, concerning the Pharisees; to the intent that the eyes of all mankind might be opened, even to the generations of generations, that they might discern that the sin of sins is hypocrisy. For other sins wound, but this sin slayeth, the conscience. Peradventure also Jesus foresaw that a time might come when certain, even among his own disciples, would err as the Pharisees had erred, shutting their eyes against the truth, as being unfit for use and not convenient. And he that came to make a spiritual Israel, a nation of priests and ministers for mankind, was it not most needful that he should thus as it were mark out and brand with censure the special sin of priests? He also that came to redeem all the children of men from all evil, was it not most necessary that he should make clear in the sight of all men what was the greatest evil? For if men knew it not, how could he redeem them from it? And well I know that, if he had not assailed the Pharisees as he did, then these same Greeks who now say that "Jesus transgressed the bounds of seemliness," would in that case have said (even as Jonathan the son of Ezra said) that "Jesus knew not the evil in human nature." Notwithstanding at this season we thought not of these things; but we feared what should betide to our Master if the Pharisees took him and cast him into bonds.

But a certain man of the Pharisees, Joseph by name, of the town of Arimathæa, clave unto Jesus; and although he dared not openly consort with us, he sent a servant after us, when we came forth from the Temple, to bid Jesus not abide in the same house this night as last night, because, said he, "the Pharisees purpose to take thee." He also warned Jesus not to come into Jerusalem on the morrow. But if Jesus desired to have some chamber in the city wherein to keep the Passover, Joseph promised that he would provide one. So much I heard myself; for I was nigh to Jesus when the servant of Joseph brought the message; but the answer of Jesus I heard not, save that he thanked the messenger courteously.

In the meantime we had passed out of the gate of the city, and had begun to climb up the side of the hill called Olivet; and by reason that we were in the depth of the valley, the sun had by this time set for us. But when we had gone some space up the side of the hill, as we turned round to take breath and rest, behold, the sun had not yet set, but was just beginning to sink; and the western quarter of the heaven was lit up with a light exceeding red and fiery, and the roofs of the temple and the towers of the castle of Herod shone as with a blood-red flame; and though our hearts were heavy with many thoughts, yet could we not choose but look. But when Jesus saw the city and the temple, whence he had but now come and wherein he was never to set foot again; his eyes were filled with tears, and he changed colour and could go no further, but sat down upon a stone and covered his face with his hands: and then he looked again upon the city and wept, mourning over it and saying, "O Jerusalem, Jerusalem, thou that killest the prophets and stonest them which are sent unto thee, how often would I have gathered thy children together, even as a hen gathereth her chickens under her wings, and ye would not! Behold, your house is left unto you desolate. For I say unto you, ye shall not see me henceforth, till ye shall say, Blessed is he that cometh in the name of the Lord."

Having said these words, he arose and went on his way, going up the hill. And we followed him, as men in the Valley of the Shadow of Death, that follow an angel of deliverance, but fear while they follow, lest at any time their guide should vanish out of their sight, and they should be left alone. Even so followed we Jesus up the Mount of Olives, and we feared much to question him concerning his words, but we feared even more to remain silent and so to be ignorant concerning the approaching peril. Therefore presently Simon Peter, with two other disciples, went to him and questioned him, saying, "Tell us when shall these things be." Jesus turned and looked upon our faces, and he perceived that we were all desirous to question him. So he beckoned to us to sit down, and he himself sat down upon a stone, and we also sat down upon the ground around him.

Then began Jesus to pour forth many prophecies of troubles near at hand and troubles far off; and he seemed like unto one upon the shore of a stormy sea covered with mists and darkness, who peereth into the night if perchance he may descry the ship wherein his friends sail tempest-tossed; even so did Jesus look forward into that which was to come, for our sakes. For though his own end was at hand, his thoughts and words were all for us. But he also had in his mind the prophecies of the prophet Daniel; who had prophesied, many generations before, that a time should come when the worship of God should fail, and a king of evil set himself up to be worshipped, and the daily sacrifice should be taken away, and the abomination of desolation set in the place thereof. Daniel likewise prophesieth that those of the nation who were of understanding should remain upright; yet even these should fall for a time, to try them and to purify them. But because the prophecies of Daniel were like unto the words of our Master, I will here set them down; for Daniel saith, "They shall pollute the sanctuary of strength, and shall take away the daily sacrifice, and they shall place the abomination that maketh desolate.

And such as do wickedly against the covenant shall he corrupt by flatteries; but the people that do know their God shall be strong and do exploits. And they that understand among the people shall instruct many; yet they shall fall by the sword, and by flame, by captivity, and by spoil many days. Now when they shall fall they shall be holpen with a little help; but many shall cleave to them with flatteries. And some of them of understanding shall fall, to try them, and to purge, and to make them white, even to the time of the end, because it is yet for a time appointed."

Now these prophecies of Daniel were fulfilled, in part, in the days of that wicked king Antiochus who is called Epiphanes, or Illustrious; but Jesus prophesied that they, or others like unto them, should still be fulfilled. Howbeit, in my judgment, he did not prophesy that these things should come to pass merely because Daniel had prophesied the like; but because, looking upon the present, he discerned the signs of the times (according to his own saying), and hence he perceived that which was yet to come. For his words were the words of Daniel; but his thoughts were the thoughts that came to him from that which he saw in the world. For when he looked upon the world, he saw love of self, and love of ease, and all manner of baseness and servility; and all the empire was given up to the worship of a man, even the Emperor Tiberius, and that man a tyrant and a man of sin, a slave to all abominations of the flesh. Wherefore death was reigning over the whole of the world. But when he looked to Israel, which was appointed to redeem the world and to lead the world to the knowledge of the true

A A

God, behold, Israel himself was blind; and they which should have been priests unto the Gentiles were as naught but pedants; and these too, given over unto all sin, hypocrites, and murderers in their hearts, and children of Satan.

Therefore it was discerned clearly by Jesus (having his eyes open to things future even as our eyes are open to things present), that a great conflict was at hand between evil and good, evil rearing itself aloft in the world to receive the worship of all mankind and driving out the true worship of God; and for a time evil must prevail. For if he looked upon us his apostles or disciples, then he perceived even too easily in our hearts the signs of weakness and instability; and for this cause he prophesied that we should all desert him and fall away for a time. Moreover, because he saw how the men of Israel thirsted for redemption, yea, and how all the children of men desired some deliverance from their present evils, therefore he knew and prophesied that, when he had departed, his place would not be left empty, neither at once nor in after generations; but in every time and in every nation false deliverers and false redeemers should arise, saying that men should obey them, and that they would deliver men. For this cause he warned us against false Christs, yea, even though they should work signs and wonders.

But as concerning the times and seasons when these several troubles should arise, he said naught; nor did he describe the manner of the wars, nor the nations, nor the armies that should make war. Now Quartus judgeth that Jesus knew not these matters; and true it is that Jesus himself spake concerning the time of his coming, saying, "But of that day and hour knoweth no man, no, not the angels of heaven, neither the Son, but the Father." Only, concerning one part of the prophecy, he said, for certain, that this generation should not pass away till all had been fulfilled. But this, saith Quartus, he knew because of the signs of the times: for as to that which he said, "Ye shall not see me henceforth, till ye shall say, Blessed is he that cometh in the name of the Lord," Quartus supposeth that Jesus himself knew not the time thereof, but only this, that it was not possible that Sion could behold him until Sion desired him : for the beholding of Jesus after his death was not to be with the bodily eye, but with the spiritual, through love and desire. Now concerning the foreknowledge of Jesus, what things he knew, and what things he knew not, I have said above that I pronounce no judgment. But true it is that at this time he spake unto us a third parable concerning the fig-tree, and said that we were to discern the coming of these evils from the signs of the times, even as men discern the coming of the summer from the fig-tree, when it putteth forth leaves. For, like as the summer causeth the fig-tree to put forth her leaves, or like as the scent of the carcase guideth the vultures to the prey, even so he taught us that the sins of men, and especially of Israel, would bring after them miseries and judgments, not by chance, but of necessity.

Therefore he prophesied that great tribulation should fall on the land of Israel, such as was not since the beginning of the world to this time, no, nor yet ever shall be. And except those days should be shortened, there should no flesh be saved; but for the elect's sake those days should be shortened. But after the tribulation of Israel, he prophesied that all the empire should be shaken, and the thrones and princedoms thereof should be cast down, and the throne of the Son of man should be set up on high in the sight of all men, and the tribes of the earth should mourn, and the Gentiles should see the Son of man coming on the clouds of heaven with power and great glory, and the elect should be gathered together by an angel as with the sound of a trumpet from all the corners of the earth. Finally he exhorted us to watch in patience, for we knew not at what hour our Master would come.

Now as concerning these prophecies, part were perchance fulfilled when our Master came to us from the grave; for then to them that watched and waited he appeared. But part also, in my judgment, yea, and a great part, were fulfilled ten years ago, when Jerusalem was trodden down by the Gentiles, and the temple was burned with fire, and Israel was scattered over the face of the earth, and many were slain, and many more sold for slaves, and such tribulation befell them as never before. But part remaineth to be fulfilled, when men's hearts shall fail them because the empire shall be shaken, and the thrones of this world shall be cast down, and the worship of the Son of man shall be set up. For albeit the empire fell not in the days of Nero, when all men expected that the end of all things was at hand; yet must the empire needs be cast down. And it is like that this shall come to pass in my days, even in the days of me Philochristus, the writer of this book. And when Israel shall turn unto the Lord Jesus and shall call them blessed that come in his name, then shall Israel see him, according to his saying. Howbeit concerning the day and the hour we have no knowledge thereof; only we know that in the end the Son of man must come with glory; and until the Son of man shall reign over the world, peace cannot be; that is to say, cannot be so as to be settled and firm. For all things move violently to their place, but easily in their place. Wherefore the ways of the world cannot be smooth, nor can the children of men and the tribes of men move smoothly and easily in the world, until the Son of man be in his place as King of the world over all men and over all nations, and until all men and all nations be in their places as his servants; and then there shall be peace for ever; but not till then.

But all this I write, having been enlightened by the Spirit. But at the time when we were sitting thus round about Jesus, listening to his prophecies, we were not yet enlightened; for the Spirit of Jesus was not yet in the world, because Jesus was yet with us. Therefore were we all greatly dismayed by his words, and our hearts quite failed us; and when he had made an end of speaking, we sat still silent; and the shadow of night, stretching over the face of the earth, seemed unto us like to a shadow of Satan encompassing both us and all the world and our Redeemer himself, in whom we had trusted that he should have redeemed Sion. Thomas at last brake silence, and said, "Alas, O Master, dost thou not remember thine own words on that other mount in Galilee, where thou didst pour blessings on us, and didst strengthen us with comfortable sayings, telling us that the meek should inherit the earth? Verily the prophecies of the Mount of Olives do not accord with the prophecies of the Mount of Blessing." By this time it was become dark, so that we could not clearly discern the features of Jesus, for the moon had not yet risen; but he seemed to turn his face suddenly to Thomas as though his words had grieved him. Howbeit, he said nothing, but arose from his place, and we followed him up the mountain even unto Bethany.

When we had been a full hour in Bethany, our Master called for Judas, that he should bear some message to Joseph of Arimathea in Jerusalem; for Judas was oftentimes employed by Jesus about such matters, being a man of understanding, and of a ready wit, and having a knowledge of the ways of men, more than the rest of the disciples. But search being made for Judas, he was not to be found; and this seemed not a little to disquiet Jesus. Howbeit, he bade me go in his stead, and bear a certain letter to Joseph of Arimathea. So I went down straightway and delivered the letter; and having received an answer written and sealed, I set forth to return to Bethany. Now the moon was by this time risen, and shining very brightly. So, because I was minded not to be seen of any of the servants of the chief priests, I kept myself in the shadow of the street as I went forth to the gate of Kidron; and it being now late, even in the second watch of the night, there were few people stirring.

But as I was now near to the street called Straight, whereby one turneth to the right hand to go unto the gate, methought I heard the sound of the voice of the night-watch going their rounds. So I drew near to the wall, and remained in a corner where I could not be seen. And straightway Hezekiah the Scribe came by, and Judas with him, walking very near the place where I was (but they discerned me not) and talking in a low voice together. And as they passed, I clearly heard Judas say to Hezekiah, "But if he should call down fire upon the guards?" And Hezekiah made answer, "Then thou wouldst have done him good service," or words to that effect: but the exact words of Hezekiah I heard not, because they were by this time gone somewhat past me. Neither could I hear what Judas said in answer to the words of Hezekiah. Only I noted, even afar off, that after they had conversed some while longer, Judas held out his right hand to Hezekiah, and Hezekiah seemed to take it as a pledge.

When I saw this, my mind misgave me that all was not well; yet did it not so much as enter into my mind, at that time, that one of the Twelve could purpose treachery against our Master; and, because of my message and my haste, I gave no thought to the words that I had heard. But I sped away to the gate, and passing through unquestioned, I went up the mountain in haste; and when I came to the top, I found John, the son of Zebedee, waiting for me, to take me to the house where Jesus lay that night; for he was not to abide in the same house as before, for fear of the Pharisees. So I came to Jesus and delivered my letter; and I found with him a certain Nicodemus, a great teacher among the Pharisees. He had come to converse with Jesus, but secretly, for fear of the chief priests. Then I delivered my letter to Jesus, and I told him how I had seen Judas discoursing with Hezekiah. But the old man, even Nicodemus, was troubled when he heard me make mention of Judas, and he turned to Jesus and said that from friends came sometimes even more dangers than from enemies; and as he had before warned Jesus against the plotting of the Chief Priests, so now again he besought Jesus not to adventure himself in Jerusalem on the morrow. Then he gave thanks to Jesus for his doctrine, and departed. But when the letter of Joseph of Arimathea was opened, it confirmed the words of Nicodemus; for he also bade Jesus not come to Jerusalem on the morrow, but to tarry till the next day. He also added (but these words Jesus read not aloud, so that I knew not of them till afterwards) that Jesus should keep the Passover on the day after the morrow; howbeit not at his house, but at another house which his servants should prepare. He also gave Jesus a sign whereby he might be guided to the house. Likewise the letter bade him beware of false friends.

When Jesus had made an end of reading aloud those last words bidding him beware of false friends, his heart was sorely troubled, and the burden seemed more than he could bear; and he went out for a while to be alone and to pray. But presently he returned and spake comfortable words to us, and cheered us with his kindness; and so for that night he lay down to rest; and some of us slept while others watched. Howbeit that night no enemy came.

On the morrow (which was the fourth day of the week) Jesus neither went down to Jerusalem, nor sent any down to make preparation for the Passover. But he remained with us in Bethany, part of the time in the house, and part in the fields round about, going with us hither and thither, and speaking more and more to us of that same Holy Spirit whereof he had spoken before; which should guide us, he said, into all truth, and teach us what to reply unto our enemies, and be unto us a comforter and a friend, yea, the source of all happiness and good. And more and more he spake concerning his departure; insomuch that, though we were unwilling, yet by this time we were constrained to suppose that our Master must be severed from us for a season, and that we must watch for his return. Yet how or in what way he should be taken from us we could not conjecture: only that he should be slain by his enemies we had no manner of belief, no, nor so much as a fear thereof, although he had so many times prophesied it to us. For the thing was hidden from us of the Lord, that we should neither believe it nor conceive it.

But the women were otherwise minded, and were very full of fears. To them it seemed that, if Jesus was indeed about to be taken from them, then it mattered not whether he were taken in a chariot of fire or by whatever other means: and they lamented over him as over one already dead. Many times did we rebuke them for their faithlessness (for so it seemed to us), but they would not cease. Judas also rebuked them even more bitterly than we: for he had come to us on the morning of that day, saying that he had been with certain of his acquaintance in Jerusalem that he might be informed concerning the plots of the Pharisees. Jesus received him kindly, even more methought than was usual; and when we sat together at meat that night, he placed Judas next unto himself,

John being on one side of him and Judas on the other, in the seat of honour.

Now so it was that, while we were at meat, behold, one of the women came behind Jesus, having an alabaster box of very precious ointment, and poured it on his head, at the same time uttering most piteous cries and lamentations. Then Judas changed colour; for his heart misgave him, as I judge, that the lamentations of the women might prove true; and besides, he was wrath perchance because the love wherewith this woman loved Jesus put his semblance of love utterly to shame. Therefore he rose up from his seat in indignation and said, "To what purpose is this waste? for this ointment might have been sold for three hundred pence and given to the poor." We also ourselves in like manner murmured against the woman. But Jesus said, "Why trouble ye the woman? for she hath wrought a good work upon me. For ye have the poor always with you; but me ye have not always. For in that she hath poured this ointment on my body she did it for my burial." Then he paused, and mused for an instant, and added a prophecy, that wheresoever his good tidings of Redemption should be proclaimed in the whole world, there also should this that this woman had done be told for a memorial of her.

Now before these words, while we had sat at meat listening to the discourse of Jesus, Judas seemed as if his heart were enlarged towards Jesus; and albeit at times he fell to pondering and musing (like unto a man doubting of two courses which to take), yet anon he would be aroused by some word that Jesus spake; and then his countenance would kindle, and he would stoop forward, us in old times, with his eyes all a-glow, listening as if he would fain devour each syllable with his ears. But now his countenance fell, and he was filled with rage because he had been rebuked by Jesus; and he went forth from the chamber, and we saw him that night no more. But as for us that remained, our hearts became exceeding sorrowful; for now indeed it pressed upon us that the departure of Jesus must needs be sad and grievous and full of sorrow, like unto death. But still, that he should die indeed, and be buried: this, even now, we could in no wise believe.

CHAPTER XXVIII

WHEN the morrow came (which was the fifth day of the week) Jesus abode still in Bethany, and went not forth to Jerusalem. Now so it was that the Passover that year fell on the Sabbath day; and because of the multitude of the sacrifices that were to be slain between the two evenings in the temple, it was a custom that certain of the pilgrims should keep the Passover on a day before the Sabbath. For it was said (though I can scarce believe it) that there were nigh upon three hundred myriads of souls in Jerusalem during the Passover week; and even though the women partook not of the feast, yet the number of lambs to be slaughtered must needs be very great. Therefore we expected that he should have gone down to Jerusalem that day, for so it had been determined with Joseph of Arimathea; and we marvelled that he did not go. But he continued speaking unto Mary and Martha and other of the women. And by this time it was noon, and yet nothing had been done.

But at the last Peter went to him and reminded him that after two days would be the feast of the Passover; and he asked Jesus where he desired that we should prepare for the feast. Then Jesus bade Peter and John go to a certain street in Jerusalem and to stand there during the ninth hour of the day; and they should meet there a certain slave of Joseph of Arimathea bearing a pitcher of water upon his head; and they were to say, as a sign to the man, "The Master saith, my time is at hand; I will keep the Passover at thy house with my disciples;" and the slave would shew them an upper room prepared; and there they were to make ready. For the space of an hour after Peter and John were departed, Jesus continued still speaking unto the women: then he arose and bade them farewell, and set his face to go down to Jerusalem.

When it was now late, the sun having set two hours or more, we sat down to keep the feast; and Judas also was with us. While we sat at meat, we spake, according to the custom, concerning the ancient deliverance of Israel in the days of Moses: but our hearts were very heavy, for we said within ourselves, "We need not a past, but a present deliverance; and, behold, it is not to be." Jesus alone was of good cheer, and rejoiced with a marvellous joy; and he spake very cheerfully and tenderly to us, and said that his heart had yearned to eat this Passover with us, for he should not eat with us again till the Kingdom of God should be established. Now at this we marvelled, but we rejoiced not; for we had learned by much experience not to rejoice at the promises of Jesus as if they were the promises of common men. Moreover we were sore disturbed by a certain saying of Jesus. For in the midst of his comfortable discourse to us, he suddenly brake off, saying that one of us, that sat there at meat with him, should betray him. And he said, "The Son of man goeth as it is written of him ; but woe unto that man by whom the Son of man is betrayed! It had been good for that man if he had not been born." And hereat we sat a while dumb and looking each at other, wondering whom Jesus might mean, and afterwards we brake out into many and passionate questionings, each asking whether he himself was to be the traitor: but Jesus made no certain answer, none at least that I heard. At the last, before rising from the table, Jesus looked earnestly upon us all, as if his heart went out to us: and he pitied us, and said that he would now give us his last gift; for this feast was as a funeral feast, and he was to die and leave us alone; therefore, before he died, he desired to bequeath to us somewhat by his last will and testament.

While we marvelled what this gift or legacy might be, behold, Jesus took bread and blessed God, and brake it and gave it to each of us, saying, "Take, eat, this is my body." After this he took wine and blessed that likewise, and bade us drink of it, saying, "This is my blood of the New Testament, which is shed for many." So we ate and drank as we were bidden, even like children that have no understanding; nor did we then discern the meaning of his words. Howbeit, even at that time we understood somewhat of his purpose; for we perceived that Jesus was pouring his love, yea, and his life, into our hearts; and our souls stretched out as it were toward the truth, namely, that Jesus, in this testament of his, was bequeathing himself to us his disciples, to be our possession for ever.

Now all the other disciples were strangely moved,

insomuch that their hearts were melted with the fervency of their love; but Judas alone was unmoved. Yea, rather he was moved indeed, but in a manner quite contrary to the rest. For when Jesus reached unto him the bread, all eyes were upon him, for we could not now refrain from suspecting him: but he ate it against his will, and as though he ate it with difficulty; and when he had eaten it, he looked angrily at us that gazed still upon him, and then he rose up in haste from the table, like unto one possessed with Satan. Now while he was eating, Jesus beheld him with a marvellous love and pity, yea, and, as it seemed to me, with a great struggle and conflict of soul, as if he were wrestling for the last time against Satan for the soul of Judas. But, when he perceived that Judas had hardened his heart against him, he sighed, and said some word unto him, but what it was I heard not: and hereupon Judas went hastily forth, and left Jesus still sitting with us. Then did our hearts misgive us yet more. For none could any longer doubt that Judas was indeed a traitor; and we bethought ourselves for what cause he had gone forth, and when he would return.

But Jesus neither stayed him, nor lamented when he had departed; but he seemed like unto one in whom all tears and sorrow had been swallowed up in a certain unfathomable depth of joy. For he looked up to heaven and offered up praise unto the Lord, the Deliverer of Israel, and he bade us join him in singing a portion of the great Hallel; for the singing of these psalms was according to the custom of the Passover. Now so it was that, in the singing, Jesus must needs utter certain words that tell how the Lord giveth life out of death: "The snares of death compassed me round about, and the pains of hell gat hold upon me. I shall find trouble and heaviness, and I will call upon the name of the Lord, O Lord I beseech thee, deliver my soul:" and then, "Turn again then unto thy rest, O my soul, for the Lord hath rewarded thee. And why? Thou hast delivered my soul from death, mine eyes from tears, and my feet from falling. I will walk before the Lord in the land of the living." While he sang these words, it was a wonder to see the face of Jesus, with what a brightness he looked up to heaven, and how great a trust shone from his countenance; insomuch that, as we gazed upon him, our hearts also seemed lifted up with his. But Jesus went on, until he came to those following words of the Hallel which say how "The right hand of the Lord hath the pre-eminence: the right hand of the Lord bringeth mighty things to pass. I shall not die but live, and declare the works of the Lord. The Lord hath chastened and corrected me, but he hath not given me over unto death. Open me the gates of righteousness, that I may go into them and give thanks unto the Lord."

At the last, when we sang of the stone refused of the builders but become the head stone of the corner, he sang with an exceeding clear voice, not loud, but very piercing, so that it seemed to cleave us to the very heart; and behold, our voices became lower, even as his became clearer; and we feared to sing the same words as he sang; but we were rapt with wonder as we looked upon his countenance; for it was as the countenance of an angel seeing the very glory of the Most High and gazing upon Him face to face. And when he sang the last words of all, "God is the Lord who hath shewed us light, bind the sacrifice with cords, yea even unto the horns of the altar. Thou art my God, and I will thank thee; thou art my God, and I will praise thee"; then indeed it came to pass that all we that listened to him were lifted up in spirit with him in an ecstasy, being delivered from all our doubts and cares and fears, looking down on them as petty things; and it was even as if Jesus were holding us by the hand and carrying us up with himself above the firmament, to the seventh heaven and beyond, yea even to the Throne of the Blessed.

That instant, a knocking was heard at the door, and one entered in haste and as if in terror; and he went up to Jesus and whispered in his ear. Then the glory faded from the face of Jesus, and he became sad, and straightway gave commandment to depart. But as we went forth from the chamber to the roof (for the guest-chamber was an upper chamber and upon the roof, as was the custom in my country), we heard from the slave that a guard had been sent forth by Annas to seek Jesus, and that Judas of Kerioth was thought to be with them, to guide them to the place where Jesus was. So we went down immediately from the upper chamber where we had been at meat; and behold, as we passed from the brightness of the moonlight, which shone upon the roof, down into the darkness of the shadow of the street, we seemed to have passed out of life into death, and to have been cast down from Paradise to the depths beneath the earth.

Now when we were all come down from the house into the street, Jesus stood for a while in the midst of his disciples looking up to the sky; and he seemed for an instant like unto one doubting whither he should go. For first he made two or three steps toward the temple and the tower of Antonia, as if to go thither (but this would have been certain death, for the guard was coming thence, and we should have met them); but then he looked at us and seemed to change his purpose. For he turned towards the gate that leadeth to the vale of Kidron. Now why he did this we knew not at that time; but afterwards we judged that he was moved at first to go to meet the guard that he might give himself up at once unto death; but when he had thought thereon, it seemed better for our sakes that he should still remain with us a few hours longer. Perchance also he wished to commune with God alone upon the mountain of Olivet; for he ever loved the loneliness of mountainous places and nightly prayers. Moreover Quartus writeth to this effect, that "though Jesus knew that he was to die, yet the manner of his dying, and how he should be taken, was not known to him: therefore he would not prevent the hand of the Lord; but would avoid the peril by all honourable means even till the last, leaving the decision with the Lord."

As we drew nigh to the gate of Kidron I was near him, and I heard him repeating some saying of Scripture to himself; and at the last, he spake aloud and said, "All ye shall be offended because of me this night, for it is written, I will smite the shepherd, and the sheep shall be scattered." But when he marked us, how exceedingly we sorrowed at these words of his, then he began to encourage us again; and he spake some words how that he would return to us, or guide us hereafter. Now what he said exactly I know not, for I was a little behind the rest. But he looked around him in the narrow street, as though that were no place for him to abide in : and then he added some words concerning Galilee, which I did not clearly hear. Howbeit, it seemed to me that he said he should manifest himself to us hereafter, not in Jerusalem but in Galilee.[1] And so also most of the disciples interpreted his words. But we all with one consent cried out that we would never desert him nor go from his side; and he listened to us gently, even as a mother listeneth to the prattle of a little child which prattleth concerning the things which he will do when he cometh to man's estate. Even so listened Jesus to our speech ; but when Peter was vehement, even above the rest, in protestations, Jesus interrupted him, and said that before the morrow's sun had risen, yea, before cockcrow, Simon Peter should have denied him.

By this time we were come to the gate of the Kidron valley; and methought certain of the servants of the chief priests, which stood together at the gate, were advised of the intent to arrest Jesus, and were fain to lay hands on him. Howbeit, many were coming in and going out, and we that were going with Jesus joined ourselves together around him, insomuch that the guards suffered us to pass; for they could not then have taken him quietly, nor without a tumult; which thing they purposed to avoid. And so it was that, as we closed ourselves together for to encompass Jesus and to guard him, my place was very nigh unto Jesus, even next upon his left hand ; and as we went down the steep path which leadeth across the brook Kidron, I chanced to stumble;

[1] See Note IV.

and Jesus took me by the right hand to stay me from falling. And the touch thereof remaineth with me unto this day; for his hand was not again to touch my hand upon earth.

When we were now going up the hill on the other side of the brook (being by this time quite out of the shadow of the city walls, so that we could see all things in the moonlight very clearly), we perceived that Jesus was still meditating on prophecies; and ever and anon he looked upon us, as though his care for us were a burden on his soul. And perchance he desired to prepare us to live without him in the world; and not to depend upon the exact words of his precepts, nor to make therefrom a rule nor a law unto ourselves, but to obey the Spirit only; making new rules and laws for ourselves if need were, even as the times might suggest and the Spirit might bid us. For he said unto us, "When I sent you without purse, and scrip, and shoes, lacked ye anything?" And we said "Nothing." Then said he unto us, "But now he that hath a purse let him take it, and likewise his scrip." Here he paused awhile, and then he added these words: "And he that hath no sword let him sell his garment and buy one. For I say unto you that this that is written, must yet be accomplished in me: 'And he was reckoned among the transgressors.' For the things concerning me have an end." Hereat we wondered, that Jesus (who had ever spoken against smiting with the sword) should bid us buy swords. Howbeit, we answered that we had two swords with us. Straightway Jesus ceased from walking, and stood quite still for an instant; and it seemed as if he marvelled at our want of understanding, but yet perceived that he must needs be content, for he could do no more to help us. Therefore he said nothing, but presently continued to walk on as before. But, as I now suppose, his meaning was to prepare us for much tribulation, and that we should, in the days to come, use all means and all faculties in his service. Howbeit, even to this day, I understand not altogether that saying about the buying of a sword. But as I judge, Jesus had invisible things in his mind, and he spake of the stores and treasures, and of the weapons also, that were like to be needed in the great and terrible war which we were to wage against Satan in the days to come.

Against this, Xanthias urgeth (and methinks not without shew of reason) that the scrip and purse whereof Jesus made mention in Galilee were not invisible things, but visible: but, if they were visible, so also must the sword needs be, whereof Jesus made mention in the same saying. But Quartus replieth that when Jesus, being still with us in the flesh, sent the disciples forth in Galilee without purse and scrip, he would have them to go forth not only without visible purse and scrip (which indeed they did), but also without the spirit of the purse and the spirit of the scrip, that is to say without forethought and provision, the better to awaken them to whom they were to preach the Good News : and this, saith Quartus, was the main part of the precept of Jesus. But now that he was to be no longer with us in the flesh, he changed his precept, bidding us use the spirit of the purse and the spirit of the scrip : and " after those words," saith Quartus, " that ye might the better understand them, Jesus paused " (which indeed he did, for I took note of it) "in the midst of his saying, and bade you buy a sword, supposing that ye would know assuredly that he (who ever hated the sword) could not mean a visible sword, but an invisible : even that two-edged sword which Jesus brought into the world to do battle against evil withal. And belike," saith Quartus, "Jesus meant that, after he should be taken away, we were never to be content to defend ourselves against evil, nor to lead harmless lives in peace and quiet (as the Essenes are wont to do) ; but that we were evermore to do battle against evil, and to assail it, and to give up all things sooner than cease to make war against it."

At this, time came down one from Bethany to tell us that the servants of the chief priests had beset the house of Mary and Martha, and others were watching on the road for to take Jesus if he should come up the hill. Therefore Jesus turned aside from the road and went unto a place whither he had also beforetime gone with us : it was a small vale, wherein grew many olive-trees, insomuch that it was hence called the Press of Olive Oil, or Gethsemane. When Jesus came to this place, we would fain have still accompanied him ; but he suffered us not, but bade us stay where we were, and there to watch and pray, lest we entered into temptation : for these were his very words to us. But taking John and Peter and James, he himself went forward about a stone's cast ; and we noted that, after a short while, he parted from them, though they were fain to stay him (for we could hear all things as well as see, because the night was very calm, and no less still than bright) ; and he went on yet another stone's cast or somewhat less, and the three disciples sat down where they were. Then Jesus stretched out his hands unto the Lord and prayed with exceeding earnestness; and to us, where we stood, he seemed as one in a sore agony; for at one time we could discern him standing erect, but at another time kneeling or prostrate upon the ground; and though he spake not loud, yet could I hear words that made my very flesh to shiver and creep; for he cried unto the Lord and said, "Father, if it be possible, let this cup pass from me." These words he said more than once, so that I could not but hear them; and a sickness of heart and an horror fell on me that such an one as Jesus of Nazareth should come to such a pass, and should ever need to say, "if it be possible."

Now so it was, that in spite of our sorrow and anguish of heart, all we that watched with Jesus at this time were so pressed down with a strange slumber that it was not possible for us to resist the burden thereof upon our eyelids; and oftentimes we would walk up and down and speak each to other for to shake off the leaden weight from our eyes; but we could not, no, though we were angered, and reproached ourselves aloud. For we had not slept much during three nights past or more, because of the need of watching for Jesus; and besides, the very unexpectedness of all that sorrow which had of late encompassed us round on every side, caused us to feel like unto them which wander in the wilderness of a dream or vision of the night, insomuch that we scarce knew whether we were asleep or awake : and the anguish of Jesus itself was unto us as it were but a part of a bad dream. For we could not attain to understand his sorrow, nor to share in his burden. Only we knew that he sorrowed not for fear of death. But we knew not at that time the secret of his agony, how he was at that instant wrestling with Satan for the salvation of all the children of men. Yet so indeed it was. And though the suffering of Jesus was seen of men when his body hung upon the cross, yet meseemeth it was seen of God when he was prostrate upon the ground in Gethsemane, and his soul was crying unto the Lord and saying, "if it be possible."

Loth am I to write many words concerning that which is above all reach of words, yea, and above all reach of the thoughts of men; yet will I here set down that which was said unto me concerning this matter by a certain Alexandrine, a friend of Quartus, who was a man of an understanding spirit and of discernment above the common. This man, when I once marvelled aloud, in his presence, as to the cause of the agony of Jesus, made answer to me and said, "What was it, thinkest thou, that caused Jesus more pain and sorrow than aught else?" So I replied, "Without doubt, the sins of men: for he often spake as if it were a pain to him, even to forgive the sins of men." But the Alexandrine replied, "As it seemeth to me, Jesus did not merely forgive sins twice or thrice in a week, nor in a day, no, nor even in an hour: but his whole life was a state of forgiving, and a state of bearing sins and of carrying iniquities, and of making himself one with sinners. For this end it was needful that Jesus should have strength to trust in men and to hope for men: for without trust and hope thou knowest it is impossible for thee to lift up a sinful man in forgiveness, howsoever great may be thy love for the sinful.

"Therefore, even as the Gentiles fable that Atlas doth

bear up the pillars of the earth, even so, methinks, Jesus of Nazareth knew in himself that he bare up the pillars of the invisible Jerusalem, the city of the souls of men; and so long as he had strength to trust and hope, so long he knew that the invisible city stood and was to stand; but, if he should fail in trust and hope so that he should fall (even for a single instant), then behold, in that same fall of the Son of man fell all the world, yea, all the souls of men, and all the Temple of the Congregation of the children of God; and so the universe became the hunting-ground of Satan, and the children of men his prey, and God was not. Peradventure, therefore, the burden of Jesus was this bearing of the sins of men, and especially of the sin of Judas and the infirmities of you his disciples, and the thought of the impotence of good to conquer evil. Moreover perchance there rose up before him the image of the morrow, when he should hang upon the cross, and when the strength and force of life should leave him, and there should be no one to succour, no one to comfort; and a vision from Satan stood before him, and he heard a voice that whispered evil things : 'If now thou shouldest lose thy trust for an instant? and the pillar should be snapped? and the invisible city should fall? and the gates of hell should prevail over the gates of heaven?'"

This then is what the Alexandrine said unto me concerning the suffering of Jesus : but it needeth not to say that at this time we understood naught of these things : only we perceived that some terrible thing was at hand. But about the space of an hour or more, as I judge, had passed since we first heard Jesus say, "if it be possible"; and now methought Jesus was less disturbed in praying. And presently we saw him standing upright, very clearly to be seen in the light of the moon, which streamed upon him through the olive branches; and these words were borne to our ears through the stillness of the night, "O my Father, if this cup may not pass away from me, except I drink it, thy will be be done." But some of the disciples told me afterwards that at this time they saw a shape, as of an angel clothed in white, ministering unto him. But I saw it not, for it may be that I was at that time slumbering: for soon after I had heard Jesus speak these last words, there fell a deep sleep upon me and upon the rest of the disciples that were nearest to me. Afterwards they all slumbered and slept, even the sons of Zebedee and Peter also; and perchance this thing was from the Lord, to the intent that Jesus might bear all his burden alone.

After this, I remember no more, save that I had a vision of the night in my slumber, wherein I saw Jesus of Nazareth clothed in bright raiment, glorious to behold. He stood and prayed upon the summit of a mountain. Howbeit in my dream it seemed to be not Mount Olivet, but the Mount of the Law in Galilee. And as I looked upon him, his stature grew larger and his raiment brighter, till the brightness thereof filled the sky, and set it all in a flame. With that I awoke on a sudden, and opening mine eyes, I perceived that there were flames indeed around me; then, leaping up, I found myself in the midst of torches, and armed men compassing me round. Yet could I discern, through the midst of them all, Jesus, with a calm countenance, stooping over John and Peter and James, and arousing them from sleep.

Now all that came to pass thereafter was finished in a few moments, though it take long to tell. For Judas, who was the guide of the armed men, ran swiftly before the rest up to Jesus and said, "Hail, Master," and saluted him. And, as I was told by them that were nigh to see, Judas seemed as if he knew not, even at the last, what would come to pass, nor scarce what he himself was doing. For he embraced Jesus and pointed to the soldiers that followed behind him, as if half expecting that Jesus would call down fire upon them. But Jesus looked upon him as if looking upon a stranger, and made him such answer as to shew that he perceived his treachery; whereat Judas drew back, they said, as one distraught. Then Simon Peter drew a sword and struck a blow at one of the soldiers; and the rest of us ran up to have joined in the fray. But Jesus straightway rebuked us, and bidding Peter put up his sword, he yielded himself up to the soldiers. Yet even to the last he was as a son obeying the will of the Father, and not like unto one acting from constraint; for I myself heard him say unto Simon Peter, "Thinkest thou that I cannot pray to my Father and He shall presently give me more than twelve legions of angels? But how then shall the Scriptures be fulfilled, that thus it must be?"

Now up to this moment we had not yet fled; for we could not even then believe that our Redeemer, the Messiah, the Son of the Living God, would be led captive; yea, even though he resisted not, yet were we assured that the Lord God of Israel would stretch out His hand to deliver His Holy One. So we still waited and were in expectation. But when at last the servants of the high priests laid their hands on him, and the soldiers bound him and dragged him roughly away, and yet no fire from heaven came down upon them, neither did the earth open her mouth to swallow them up; then we all forsook him and fled.

CHAPTER XXIX

THOUGH we had so basely fled from our Master, yet away from him we were not able to rest. Therefore we followed after the guard down the mountain, even into Jerusalem, and mingled with the concourse that was gathered together before the doors of the High Priest's house. Near me was John the son of Zebedee; who, having some acquaintance in the household of the High Priest, gained access into the house; and Peter also with him. But I remained without; and I conversed with the people, making as if I were no Galilean, but a citizen of Jerusalem. For I perceived that the most part of the multitude were men of Jerusalem, some indeed citizens, but the greater part servants of the chief priests, and money-changers, and cattle-dealers; who had been gathered together of set purpose by the enemies of Jesus.

But when I asked one why he hated Jesus (for the man had declared aloud that he trusted that day to see Jesus on the cross), he replied, "Because this Galilean marreth our trade, and taketh away our living; for behold, these three days men buy no beasts for sacrifice from my stalls in the temple." And another said, "Yea, and he maketh no secret that he purposeth to destroy our religion, and change our customs which Moses appointed : for he saith that he will destroy this temple, and boasteth, forsooth, that he will raise up another equal to this in three days." Now this saying of Jesus (which indeed he had not said, for I have set down his words exactly above) had been carried from mouth to mouth throughout Jerusalem ; and the chief priests had everywhere caused it to be rumoured that the intent of Jesus was to destroy the temple with fire during that Passover. Therefore the hearts of many of the devout and sober people were turned away from Jesus.

After we had waited about two hours or something less, a certain Scribe came up to a servant of the chief priests, who was conversing with me ; and the Scribe asked the man concerning the multitude, for what cause it was gathered together : and the man said, "To see the false prophet, named Jesus of Nazareth, who is to be condemned to death." "Nay," said the other, "then thou losest thy labour. For if a man be tried for his life, he may not be tried on the day before the Sabbath ; for the Law alloweth appeal on the morrow. Therefore if, as thou sayest, Jesus of Nazareth is yonder being tried, it cannot be that he is tried for his life." Hereat I rejoiced greatly, for I bethought myself that it was even so as the Scribe had said, wherefore it could not be that Jesus was to be tried for his life. But when I drew nigh unto them (for the press had parted us for an instant) : "I give thee a yea for thy nay," said the other, "for thou knowest the Law, but I know my master Annas ; and he is not the man to allow a little matter of a day to stand in his way; nor to permit the booths and shops in the temple (whence cometh profit to the priests) to be destroyed by false prophets and Galileans to boot." Then indeed my heart misgave me that it was to be no trial, but only a murder.

Just then one came down the steps leading from the High Priest's house, and the people ran together towards him to know what had been done. He stood still, and made a gesture that they should keep silence; and then in a clear voice he spake to the multitude and said, "The council hath pronounced that Jesus of Nazareth is a man of death." Hereupon there was a general shout, for all knew that to be "a man of death" meant to be condemned to die: and straightway a cry arose, "Stone him, stone him; bring him out that we may stone him." But the man checked them that shouted, saying that the accused must first be led to the judgment seat of the procurator, Pontius Pilate, for without his judgment it was not lawful that any should be put to death.

Then my heart revived a little again; for it seemed there was still some hope. But seeing Simon Peter come forth from the High Priest's house, I pressed through the throng if perchance I might come at him, to ask him touching the trial, and what the witnesses had testified, and how Jesus had borne himself. But Peter seemed not to see me; and even when I called him by name he would not hear me. At last, by dint of striving, I came near him in the throng and caught hold of his garment, and stayed him by force. Then, indeed, he stayed; but as he turned round and his face looked upon my face, behold, I saw in his countenance shame, and remorse, and despair; and he assayed to speak, but could not, and wrung my hand in silence. Then waving me off that I should not any more stay him, he hasted away, and I durst not follow him; for it was evident to me that the prophecy of Jesus had been fulfilled, and that Simon Peter had denied our Master.

I turned back into the throng, for my intent was to have remained standing without, till such time as Jesus came forth. But I heard the servant of the High Priest say to one of his acquaintance that the procurator was not one to have his sleep broken by business at so early an hour; "Therefore," said he to his companion, "go home to thy house, and warm thee, if thou wilt; for there will be naught to see these three hours." Then it came into my mind that the mother of Jesus, and likewise Mary Magdalene, and the other women, were all this while in Bethany, neither knew they aught of that which had befallen Jesus; and it was fit they should be told. Therefore I went forth by the gate of Kidron and up the Mount of Olives even to Bethany; and there I writ a few words, telling what had befallen, and left it in the hand of one of the servants of the house; for to go in myself and to tell the tale, and to look upon their sorrow, I durst not do it. This done, I hasted back for to go down to the house of the procurator, making sure to have arrived thither long before they had made an end of the trial. But when I was gone but two or three hundred paces from Bethany, one of the women ran after me with tears and lamentations, beseeching me to return and to tell them all; and she constrained me. So I returned and told them all; and the memory of their lamenting remaineth with me unto this day.

Thus passed a long time, a very long time as it seemed to me; but at last I withdrew myself from them perforce, and hasted down the mountain. But when I was come to the palace, behold the trial was over; and I saw the rear part of a moving throng, and one told me that they were taking the prisoner to be crucified at Golgotha. Then my heart within me seemed to burst; but though I was faint before with long watching and weariness, I was not faint now, but sped after the throng. Many times did I strive to press in amidst them, if perchance Jesus might look but once upon me, or I might see his face, or so much as catch a sight of his garment as he walked; and I wept and was ready to curse myself that I had gone from the High Priest's door before I had seen my Master's face. For now I could not see him, no, nor anything of him, save now and then the cross, which, as they told me, he was carrying upon his shoulders; but I heard the men in the crowd saying what insults had been offered to him, and how he had been scourged and mocked and spit upon, decked with a crown of thorns and a sceptre of reed; and I was as one distracted, in whom there is no power of thought.

By this time we had passed out of the city through the western gate, and the fore part of the multitude was come to the place of execution; and they that went before me came now to a stand; and I saw the cross lifted up for an instant, to the intent, as it seemed, that it might be laid upon the ground; and one near me said, "Now they are making ready." Then I gnashed my teeth, for I could do naught else; but I was ready to curse God (blessed is He), for I knew right well what that "making ready" meant; and a deep silence fell on all the crowd; and I could hear the blows of the hammer upon the nails; and every man held his breath, if perchance there might come the sound of a shriek or a groan. But no such sound came to the place where we stood.

Presently arose a very loud shouting from the multitude that stood before me, and behold, the cross was reared up so that the top thereof was a little above the heads of the people; and from afar off I could just discern Jesus. But I saw not his face; for his head was bowed forward and his hair, hanging over his forehead, hid his eyes. But when I thrust myself forward to have approached nearer, I could not for the press. At the same time there rang in upon mine ears a very storm of mocking and reviling and cursing against Jesus from all the bystanders, yea, even from the women and little children (with such a venom of slander had the Chief Priests poisoned the minds of the people); insomuch that I seemed to stand alone among a host of the children of Satan; neither could I endure any longer to behold such a sight, amid such beholders, and to be of no avail. Wherefore I became as one possessed; and I turned my back upon the cross and forced my way out of the crowd; the people calling after me and mocking me, and plucking me back by the cloak as I fled.

But even as my body fled away, my soul was drawn back unto the cross; and I feared to go back lest I should see Jesus, and I feared to go forward lest I should never see him. And these two fears were as two devils that possessed me, driving me hither and thither about all the hills and valleys of that neighbourhood for the space of two hours or more ; and during all that time the fear to go back was the stronger. But about the eighth hour of the day, as I wandered like unto one dreaming, not knowing whither I went, behold, I stood on the top of a certain hill ; and thereon was a flock of sheep quietly pasturing, and the shepherd-boy piping to them, and sunlight was all around. But casting mine eyes downward, I saw very far off, under a dark cloud, the multitude still standing round Jesus, and three crosses in the midst (for other two were crucified with him) ; and all in so small a space that it seemed no larger than a man's hand.

Then came my misery back to me with a shock ; and it seemed a wonderful and an horrible thing that in a little corner of the earth the Almighty should suffer such a one as Jesus of Nazareth to be slain on the cross : and yet, behold, the sun shone and the shepherds piped to their sheep, and there was peace upon the mountains, and all as if nothing strange were happening below. But soon these and all other thoughts were swallowed up in one remembrance, namely, that if I would see Jesus alive, not many minutes now remained unto me ; for the sun was sinking towards the west, and I knew that he could not be suffered to remain upon the cross when the Sabbath began ; for that had been against our customs. Therefore I ran down with exceeding speed, and came again to Golgotha about the tenth hour.

When I was now within two or three furlongs of the place, I perceived that some of the people were already coming away ; for the Passover was near at hand, so that they must needs go to their homes. So I ran on, and came to the place where the multitude was standing. And because the throng was diminished, I was now able to come very much nearer to the midst of the multitude, not more than a stone's cast from the cross. But alas for the sight I saw! For though I was so close, I could not discern anything of Jesus as he once had been; because his head was bowed forward even more than before, and moreover there was an unwonted darkness over all the place. The people were very still, nor was there now any more sound of cursing or mocking; for of them that still remained round the cross some were the friends of Jesus, and others had been greatly moved (so it was told me afterwards) by the manner in which he had borne himself upon the cross; insomuch that even the soldiers which kept guard mocked him no more, but stood watching in silence. But I came forward to the furthest that I might, and placed myself where haply he might see me; and I would fain have called unto him; but I durst not, lest I should trouble him, for he was very still. But when I was now come so close unto him that I might almost discern his features in spite of the darkness, behold it was as if a trembling ran through all his limbs, and he raised his head a little, and a voice came forth, which, whoso heard, could not forget for ever: "My God, my God, why hast thou forsaken me?" Then there was another cry exceeding long and loud, and a second trembling running through all the limbs even to the neck and face; and then a stiffness as of death.

Now up to the very last I had not given up all hope that Jesus might yet come down from the cross, shewing forth some mighty work worthy of a Messiah; nor did I indeed know how much hope I had had, till this moment wherein all hope perished. But now, when I turned myself to go away from the cross and to leave Jesus for ever, all things seemed ended, and I felt as one alone in the world; yea, I knew not whether there were a God, or whether I myself lived, or all life were not a dream. Thus I went forward, as one in a trance; when on a sudden I heard the voice of Hezekiah the Scribe: "Art thou not yet convinced of thy folly? Behold, it is written that thou shouldest not put thy trust in any child of man. For when the breath of man goeth forth, he shall turn again to his earth, and then all his thoughts perish; even as this thy master, the false prophet, hath perished. But blessed is he that hath the God of Jacob for his help, who keepeth His promises for ever. But thy master, how keepeth he his promises? Unless perchance," and here he lowered his voice and looked jealously at me, " unless (as is reported to us) ye Galileans hope to steal his body from the grave and so to feign that he is risen; but that shall not be. For though your patron Joseph of Arimathea may have his will to-day, yet will we take good order that we have our will to-morrow. For the body of a false prophet deserveth not honourable burial."

I could endure his words no longer, but ran past him as one mad. But, when I was now rid of his presence, passing back into the city by the western gate, my mind ran on all such things as I had done with Jesus on the day before, and my feet turned of themselves toward the house where we had kept the Passover together. Thence, but still as one in a dream, scarce knowing what I did, I bent my way towards the gate of the valley of Kidron. Here I was musing how, but yesterday, in this very place, I had walked by the side of Jesus, even at his right hand, and how the touch of his arm had held me up in my stumbling; when behold, I started back as if I had seen a spirit. For the voice of one close to me in the twilight whispered with an hissing sound, "He is not dead." I looked, and behold, Judas stood before me. His face was pale and his eyes glared, and passion so wrought his features that they moved and quivered, as if against his will, like unto the features of one possessed by Satan. When I drew back from him, at first he would have stayed me; but seeing that I loathed him, he also drew back and said, "Nay, be not afraid, I cannot betray another. But he is not dead. Hast thou not seen him?" I marvelled at him, but said nothing, only shaking my head. Then Judas replied, "Think not that I have slain him; he liveth: he hunteth me to death; these three times have I seen him. I have not slain him. Why then doth he yet hunt me? But thou, thou didst love him, be thou at peace with me." Saying these words, he came forward again to have taken me by the hand; but I could not. Then he turned away and laughed such a laugh as I pray God I may never hear again. But as he departed, he cried aloud, "Thou rememberest his words, 'It were better for him that he had never been born': verily he was a prophet." Then he laughed again, even such another laugh as before; and he cursed the God that had made him. With that he went his way, and I saw him no more.

For a while I stood where I was, as if in a trance, almost expecting that the words of Judas should prove true, and that Jesus should come forth to me out of the air around me. Then I passed through the gate of Kidron; and, crossing the brook, I began to go out by the way which leadeth to Bethany. But ever as I went up the mountain, I pondered over the words of Judas, "He is not dead, I have seen him:" for I could not forget them, nor put them away from my mind. And behold, whithersoever I looked in the twilight, all things bore witness unto Jesus and seemed to say the same words, "We have seen him. He is not dead." For if I looked back at the city gates, then I remembered how Jesus had lately passed through them in triumph; and if I looked on the road before me, then every tree and rock seemed to testify that Jesus had but now been there again and again, in his passing between Bethany and the city; and at one place he had spoken a certain parable: at another, he had sat down and rested; or at a third, we had asked him certain questions and he had answered them. Thus the whole of the mountain and all things thereon seemed to cry aloud with one consent, "He is not dead"; but my heart cried back again, "Nay, but he is dead indeed."

When at last I came in my wanderings nigh to the top of the mount, even to the stone whereon Jesus had sat down in the midst of the disciples and had prophesied of his coming, then could I no longer refrain myself; but I threw myself on the ground in a passion of tears and sobbings, beating my breast and rending my garments. And when I desired to cry unto the Lord in my agony, behold, the words of Jesus on the cross came into my mouth; and if I tried to fashion some other prayer, no other words would come to me, but I could do naught but repeat them over and over again, crying unto the Lord and saying, " Why hast Thou forsaken him ? Why hast Thou forsaken him ? " So speaking, I scarce refrained from doing even as Judas had done, so as to curse the day wherein I was born ; and I became again as one distraught. But after a time (but how long a time I know not) a darkness came down upon mine eyes, and all things swam around me, and I fell to the ground as one without life.

When I came to myself, behold, I lay upon my back and looked upward, and the moon was shining high in the heavens above me. So I thought how the same moon had shone down with the same brightness yester-night upon my Master in Gethsemane. "And now where is he ?" I ceased from that thought, and went back in my mind to thoughts of the past. Then I remembered what a splendour, even such as I now saw, had shone upon our Master's face when he came down from Mount Hermon, and when he came up from Jericho to Bethany, and also when of late he gave us the bread and wine at our last supper together. Also there came into my mind the words that he had spoken, when this brightness had been upon his countenance : how he had then prophesied, and more than once, that he should be slain ; but we had never believed him. Yet his words had come to pass. Then I asked within myself how it was that Jesus had foreseen his own death and prophesied it so oft, yet had never been dismayed nor even disturbed by the thought thereof; and I remembered that whensoever he had spoken of his death, he had spoken also of a certain rising again, or coming : and I said aloud,

"If Jesus prophesied his death truly, why might he not also prophesy truly concerning his coming again?"

But against this hope there set themselves those last words which had come from the mouth of Jesus on the cross, "My God, my God, why hast thou forsaken me?" Now these words are the first words, and as it were the prelude, of one of our psalms. So I began to repeat to myself the words of the psalm; which beginneth with sadness, yea even from the depths of sorrow, but these words follow afterwards: "I will declare thy name unto my brethren: in the midst of the congregation will I praise thee. For he hath not despised nor abhorred the affliction of the afflicted; neither hath he hid his face from him, but when he cried unto him he heard." So I wondered whether Jesus, in speaking those last words, had in his mind all the words of the psalm, and "Perchance," I said, "in saying the first words, he signified (in his sore weakness when the breath was departing from him) that he desired to say the whole; for the first words are but as a title to the whole. Wherefore, perchance, beneath the sense of the forsaking, there was a deeper sense that God did not despise the affliction of the afflicted." Then I mused again concerning the words of the Psalm, and especially on these, "When he cried unto him, he heard." And I looked up to the moon and the stars in heaven, which are the work of the hand of God, and I asked whether it was possible that the Maker of so beautiful an order in heaven should suffer disorder to prevail upon the earth; and my heart said that it could not prevail for ever. "Therefore," said I, "God must needs have heard Jesus of Nazareth when he cried unto Him. Yea, though He seemed not to hear, yet must He have heard indeed. Yea, even though Jesus be dead, yea, even though Jesus be not the Messiah, yet surely the Lord must have heard Jesus; for not to have heard him, would have been not to be God."

Then rose I up and stood and stretched out my hands in prayer unto the Lord with whom all things are possible, that He would shew forth His mercy upon me; and behold, when I tried to pray, my lips would shape forth no other prayer, but that He would bring back Jesus unto us, even though it were for a moment of time, that we might look upon him and know that he still lived. And at one moment I rebuked myself because the thing seemed impossible; but the next moment that prayer rose up again, and no other. But when I had prayed, I lay down again, for I was very weary; and because I was now more at peace within myself, there came upon me a sweet sleep.

In my sleep I dreamed; and the Lord sent unto me a vision of the night, whereof the former part was like unto the vision which I had had the night before, but the latter part was different. For again, methought, I saw Jesus standing on the top of a mountain in great glory; and albeit his face was like the face of him that hath passed through much tribulation, yet did the glory prevail over the sorrow, and he rejoiced as one triumphing over Satan and Death. As I looked, methought Jesus was lifted up in a chariot from the mountain towards the clouds, and angels accompanied him as he rode upward; and a sound of solemn music came down from above to greet him. The heavens opened, yea, even to the seventh heaven, and there appeared the likeness of a throne on the right hand of the Majesty on high; and ten thousands of thousands of saints were about the throne, with palms in their hands, singing hosannas unto the Son of David. But even as the chariot rose higher and higher, the music waxed louder and fuller; till at the last, when the chariot was now nigh unto the throne, behold all the harps in heaven rang out hosannas with such a peal of praise as made me start out of my vision; and I awoke, and it was a dream.

CHAPTER XXX

WHEN I awoke, it was now hard upon the third hour of the day, and the sun from behind Mount Olivet was shining brightly down upon the city. All things below were full of beauty and glory, nor would a stranger have known that the stain of innocent blood was upon the place; so fair shone all the city rejoicing in the Sabbath sun. When I looked thereon, the memory of my dream vanished, even as the mists which I saw rolling upward from the side of the mountain and vanishing into the pure air. My misery returned upon me again; and I felt once more alone and without God in the world. But I resolved to go up straightway to Bethany, if perchance I might there find the apostles in the house of Mary and Martha. When I was come thither, I found them all, save Judas; and I entered in and sat with them in silence; and for a long time we neither prayed nor spake together, nor so much as lamented aloud; but there we sat speechless and comfortless; for the hand of the Lord was heavy upon us.

At the last spake certain of the women, saying that they had brought spices, such as are used in the embalming of bodies, and that they purposed to go early on the morrow for to embalm the body of Jesus. Then I asked where he was buried; and they told me, "in a garden of Joseph of Arimathea, nigh unto the place of crucifixion." After that, I asked whether any had stood near, and in view of the cross while he was suffering; for I had been thrust away by the crowd. Then John the son of Zebedee answered and said that he had been nigh, and that Jesus had borne all the anguish with a marvellous constancy. He told me also of certain other words which Jesus had spoken while he was on the cross, and that a soldier, after his death, had wounded his side with a spear; but when I asked him whether he had heard Jesus speak also those words which I had myself heard, namely that God had forsaken him, then John said nothing, but only moved his head as if to say that it was so; and the rest also were silent, for we feared to think on those words.

After we had all thus sat silent for a while, one of the women began to speak again and to say that all things had happened according to the words of Jesus; for he had said that he should be slain; and he had blessed Mary, in that she had anointed his body for the burial. Then another of the women began to bring to our mind how Jesus had long ago prophesied that the time should come when we should desire to see one of the days of the Son of man, and should not find it. And another spake how, at another time, when we were in the country round about Hermon, he had prophesied that he should be slain; therefore, said she, he was a true prophet. But Thomas made mention of the saying of Hosea, whereof Jesus had oftentimes been used to speak, "Come and let us return unto the Lord, for he hath torn and he will heal us; he hath smitten, and he will bind us up. After two days will he revive us; in the third day he will raise us up, and we shall live in his sight." Then said Thomas, "A part of the sayings of Jesus hath indeed come to pass"; and he added no more. But all we that were in that chamber sitting together, knew what Thomas had in his mind to say (for it was in our minds also), namely, that the rest of the words of Jesus were not to be fulfilled. So again we sat silent; for indeed our souls were wholly given up to meditating on those words of Jesus, "after two days he will revive us"; and each knew that the others were meditating on the same; yet durst none of us say so much as a word, nor so much as confess to himself that the words could import anything now; for about that matter we feared even to hope.

But by degrees our tongues were loosed, and we began to speak more freely concerning the goodness of Jesus, how exceeding gentle he was at all times to the young and simple, and to the poor and oppressed; how full of peace and cheerfulness; how thoughtful for others, how forgetful of himself. Then we spake of his marvellous power in the forgiving of sins, and in the healing of diseases, and in the casting out of unclean spirits. And one said that with all these faculties he joined a marvellous grace of modesty and humility, so that no child could carry himself with less of pride or ostentation. "Yea," said another, "and yet withal, though he were never so simple and humble, he ever spake of himself, none the less, as the haven and refuge for men, saying such words as these unto us, 'Come unto me, and I will give you rest,' and again, 'Take my yoke upon you:' moreover he bade us take his voice as our Law in the stead of the Law of

Moses, saying, 'It was said to them of old, do this, but I say unto you, do that.' Therefore are we of all men most miserable in that, having received from God the very source of light and life, now we are deprived thereof." Then Peter said, "Yea, verily we have none else to whom we can go, for Jesus alone hath the words of eternal life; and without him we have no life." But said another, "If God be good, how could it be that He should have forsaken Jesus, so that he cried aloud, 'My God, my God, why hast thou forsaken me?'" Then Nathanael spake and said (the very thought that was in my heart also) that perchance Jesus used those words, desiring briefly to pour forth all the trouble and all the trust of his heart; for, said he, "These words are as it were the title of the psalm, and the psalm beginneth with trouble, but it endeth with trust." To this the rest agreed that it might be so; but we all felt within ourselves that this was small comfort: for we needed not only to think that it might be so, but to know that it was so.

Then one said that the Kingdom of God and the Redemption of Sion were now as far off as ever. But Mary of Magdala said with great vehemency, "that she mourned not for the Redemption of Sion, but because the breath of life was taken out of the world, for without Jesus there was no more truth nor righteousness. He trusted in God, would not God deliver him? Was he not the Son of the living God? If, therefore, the Father live, how can the Son be dead?" She added yet other words still more passionate, as if God were no God unless Jesus were restored to life. We chid her, and would have stayed her speech: for, though she did indeed express the very feelings of our hearts, yet were we afraid to see them put into plain words, and besides, we dreaded the pain of new hopes. For to hope that we should look again on Jesus, and afterwards to fail of that hope, had been to have had Jesus snatched from us a second time.

By this time the sun had set, and the women began to make ready the spices for the embalming. But I (because it had been reported to certain of the disciples that the chief priests purposed to set a guard round the tomb) determined to go down that I might see whether the tomb were beset with guards or no, and whether the women could have easy access to it. I easily found the place in the light of the moon, and it was even as the women had said; for the garden of Joseph lay not more than three stones' cast from the place where Jesus had been crucified. So I stood for a while looking on the stone, which was at the mouth of the tomb, and no man else was in the garden. But while I stood near the tomb, very nigh unto the mouth thereof, I heard a sound on my right hand; and when I turned round, behold, a light; and the lights grew many as I looked, and I perceived that there were torches approaching. So I went back some distance, and still the torches came nearer; and the men were, as it seemed to me, servants of the chief priests, but I discerned also the face of Hezekiah the Scribe; and they all stood round the tomb, and I also stood and watched them from afar off, to see what they would do. But I could not remain; for they sent out watchers on all sides calling to one another in a circle, like unto men keeping sentinel, for to spy whether any one were near.

Then I fled perforce and in haste; and though I fled straightway, yet could I not contrive but the watchers perceived me and chased after me and went near to take me. But I escaped out of their hands, and went up to Bethany to bear word unto the women. And when the women heard these things they were sore distressed. Howbeit they resolved that in any case they would go forth to the tomb very early on the morrow.

But before we lay down to rest that night, we spake again of Jesus, and concerning all that he had said and done; and we continued our discourse late into the night, and were loth to break off; for while we discoursed together of former times, we seemed to have Jesus again in the midst of us. But at the end, when we were now ceasing, the Spirit of the Lord fell upon Mary of Magdala, and she lifted up her voice and sang as the Lord moved her, and the words were even from the psalm whereof we had been but now speaking, while discoursing concerning the forsaking of Jesus by God. Now the song describeth the suffering of the Messiah. Therefore when she came in her singing to these words, "They pierced my hands and my feet; I may tell all my bones; they stand staring and looking upon me. They part my garments among them, and cast lots upon my vesture": then we wept, remembering the sufferings of Jesus. But when she sang the next words, "But be not thou far from me, O Lord. Thou art my succour, haste thee to help me. Deliver my soul from the sword, my darling also from the power of the dog. Save me from the lion's mouth : Thou hast heard me from among the horns of the unicorns. I will declare thy name unto my brethren; in the midst of the congregation will I praise thee. For he hath not despised, nor abhorred the low estate of the poor; he hath not hid his face from him; but when he called unto him he heard him": then we wept no longer, but we marvelled while we looked on her, and while we hearkened to the words of her singing: for she sang as one taught of God, so that we durst not stay her; yet we thought in our hearts, "Notwithstanding when Jesus called unto Him, He heard him not." And when we thought on this we besought her that she would cease.

Howbeit she ceased not, but began to sing yet another psalm, a part of the great Hallel; even the very words that Jesus himself had sung to us on the night before he suffered. And the other women joined with her, and they sang so that the sound thereof pierced to our very souls. Then could we endure it no longer, but covered our faces with our hands. But they continued singing, "I shall not die, but live, and declare the works of the Lord. The Lord hath chastened and corrected me, but he hath not given me over unto death. Thou art my God, and I will thank thee; thou art my God, and I will praise thee."

Now while they were singing, I had closed mine eyes; and lo, there rose up before me a vision of the upper room where we had supped together with Jesus on the night that he was betrayed: and I seemed to see the face of Jesus himself; yea, though I was not asleep nor in a trance, yet did I see Jesus himself sitting again as if at meat with us. Therefore was I loth to open mine eyes; for I feared that, when I opened them, I should no longer see what I saw. But when the women had made an end of singing, then opened I mine eyes, half expecting that it might prove no vision, and that Jesus would be sitting before me in the midst of us. But I saw nothing; nor were the women any longer with us, for they were gone forth into another chamber to finish their preparations for the embalming. For they desired to visit the sepulchre very early in the morning, and it was by this time the third watch of the night. About the space of an hour, I remained in the chamber with the rest: then I heard the footsteps of the women as they passed forth from the house. I tried to sleep, but could not; for ever in my mind was present the thought of Jesus in the tomb, waiting the approach of the women to embalm him. So my heart went forth with the women upon their errand, and I reckoned over the time and said ever and anon, "Now they are come down from the mountain; by this time they are nigh to Golgotha; now they are in the garden; now they are at the tomb." Then I saw before mine eyes the women embracing the dead limbs of our Master. "And now," said I, "the stone is rolled away and they have entered in : they weep, but he answereth not, neither heareth; his eyes move not nor make any answer to their eyes; they clasp his hands, but his hands clasp not theirs again."

When I thought on these things I arose in sore extremity nigh unto despair, and went up to the house-top. Above the mountains of Moab, to the east, there was a faint token of dawn. I thought of the coming day, and I loathed it; for without Jesus the light seemed unto me as darkness. Moreover when I strove to pray, Satan tempted me very sorely, so that I could not pray : for I said, "Behold I am without Jesus : but God without Jesus is to me as no God." Then fell I flat upon my face and wrestled with Satan in prayer, and I besought the Lord again and again that He would give Jesus back to us, yea, though it were but to look on him for one moment, that we might be assured that all was well with him. How long I prayed I know not, but it seemed to me many hours; and sometimes I stood in my praying and watched the dawn growing brighter; and even as the dawn grew, my fears and doubts grew with it; but at other times I lay prostrate and shut out the light. So at last the sky began to brighten towards sunrise; and still I was crying unto the Lord from the depths, according as it is written, "I wait for the Lord; my soul doth wait, and in his word do I hope. My soul waiteth for the Lord more than they that watch for the morning, more, I say, than they that watch for the morning."

Now while I lay grovelling in the very deepest of the depths, beseeching the Lord to destroy me if I might not have peace, behold, a sound as of many feet below, without the house, and then a knocking, exceeding loud; and one asked from within, "Who is there?" And the answer came piercing the air, "HE IS RISEN! HE IS RISEN! JESUS IS RISEN FROM THE DEAD!" Now at first I thought that the voice was the voice of an angel; but when I considered, and heard how answer was made, and the door forthwith opened, and a sound as of feet entering, then straightway I knew that it was the voice of one of the women come back from the sepulchre. Immediately, therefore, going down, I found all the household stirring, and the women returned, and all the disciples gathered together, and standing round the women, questioning them, and listening to their words.

Then the women told us how they had gone down to Golgotha, even to the tomb; and when Mary of Magdala was now nigh, even at the mouth of the tomb (for she walked somewhat before the rest), behold, the great stone at the mouth of the tomb was rolled away. Then she called aloud for despair, and her companions hasted to her; but when they were now come to her, as she was even now adventuring to enter into the tomb, of a sudden Mary cried out again, saying, "Behold, an angel of the Lord!" And lo, there appeared to them (even to all the women and not to Mary only) an angel clothed in white; and they all heard a voice which said, "He is not here, but is risen." And, said Mary Magdalene, the voice added that we were to return to Galilee, and there we should see him; but another of the women said that the voice seemed to her also to speak of Galilee, but she heard not those other words which Mary heard.[1] Also some of the women had seen two angels, but others only one. But as concerning this at least, all the women were agreed, namely, that they had seen a vision of angels, and that they had heard a voice which cried out, "He is not here, he is risen."

Now when we had spent much time in questioning and hearing the women, I desired to go down forthwith to the sepulchre, for to see it with mine own eyes: but the women stayed me, and said, "It were better to wait; for Peter and John are already gone down." So I waited, but in sore trouble of mind; for at one time

[1] See Note IV.

I believed, but at another time I doubted. For as concerning the tomb, it came into my mind that it was like enough that the servants of the chief priests (whom I had seen in the garden during the night) might haply have broken open the tomb and stolen away the body; but then on the other side there was the vision of the angels and the voice; and besides, it was being borne in upon my mind, and upon the minds of most of us, that Jesus must indeed arise from the dead, for thus should both the words of the prophets be fulfilled, and his own words also; but otherwise they could not be fulfilled. So I waited till John and Peter should return.

But while I was still waiting and marvelling that they tarried so long, there came in certain of the disciples; these were not Galileans, but abode in Jerusalem, and they asked us whether we had seen aught that night. We said " No." Then said one of them to us, " Last night, in returning from beholding that which came to pass at Golgotha, about two hours after sunset, Miriam, my sister's daughter, saw her father (who hath now been buried these six weeks) risen from the grave and standing wrapped in the grave-clothes near her bed; moreover two other women of mine acquaintance saw the bodies of their little children, fresh and blooming as if they were verily alive; and another, a certain young man named Mattathias (but he is not known to me), is said to have seen his brother, who hath been buried more than a year, standing as if alive, so that he even approached him and called him by name. And other wonderful sights have appeared to very many." And his companions confirmed all his words, saying, "The like also we ourselves have heard."

While we marvelled at their words, the two disciples, Peter and John, came into the chamber. But they had seen nothing; only the stone rolled away, even as the women had said, and the tomb void of the body. Then one of the disciples brought again to our minds how that Jesus, even before his death, had bidden us go into Galilee, saying that he would there manifest himself unto us; and when we questioned Mary of Magdala, she constantly affirmed that the voice of the angels was to the same effect. Therefore I resolved that I would set forth that very day to go to Capernaum. For a hope was now waxing strong within me that I should after all see Jesus again. So I set out without delay, with certain other of the disciples; howbeit the greater part would stay in Jerusalem yet a few days.

CHAPTER XXXI

WHEN we came to Capernaum, on the evening of the third day, we spent the rest of that day in praying and praising God; and we fasted and besought the Lord that we might see Jesus according to His promise. And so we spent the next day likewise. But on the morrow, which was the fifth day of the week, it being now a full week from the time when Jesus had broken bread with us on the night when he was betrayed, we determined that we also would break bread together, even as he had commanded us, in memory of him. And about the sixth hour of the day, when we were seated together in an upper room praying to the Lord, there came in Peter and James and other of the disciples, but now returned from Jerusalem. And Peter related how the Lord Jesus himself had appeared to him; and James said that he also had seen the Lord Jesus. Now at first I feared lest it might be the will of the Lord that Jesus should reveal himself to none save the Twelve; but I understood that Mary of Magdala also had seen him.

Then two other of the disciples, and they not of the number of the Twelve, related to me how Jesus had appeared to them also, at the breaking of bread. For they had walked forth together conversing much about Jesus of Nazareth, and about the hopes which they had had that he should have redeemed Israel. "And so it was," said one of them (for I will set down the story as it was told me by one of the disciples, whose name was Cleophas), "that we had just made mention between ourselves of the voice and the vision of angels; making mention thereof as of an idle tale. And it was the hour of prayer. And because of the extremity of our sorrow we both fell on our faces, and poured out all our desire before the Lord, beseeching Him for the Redemption of Israel. Then the Lord Jesus had compassion on us and came to us. For when we rose up from praying, we heard a voice from the Lord Jesus himself, chiding us for our folly and slowness of heart in not believing all that the prophets had spoken; for that it was needful that Christ should have suffered these things, and thus to enter into his glory : and lo, at an instant the whole of the truth of the Scriptures lay before our eyes, and all the meaning of the words of the Lord Jesus withal.

"As we went forward, our hearts burned within us while the Lord revealed unto us the Scriptures and all the meaning of his prophecies ; but still our eyes were not opened to discern that he himself was present with us ; yet we perceived that there was a divine presence near us. But when the sun was setting and we drew nigh unto the village whither we were going, our hearts became faint and dull, as if the presence were departing from us. Therefore we knelt down once more and besought the Lord that he would continue to us the strength of his presence. Notwithstanding even now our eyes were not opened that we should discern him.

"But in the evening, it being now late, when we were sat down to eat bread together, our hearts being full of the presence of Jesus, we brake the bread and blessed it, even as Jesus had broken and blessed, and then we said aloud, according to his word, 'Behold, the body of the Lord;' and lo, at that word the cloud was removed from our eyes, and first my companion, and then I also, discerned Jesus on the other side of the table, reclining as if at meat (even as he reclined when he last brake bread with us), and with his hands stretched out as if in the breaking and blessing of bread. Now for a while (but I knew not how long, except that it was not very long), Jesus remained with his hands still outstretched as at the first, looking at us with a very loving countenance, but saying naught; and we sat upright as men astonied and speechless, and not able to move for astonishment; but when we rose up for to have embraced him, straightway Jesus vanished out of our sight."

All we that were in the chamber rejoiced when we heard Cleophas saying these things. Only Thomas believed not; for the thing seemed unto him too beautiful to be verily true, and he said, "If I believe that Jesus is risen from the dead, and afterwards find that it is not so, then shall my misery be increased twofold: therefore will I believe not." And he added moreover, "Except I shall see in his hands the print of the nails and put my finger in the print of the nails and thrust my hand into his side, I will not believe." We were grieved at the words of Thomas: howbeit none rebuked him, for we knew that he spake out of his exceeding love of Jesus. But we besought him to break bread with us that evening, according to the commandment of Jesus.

So about one hour after sunset, we were assembled all together in the upper room (it was a room in the house of Peter, wherein Jesus was wont to sit at meat with us in past times), and Thomas also was with us. But the door was shut and made fast for fear of spies; whom the Scribes in Capernaum had begun to set over us for to watch us. When all things were now ready, first we sang a psalm, even the same psalm that Jesus had sung on the same night in the week before, when we kept the Passover together. Then Simon Peter offered up prayers and praises to God, and made mention of the comfortable words of the Lord Jesus, how he had said that he would never leave us nor forsake us, but that wheresoever two or three were gathered together in his name, there would he be present among them. Last of all he spake of the testament of the Lord Jesus, how he had bidden us break bread and drink wine in memory of him, that we might partake of his body and his blood. Then began Simon Peter to break bread and to reach it to each of us, and at the same time he said, "This is the body of the Lord." But behold, in the midst of his giving of the bread, Peter made a sudden pause and was silent, and his eyes were fixed, and he gazed steadfastly upon the place which had been left empty at the table; for Jesus had been wont to sit there in times past, wherefore in that place durst no man sit. Then I turned round hastily to look, and behold, Jesus was there; as clear to view as ever I had seen him in this life, only very pale, and there were the nail-prints in his hands, and methought there was a wound in his side; and the brightness of his love and compassion passed sensibly forth from his eyes to mine, and all my soul went out to him as I looked; but I could in no wise speak, nor did I desire to speak; for I had thoughts deeper than all words.

Now not a hand moved, not a word was spoken: and there was such a silence as if one could hear and count the footsteps of time; neither could I turn mine eyes from Jesus till I heard Thomas weeping beside me; but he threw himself on the ground, stretching out his hands to Jesus, and reproaching himself for his faithlessness; and at the same time, pressing the bread, even the body of the Lord which he held in his hand, he cried out saying, " My hand hath touched; yea I have touched; I believe, I believe." But neither he nor any of us durst adventure to go to that part of the table where Jesus sat; but when I looked again, behold his hand was stretched out (even as the two disciples had described their vision of Jesus) as if he brake and blessed the bread that was his body; and Thomas also heard a voice (but I heard not the voice) saying that he was to touch with his hand, according to his own saying, and to be no more faithless, but believing. After this Jesus vanished from our eyes, and neither in his coming nor in his departing was the door opened, but it remained shut·fast; whereat we all marvelled.

From henceforth old things seemed to pass away, and all things became new unto us. For whithersoever we went, and whatsoever we did, we knew that we had the presence of Jesus with us, even when we saw him not. But oftentimes he revealed himself to us, and we saw him plainly; and this too not only in the house and sitting at meat (albeit he oftentimes, and methinks most times, revealed himself to us in the house), but sometimes also abroad in the fields, or even on the lake. Yea I myself was once present when a storm came down upon us on the lake, and the winds sent up such waves as were like to have covered our boat, and we cried unto Jesus in our terror; and behold, the storm ceased, and the clouds parted asunder, and we saw Jesus walking on the waves and stilling them under his feet. And to others of the disciples he appeared at another time, when they had been toiling the night long at fishing, and had caught nothing; and he gave unto them a draught of fishes exceeding any that they had ever before taken.

But the most of the manifestations of Jesus were vouchsafed to us when we brake bread together; after which manner also he revealed himself unto James, as I have heard. For James had taken an oath that he would neither eat nor drink until he had seen Jesus risen from the dead. Therefore on the night after the vision of angels which had been seen by the women, James was in the house at Bethany with Simon Peter and John, and the table was spread for supper; but James would not eat. Then suddenly Jesus was seen sitting in the midst of them, breaking bread and blessing it, and bidding James to partake thereof.[1] But, as I have said, Jesus appeared to us at other times and in other places, and not merely in the breaking of bread; and sometimes in visions without a voice, but at other times in a voice without any vision, and sometimes also, as it has been reported unto me, by signs and tokens (without either voice or vision), and even in the guise of strangers; and all this for the space of little less than a year, insomuch

[1] See Note V.

that, if any one should adventure to set forth all the manifestations of Jesus, and the time and place and manner of each, I suppose that the world itself could not contain the books that should be written. Therefore passing over these, I will relate how Jesus appeared in Galilee on a certain mountain to more than five hundred of the brethren at one time.

It was on this wise. A year, or not much less, had passed away since the rising of Jesus from the dead; and we were still tarrying in Galilee, and the Passover was at hand. Now during that year the number of the disciples had been increasing, but not much; for we had not at that time been moved to proclaim the Resurrection of Jesus. But as the Passover drew nigh, Jesus began to manifest himself less often to us; and he made known to us by the mouth of Peter and of other of the disciples that the time was at hand when he should ascend up to heaven. Then there arose a questioning among us whether we should go up to the Passover or not; for some said that Jerusalem was an accursed city (because the doom of our Lord had gone forth upon it), and that we should not go up; but others said that we should go up; for the Lord would there reveal his will to us. Then it seemed good that the disciples should meet together on a certain mountain in Galilee, whereto Jesus had often resorted aforetime; and there we were to consider of these matters and to ask counsel of the Lord. Now when we were assembled to the number of five hundred in all, women and men together, behold, as we were all offering up prayers with one consent in the name of the Lord Jesus, there was a cry, "Behold him." And Jesus appeared unto us, of the same aspect as before, but fainter, and as it seemed standing at a distance from us ; insomuch that some that had not before seen Jesus risen from the dead, were in doubt; and others said they saw nothing. But when we prayed more earnestly, behold, Jesus came closer to us, so that all, or almost all, could discern him ; and he waved with the hand as if bidding us go southward. Afterwards the Lord spake by the mouth of Peter, saying that we were verily to go to Jerusalem. And so it was determined.

Now in the meantime, while we were waiting till the Feast of the Passover should come round, our hearts began to burn within us as if something great must surely come to pass, and the time must be at hand when we should go forth to preach Jesus to the world. For words may not describe with how great a joy we lived during those days one with another, and what a passion of love knit our hearts together ; and it seemed a sin that so much joy and happiness should not be imparted to others besides ourselves only. For at this time we, the disciples of Jesus, were as it were in Paradise, and joy went ever with us. For if we sailed upon the lake in our fishing-boats, Jesus was there ; or if we remained in Capernaum, working in the gardens, or on the quay, or about the booths, or went out into the fields, Jesus was there ; and when we met together in the evenings to break bread in memory of him, or in the early dawn on the first day of the week, to renew the remembrance of his rising again, then verily Jesus was not only there, but also often visibly there ; insomuch that while we touched his body with our hands, and while we drank of the blood from his side, we were able at the same time to feast our eyes upon the brightness of his countenance. Yet with all our joy we were not yet moved to go forth to preach the Good News. For it seemed sufficient for that present time that we should take delight in the presence of Jesus, and suck in strength from often beholding him visibly present among us.

Howbeit, though we were still as children clinging to the mother, and not yet able to walk alone, notwithstanding day by day we were learning some new thing concerning the will of the Lord: and the teaching of Jesus, which had in times past been hid from us, began now to appear more clear, and our eyes were being opened also to understand the Law and the prophets; and we all now understood that it had been the will of God from the first that Jesus should die upon the cross and give his life as a ransom for many. Moreover, we began to perceive that a time might be at hand when the Lord Jesus would depart from us, and seem to leave us alone upon the earth to preach the Kingdom of God: and we no longer feared to be alone, for we knew now that the Lord Jesus could never really leave us.

So we came up to Jerusalem. And it came to pass on the day of the Feast of the Passover, Jesus once more revealed himself visibly to us; and by the mouth of Peter he spake concerning that which was to come, and said that he must now be lifted up from among us: howbeit his Spirit should abide with us, and thence we should receive the power of forgiving sins. Some also said that they saw Jesus open his lips like unto one breathing forth breath upon another; as if he then breathed upon us the spirit of forgiveness: but this I saw not, nor anything that Jesus did, save that he blessed and brake bread, after his wont.

Now after the Passover we waited patiently at Jerusalem for nigh forty days; and all that time Jesus revealed himself not to any one of us, neither by sight nor by voice: and we questioned much among ourselves whether we ought to delay longer, for our hearts were desirous to preach Jesus. But when the feast of Pentecost was now at hand the word of the Lord Jesus came to us, saying that we should go forth to Mount Olivet, even to Bethany. And we went forth even as the Lord led us: yet he spake no word more to us; and it was now the tenth hour of the day. And after that we had walked for some while this way and that way upon the uplands of that mountain (even where our Master had walked in times past), and when we had spoken much together concerning all that he had said and done in these same places, behold, we came unto a hollow cleft in the mountain, whither no path led, nor was any habitation of men nigh unto it. Now by this time it wanted but a little of sunset: yet were we loth to go back to Jerusalem till we should have understood what the will of the Lord might be. So Peter said, "Sit we down here, and let us pray that the Lord may reveal his will unto us."

So we sat down and prayed; but we saw nothing, neither did the Lord speak by the voice of any of us. So we waited yet longer; but nothing came, vision nor voice nor sign; and by this time the sun had set. Notwithstanding it was not yet dark, for there was a wondrous brightness in the west, and behold, all the clouds and air above us were filled with a glorious appearance as of amber, and sapphire, and gold, and flames of fire. Then Peter stood up and stretched out his hands unto the Lord Jesus, and looked up to the heaven and said, "Thou, O Lord, didst promise that wheresoever two or three were gathered together in thy name, there wouldst thou be in the midst of them. Therefore, O Lord, be present now, we entreat thee." Now before the words had well passed from his lips, he ceased on a sudden, and his eyes were fixed, and his hand pointed to the sky, and John also cried out, saying, "He goeth up: lo, I see the Lord Jesus going up to heaven." Then I looked where John pointed, and lo, I also saw the Lord. But his face was no longer pale as before, nor were the prints of nails any more to be seen in his hands and feet, neither could I now discern his features so clearly as was usual: for his whole form seemed robed in a vesture of glory, and a crown of light about his head, and he sat upon a throne of sapphire. For the space of a minute or more we all gazed fixed in wonder; but then the throne rose slowly upwards, and with it rose likewise the angels, like unto flames of fire, round the sapphire throne; and so the glory grew fainter and more distant, and at the last a cloud or a darkness passed over it, and received it out of our sight.

But when the glory had now quite departed, we remained a long while steadfastly looking up to heaven, yea, even to the darkness of heaven, if perchance the glory might yet return to us. For we knew that we were now bidding farewell to the Lord Jesus for ever. But at the last Peter spake to us and said, "Be not sad, brethren, because Jesus is gone from us: for I heard the word of the Lord coming unto me, even from the angels about the throne of Jesus, and the message of the Lord unto us is this, 'Why stand ye gazing up unto heaven? This same Jesus which is taken up from you into heaven shall so come in like manner as ye have seen him go into heaven.'"

Then we returned thanks to God, praising and magnifying Him whose mercy endureth for ever; and we returned to Jerusalem rejoicing and singing songs of praise. But in the evening, when we sat together at meat, Simon Peter said that it behoved us, while we returned thanks to God for the gift of the Law (for it is a custom of our nation to do this on the evening before the morning of Pentecost), to return thanks yet more for the gift of the grace of Jesus; and he also besought the Lord to give us his grace even more abundantly, that the law of Jesus might be written on our hearts. So we sat late into that night conversing together and praying and singing praises unto God.

On the morrow we rose up very early and assembled ourselves together again to pray: and there were with us many disciples of several nations, devout men; not Galileans only, but also Alexandrines, and men of Cyrene, and some of Mesopotamia and Cappadocia, who all believed in Jesus. When we were now all assembled together and the door had been made fast, then Peter stood up, and thanked the Lord for that He had given to us His Holy One, Jesus of Nazareth, whom He had now taken to Himself; and he besought the Lord that, as He had taken up Jesus to heaven after the manner of Elias, so, after the same manner, He would send down some portion of His power upon us (even as Elias had sent down power upon his disciples) to the intent that all the people might know that the Lord had sent us to preach His word to Israel.

Then did the Lord hear us and answer us from heaven, even as He answered Elias by fire in the former days. For behold the Spirit from above fell upon us, and there was a sound as of many voices, even as the roar of many waters; and as the Lord touched the mouth of the prophet Esaias with fire, even so did He give unto us the Spirit of fire upon us, according to the saying of John the son of Zachariah, so that our hearts were all a-glow, and our faces kindling; and we prophesied as the Spirit gave us utterance, according to the saying of the prophet Jeremiah, "Behold I will make my words in thy mouth as fire." But herein was a great marvel; for we sang no psalms, nor did we speak in Scriptures, nor even in any articulate words; but we uttered strange sounds, whereof we felt the sense, but knew not of what language they were; for our tongues moved as the Spirit bade us. But behold, certain of the disciples that had not been moved by the Spirit to speak in tongues, were moved by the same Spirit to understand the meaning of our words; and one came up to me and said, "Thou speakest the language of Mesopotamia, even as I heard it in my childhood; and I verily understand thee, for thou speakest the very thoughts of my heart, thanking God for that He hath chosen us forth to be the servants of His son and to proclaim His Gospel to all the world." Then came another, a man of Cyrene, and he said the like, namely, that I spake in his own language, which was not the language of Mesopotamia, but the Punic tongue. Now while we all marvelled hereat, and knew not what to think, Peter stood up and said that the purpose of the Lord was that, in the times to come, all men upon the face of the earth should be of one language and of one family. "And to this end," said he, "God hath this day sent unto you this sign and token. For this day is fulfilled among you the saying of the prophets: And it shall come to pass that I will pour out my Spirit upon all flesh. For the time is at hand when all men shall know the Lord from the least to the greatest. For men shall no longer be taught of priests saying, Know the Lord; nor shall the knowledge of Him be given only to the rich and to them that have leisure; but upon the servants and upon the handmaids in those days will the Lord pour out His Spirit."

Then did we all rejoice with an exceeding joy, and we went forth openly into the temple for to magnify the Lord therein. And as I went, my heart leaping up and dancing within me for the fervour of my gladness, there came into my mind how, about three years ago, Philo the Alexandrine had spoken to me of a certain *enthousiasmos* that should fall upon the righteous: but his *enthousiasmos* was I knew not what, a passion for "mere existence," or for "that which is"; and I could not attain to apprehend so much as the meaning of it. But now I had indeed attained to the true *enthousiasmos*, which uplifteth and ennobleth and comforteth the soul, and stirreth to action, and purifieth the thought, and pervadeth every corner of the life of man, and includeth all things create and uncreate; so that my heart went out in love to all the creatures of God, and to all men without distinction, Gentiles as well as Jews, tax-gatherers as well as Scribes; yea, even to the Romans did my heart now go forth in love.

But when we were come together to the temple, the Pharisees and the chief priests and all the people marvelled at our boldness. For we were as changed men in their sight; because we no longer feared them as of old; neither, on the other hand, did we hate them, nor desire to revenge ourselves on them for that they had slain Jesus. But we pitied them; yea, we felt an exceeding compassion and love for them, as for them that wandered in darkness, while we sat in a great light. Therefore were we exceeding bold; and as for fear, we had forgotten what it meant: but we desired to pour out the good news of Christ before all men. For our hearts could not contain themselves for the abundance of joy and gladness and peace which the Lord had vouchsafed to us. So the people gathered themselves together around us. But when the Holy Spirit fell upon us, some men mocked, and called us drunkards; but the more part gave heed when Peter spake to them.

So Simon Peter spake in the ears of all the people, and said to them, even as he had said to us, that this out-pouring was for a sign to men, because the Lord was to pour out His Spirit upon the face of the earth. Moreover he added that Jesus was indeed the Christ, and that the Lord had raised him from the dead (whereof we were witnesses), to the intent that he should come again to judge the world in power; for he should assuredly prevail, and cast down all his enemies beneath his feet. When the people heard these words, they believed in Jesus; for a power went forth from the mouth of Peter and from the mouths of the other disciples, so that their words pierced into the very souls of such as should be saved. And we purified them (for we also baptized, even as John the son of Zachariah had baptized his disciples) and baptized them in the brook of Kidron. Then was fulfilled the word of Jesus of Nazareth, which he spake unto the apostles, saying that he would make them "fishers of men;" for on that day the net of the Gospel was indeed cast, and great was the draught of the fishes, so that there were added unto the Lord three thousand of them that believed.

CHAPTER XXXII

HERE must this history have an end. But I marvel how smoothly and easily the relation seemeth to have ascended from Jesus on earth to Jesus in heaven, as if by some ladder of easy ascent, and as though there were not seven heavens between. And perchance men would marvel the more, if I had been able to set down exactly the image of Jesus as he appeared to me at the first in my mother's house at Sepphoris, or when he sat with us in the fishing-boat on the lake; so that the image of Jesus as he seemed then, might be compared with the image of Jesus as he seemeth now. But I know that I have not been able to do this. For my pen hath still outrun the story: and in adventuring to describe Jesus as he appeared to me on earth, I have often failed of my intent, and have described him, not as he appeared to me on earth, but as he was hereafter to appear to me from heaven.

Oftentimes, musing on the difference between Jesus, as he was in deed and in truth, and Jesus, as we in Galilee supposed him to be, I have questioned myself and said, "Whence this waste of the life of the Lord Jesus? For if it be good for us to know him, and if the knowledge of him be eternal life, as we believe; then how much better had it been that we should have known him while he was alive, and not to have tarried for the knowledge till death had taken him from us?"

Now, looking back, I seem to discern a reason for our ignorance, or, at the least, a certain wholesome fruit springing therefrom. For methinks, had we known the Lord Jesus as he was, and all his greatness and glory, and all that was to betide him, and his resurrection, and his ascension, even then when he sat with us at meat, and went in and out with us throughout the villages of Galilee; I say, had we known even then that Jesus was to be raised from the dead, and to sit at the right hand of God, methinks we could not have loved him so dearly, nor have spoken with him so familiarly, nor have questioned him so freely, revealing unto him all our infirmities, and trusting him as a friend, yea, loving him as a very son of man, even one of ourselves.

But the Lord so ordained it that we should come to Jesus as to a great and good man, becoming infected with his spirit and imbued with the love of him as of a mortal being; and then, when he had caught our hearts as it were by guile, so that he had made himself now needful unto us even as the very breath of our lives, then began he to say unto us, "Whom say ye that I, the Son of man, am?" And lo, trying our hearts, we began to perceive that this same Son of man, who had so given life to our souls, could be none other than the very Son of the Living God.

Hence it came to pass that, when he departed from us, and when we felt a void in our hearts, and when we questioned ourselves what it was that we had lost, and what it was that we most loved and trusted and revered, yea also, and what it was that we most worshipped as divine; then behold, searching our hearts, we found that there was nothing in heaven above nor in the earth beneath, nor in the waters under the earth, no, nor in the host above the heavens, that could compare with Jesus of Nazareth. And so it was that, when we worshipped him as the Son, it seemed not unto us as if we were honouring him by calling him God; but (if I may speak as a child) it seemed rather as though we were striving to honour God by saying that God was one with Jesus. For saying this, seemed all one with saying that God was Love.

Therefore if any put this question unto me, "Why believest thou not that Romulus is God, and Liber, and Amphiaraus, and Elias, and Enoch (who all are said to have escaped death), and yet thou believest that Jesus of Nazareth is God?": my answer is this, that I believe Jesus to be God, first, because God is Love, and Jesus is Love; secondly, because God is Might and Jesus is Might; and lastly, because, if Jesus was not indeed divine, then must he needs have been a poor deluded creature, unfit and unable to do any great work for the children of men. For certainly, albeit he was the most humble and lowly of men, yet did he ever speak of himself, not as one of many redeemers, but as the redeemer of men, the refuge of the wretched, the forgiver of sins, the source of life and truth.

"But," say some, "Jesus was of a surety not Might; for he came not as a conqueror, but as one conquered." Now, methinks, concerning them that say such things, it was well said by Xanthias that "they are like unto the foolish giant Polyphemus, who could not think that

Ulysses could be Ulysses indeed, for that he was not a giant like unto himself. In the same way certain persons of gross understanding" (even of such an understanding as I myself had, before that I had been enlightened by the spirit of Christ) "suppose that Jesus could not have been the Messiah, for that he did not come into the world as they themselves would have come, nor do the works which they themselves would have done, had they been Messiahs. For they would have come into the world, forsooth, riding on the clouds, or borne on chariots of fire, or working signs in heaven or portents upon earth. Now this is even such a Messiah as Polyphemus would have devised for himself. But it was surely a much more divine thing that the Word of God should come into the world as a poor man, and the child of the poor (as if to shew that no estate of man is too low to be sanctified by the Divine Word); and that he should subdue all men unto himself, not by force nor portents, but by love, patience, and suffering; submitting himself patiently to all the laws of the world, yea even to the law of death, and yet triumphing over them all through the force of righteousness."

Thus spake Xanthias, and I assent unto his words. But furthermore, if I believed Jesus to be the Son of God when mine eyes were opened to discern him after his resurrection, much more do I believe it now; because all the years as they pass by, yea, and all the seventy nations of the earth, are as so many angels of God; which do cry aloud with a clear voice and say, "Jesus of Nazareth is our King; Jesus of Nazareth, though he be in heaven, is ruling on earth." For whithersoever I look throughout the Empire, I behold the love of Christ beginning already to rule over the tribes of the earth, though as yet it be in small beginnings. In Britain, where I now write, in Gaul, in Spain, in Italy, in Greece, in all the parts of Asia Minor, in Carthage and Egypt, yea even unto Babylon and the parts far beyond the River, the Lord Jesus now hath his worshippers.

Too long were it now to recount what I beheld in Alexandria and in Rome concerning the power of Christ and how the churches in those cities increased and are still increasing. But thus much have I noted concerning the law of Christ, that it differeth from all other laws, in that it is fitted for all nations and climates and times. It is as useful for the poor as for the rich. It loveth order and concord, and hateth disorder and tumult. It loveth truth, righteousness, and happiness; it hateth deceits and unrighteousness and misery. It doth not say unto all nations, "Take unto yourselves the customs of the Greeks," nor yet "Take unto yourselves the laws of the Romans," neither doth it prescribe any pattern of government as the best: but what saith it? It saith, "Love God and thy neighbour; and I, even I, will give thee strength to love them." For our law is none other than the Lord Jesus himself, dwelling with us again, and abiding in our hearts for ever, through faith.

Therefore is the law of Jesus in the end to prevail over other laws. For other laws are laws of fear, and they rule by constraint and hinder growth; but the law of Jesus is a law of love, and ruleth through freedom, causing all good things to grow, and making the heart to leap up with joy. Other laws need addition of rewards and punishments; but the law of Jesus assigneth fit reward, and executeth needful punishment, of itself, without help of king or lawgiver. The laws of other lawgivers will pass away with the passing of those needs for which the laws were made : but the law of love will abide for ever, for the need thereof passeth not away. And when that law shall be established, then, and not till then, shall wars cease from the earth, and all nations shall be as one : for as Moses gave Israel a law to knit the ten tribes into one nation, even so hath the Lord Jesus given us a law to knit the seventy nations of the earth into one family of God.

In this hope I rejoice, even in the midst of tribulations, for I trust that Jesus of Nazareth reigneth. Therefore shall my heart not fail, albeit the signs and mighty works of the Church seem now to be passing away, and devils be not now cast out as of old; nor are the sick so often healed; and the saints speak less oft with tongues. For if the signs of righteousness and mercy and truth abide in the Church, those other signs may perchance be suffered to pass away. But that which sometimes troubleth me more, is that, as I hear in some of the churches, the saints are overmuch given to the governing of the congregations, and the arranging of the worship of the saints, and the observing of feasts and fasts, more than to the waging of the war against unrighteousness. For though it be well to follow after peace, yet can I not forget that the Lord Jesus studied not to lead a quiet life, but spake unto us saying that he must needs send a sword on earth. And who knoweth not how he stood up with the sword of his mouth against the Pharisees in the Temple of the Lord ? The like of which contests and protestations against evil we hear not so oft, methinks, as in old times: howbeit, perchance even herein the Holy Spirit guideth us. But be this as it may, I still trust in the Lord Jesus; yea, even though there be (as I hear there be) divisions in certain of the churches, yet trust I in him. For I perceive that the Lord's ways are not as our ways; but the last are made first; and the weak become strong; and the foolish are exalted above the wise. Therefore, even as from the fall of Sion there seemeth to have come uprising to the Gentiles, even so perhaps out of the divisions of the churches may arise truth for all the world.

But as concerning the hour of the coming of the Lord, I deny not that he tarrieth long, even past all expectation. But inasmuch as the Lord Jesus himself said that he knew not that hour, for this cause I judge that no man shall know it. Only this is revealed unto me, that when the Lord shall come, it shall not be after such manner as we expect and shape forth in our minds, but the manner thereof shall be unexpected and new: better, I doubt not, than ever we hope or imagine, yet none the less, strange; yea, and perchance, at the first, full of disappointment. For I perceive that all the dealings of the Lord with men are after this fashion. He ever prepareth some good thing for us, exceeding all that we had expected; notwithstanding, with the good, there cometh also some wholesome pain or temptation that we expect not. For thus the Lord dealt with Adam in Paradise, and thus with Israel in the Promised Land; and thus also dealt the Lord Jesus with his disciples on earth. Wherefore thus also, I doubt not, the Lord Jesus will deal still with his disciples now that he reigneth in heaven.

But why speak I in conjectures concerning these unknown matters, or why yearn I thus impatiently for the hour of the Lord's coming, seeing that the Lord vouchsafeth to me, even on earth, his perpetual presence in mine heart, and the signs of his presence compass me everywhere around, so that even to live is joy? For verily to thee, O Lord, and to thy Kingdom, all things in heaven and earth do bear witness.

The faces of all children, whom thou didst call thy little ones, give back the brightness of thy countenance; the goodness of all good men testifieth unto thee, the supreme pattern of all good; yea even the bad and the weak proclaim their need of thee, O Lord our Redeemer, in whom alone is power to create goodness in the worst, and to make the weakest strong. To thy word the seed-time and harvests bear witness; the flowers also do sing of thy trustfulness and hope. If I look unto the earth, thou hast trodden and sanctified it; if to the heaven, thou hast gone up into it and dost possess it; if I think of the terrors of the depths beneath the earth, behold, thou knowest them, and hast passed through them, and overcome them, and hast broken the bars thereof; that they may no more keep captive them that shall follow in thy footsteps, passing through the darkness of the grave. Thus hast thou, O Eternal Word (by whom in ages past the worlds were created) now in these last times created the universe anew for them that love thee; so that all things do serve thee and proclaim thy Good Tidings, and the world is become unto thee as a vesture, and the elements are become thy servants: yea death itself thou hast subdued to be thy minister, and sin thou shalt subdue to be thy bond-slave.

Who is like unto thee, O most mighty Lord, for verily thy truth is on every side. Whither shall I go from thy Spirit, or whither shall I flee from thy presence? If I climb up into heaven, thou art there. If I go down unto the dead, thou art there also. If I take the wings of the morning and remain in the uttermost parts of the sea, even there also shall thy hand lead me and thy right hand shall hold me. Therefore when I sleep in the grave, I am in thy cradle; and when I shall arise up and awake, behold around me are thy everlasting arms.

THE END OF THE HISTORY

OF

PHILOCHRISTUS.

POSTSCRIPT

It had been my purpose, beloved brethren, to have continued this history from the year after the Lord Jesus suffered (in which year I left Syria and came to Alexandria) even to this present year, the tenth year after the destruction of the Holy City. Herein I was minded to have set forth how great things the Lord wrought for us in the Church of Alexandria, and the troubles that befell us there; even to the time of my going on the embassage unto Gaius Cæsar along with Philo the Alexandrine. Next it was my intent to have spoken of the Church of Rome, how it grew and prospered, and how in those days the Spirit of the Lord began to lead the saints towards wisdom in the governing and administering of the Church; lastly, the history would have told how I accompanied Julius Plautius the legate hither, even to Londinium, where now I write, where the Lord had prepared a work for me to do in building up the Church in Britain. For in this way methinks it might have been possible for you, my brethren, more clearly to discern how the Lord Jesus, though he be now in heaven, still guideth his Church upon earth.

Notwithstanding, because I am now stricken in years (being now fourscore and six years of age), and forasmuch as I know not whether I may have life to complete so great a work, it seemeth best (although I have in part already written these matters of my later life) first to make an end of this former history, especially considering the troubles now imminent in Britain from the barbarous people, and to defer the rest to a more convenient season.

Farewell.

SCHOLIA

SCHOLIA

I

These words of the Lord Jesus are not indeed found in our Gospels; but they have been handed down by tradition.[1] *Nor have I been able to find in the history of Philochristus any sayings of the Lord Jesus, save such as have been either handed down by tradition or else recorded in our Gospels.*

Moreover, the writer (as it seemeth to me, having diligently compared this history with the Gospels of the holy Evangelists Matthew and Mark and Luke) maketh mention of all such miracles as are found in all the three Gospels (though the raising of Jairus' daughter and the healing of the woman with the issue be but briefly mentioned): but if any miracle is found in one or in two Gospels only, concerning that he is silent. And this he seemeth to do not by chance, but of set purpose, as if he were minded to speak of those miracles only which are common to the first three Gospels. But Anchinous the son of Alethes maketh conjecture that Philochristus had in his mind a certain Original Gospel (whether it were a book or tradition) of exceeding antiquity; whence also the holy Evangelists drew that part of their several relations which is common to the first three Gospels.

[1] They belong to the twenty traditional sayings "which seem to contain, in a more or less altered form, traces of words of our Lord."—(*Westcott's Introduction to the Study of the Gospels*, p. 453).

II

Here again the writer of this history addeth nothing to our knowledge: for of all the words that Philo the Alexandrine uttereth to Philochristus, there is scarce one that may not be found in the writings of Philo, such as we now possess.

The like observation also is to be made concerning that which Philochristus reporteth of the sayings of the Scribes: whereof there is scarce one but I have found it (or the like of it) among these sayings of the Teachers of Israel which have been handed down to us even to this day.[1]

III

Whereas Philochristus reporteth that a certain Scribe in his days spake of "eating the Messiah," I find no such saying current in those days. But true it is that, many years afterwards, Rabbi Hillel (but this is not the same as Hillel the Great, who lived in the generation before Philochristus) said these words: "There is no Messiah for Israel, since they have already eaten him in the days of Hezekiah."[2] Moreover the saying of Moses, how that the nobles of Israel "saw God and did eat and drink," is, without doubt, explained by some of the Teachers among the Jews to mean that the Shekinah was as meat and drink to the nobles. But whether this saying was current in those days, or whether Philochristus erreth here also (as elsewhere), certain it is that many of the sayings of the Scribes reported by Philochristus were not made known nor published till very long after ; and meseemeth he hath perverted the doctrine of the Scribes with intent to cause the reader to have them in derision.

---

[1] "Sayings of the Jewish Fathers," by C. Taylor, M.A., published by the Cambridge University Press. [2] Ibid. p. 74.

But Anchinous the son of Alethes saith that, howsoever the sayings of the Scribes (whereof Philochristus maketh mention) have not been handed down to us as spoken in those times; yet the cause is, saith Anchinous, that few sayings of those times have been preserved. But if they had been preserved, then, saith he, we should have found that Philochristus described the teaching of the Scribes with exactness; even as the Gospels also bear witness that the Scribes in those days strained at gnats but swallowed camels; and overmuch esteemed the tithing of mint and anise and cummin, and the purification of pots and platters; and counted an oath that was sworn by the gold of the Temple, as being weightier than an oath that was sworn by the Temple itself.

IV

Herein it is marvellous to see with what a persistence Philochristus cleaveth only unto that part of the first three Gospels which is common to all the three; so that one might go near to suppose that Anchinous was right, in that he conjectured that Philochristus doth this not by chance, but of set purpose; having before him, perchance, some book or tradition which contained no more than this. For whereas Philochristus saith that the women heard some mention made of Galilee, but what it was, they agreed not exactly among themselves: I will here set down, in order, the three relations:—

1 (*Saint Matthew, xxviii. 7*) "And behold HE GOETH BEFORE YOU INTO GALILEE; there shall ye see him: lo I HAVE TOLD YOU."

2 (*Saint Mark, xvi. 7*) "HE GOETH BEFORE YOU INTO GALILEE: there shall ye see him, as HE SAID unto you."

3 (*Saint Luke, xxiv. 6*) "Remember how HE SPAKE unto you WHILE HE WAS YET IN GALILEE."

But as to the Gospel of the holy Apostle John, I have not been able to find out whether any part of it were known to Philochristus. Howbeit Anchinous saith that Philochristus, although he make no mention of any of the acts, nor of the long discourses, nor set dialogues of that Gospel, nevertheless useth the doctrine of that Gospel as the foundation of the whole of his history. Notwithstanding, saith Anchinous, Philochristus seemeth not to attribute this doctrine to John the son of Zebedee (who ever speaketh after a different manner, and rather as one of the Sons of Thunder, or as the writer of the book of Revelation, than as the writer of the Fourth Gospel), but to Nathanael and Quartus.

V

Here Philochristus is unlike himself. For whereas he is wont for the most part to omit miracles, albeit the Gospels relate them, here on the other hand he inserteth one, albeit the Gospels omit it. Howbeit, true it is that the holy Apostle Paul seemeth, in his first epistle to the Corinthians, to make mention of some manifestation of the Lord Jesus to the holy Apostle James. And the same is mentioned in certain traditions.

But it is to be noted that, in the whole relation of the Resurrection of Jesus, Philochristus departeth from his usual course. For he reporteth many manifestations whereof mention is not made in all the three Gospels, nor even in two, but in one only; and he speaketh of others also innumerable. Howbeit he maketh no mention of that manifestation wherein the Lord partook of fish and honey with the Disciples.